# The
# Crossword
# Companion
## and Solver

# The Crossword Companion and Solver

Compiled by Phil Larkin

ISBN: 1 86476 024 9

Axiom
Australia

# CONTENTS

# THREE-LETTER WORDS

| | | | | |
|---|---|---|---|---|
| A | daw | gam | jib | nob |
| ado | dib | gar | | nog |
| aft | dub | gas | K | nub |
| aga | dun | gat | kef | |
| ait | duo | gel | keg | O |
| auk | dux | gem | ken | obi |
| ave | | gen | key | ohm |
| awe | E | gig | kip | ope |
| awl | eau | gip | | opt |
| awn | eff | gnu | L | ora |
| | eke | guy | lac | orb |
| B | ell | gyp | lag | ova |
| bap | ems | | lam | |
| ben | ens | H | lax | P |
| bey | erg | hag | lea | Pan |
| | | hap | lei | pax |
| C | F | haw | ley | ped |
| caw | fay | hew | lie | phi |
| cay | fee | hex | lox | pod |
| chi | fen | hie | lug | poi |
| cob | fey | hob | lux | pox |
| col | fez | hog | lye | |
| coo | fid | hot | | Q |
| cor | fie | hoy | M | qua |
| cos | fig | hum | mad | |
| cox | fit | | maw | R |
| coy | foe | I | mew | rad |
| coz | fop | ilk | moa | rah |
| cum | fug | ink | | raj |
| | fur | ion | N | ret |
| D | | | neb | Rex |
| dab | G | J | nit | rho |
| dap | gad | jay | nix | roc |

| | | | W | Y |
|---|---|---|---|---|
| roe | soy | tug | | |
| | spy | tun | wad | yam |
| S | | tup | wag | yap |
| sac | T | two | war | yaw |
| sag | tad | | web | yen |
| sal | Tao | U | wen | yes |
| sib | tau | urn | wet | yew |
| sic | taw | | who | yip |
| ska | ted | V | why | |
| soh | tod | vie | wok | Z |
| sop | tor | vim | woo | zit |
| sot | toy | vis | wry | |
| sou | tub | vox | | |

# FOUR-LETTER WORDS

| A | aril | bice | bore | cane |
|---|------|------|------|------|
| abet | arms | bide | bort | cans |
| acme | army | bier | bosh | cant |
| acne | arum | biff | brad | cape |
| adit | aura | bilk | brae | capo |
| aeon | aver | bine | brag | carl |
| agar | avid | bise | bran | carp |
| agio | avow | bite | brer | caul |
| agog | awry | bitt | Brie | cavy |
| ague | axel | blab | brig | cede |
| ahem | axil | blah | brio | ceil |
| ahoy | axis | bleb | bubo | cell |
| alar | axle | blip | buff | Celt |
| alee | axon | blob | buhl | cere |
| alga | ayah | bloc | bund | cess |
| alms | | blue | bung | char |
| aloe | B | blur | bunt | chew |
| alto | bach | boar | buoy | chez |
| alum | back | bode | burg | chic |
| amah | bait | body | burl | chit |
| ambo | bald | Boer | burr | chow |
| amok | bane | bogy | busk | chub |
| amyl | base | bola | buss | ciao |
| anil | bast | bole | butt | cist |
| ankh | baud | boll | byre | cite |
| anna | bawd | bolt | byte | clad |
| anon | bawl | bonk | | clam |
| apex | beam | bony | C | clan |
| apse | beer | book | cadi | clef |
| aqua | berm | boom | cage | cleg |
| arak | beta | boon | calf | clew |
| area | bevy | boor | calk | clip |
| arid | bias | bora | call | cloy |

| | | | | |
|---|---|---|---|---|
| club | cyme | doab | dyke | exam |
| clue | cyst | dodo | dyne | eyas |
| coal | | doff | | eyed |
| coax | D | doge | E | eyra |
| coca | dace | dolt | earl | |
| coco | dado | dome | earn | F |
| coda | daff | dory | east | face |
| coif | daft | dosh | easy | fade |
| coir | dais | doss | ebon | fain |
| cole | damn | dost | echo | fair |
| colt | damp | dote | ecru | fame |
| cone | dank | dour | Edam | fane |
| conk | date | dove | eddo | fare |
| cony | daub | doxy | eddy | farl |
| coop | dawn | doze | Eden | faro |
| Copt | daze | drag | edit | fate |
| corf | debt | dram | eels | faun |
| corm | deep | dray | egad | fawn |
| cosh | deft | dreg | Eire | fays |
| cote | deil | drub | emir | faze |
| coup | dele | drug | emit | fear |
| cove | dell | drum | enol | feel |
| cowl | deme | duad | epic | fend |
| coxa | demy | dual | epos | feud |
| craw | dene | duct | ergo | fiat |
| crib | dent | dude | Erin | fico |
| crud | dewy | duel | erne | fief |
| crus | dhal | duly | Eros | fife |
| crux | dhow | dumb | Erse | file |
| cull | dibs | dump | erst | film |
| culm | ding | dune | espy | find |
| curd | dint | dung | etch | fino |
| curt | dirk | dunk | Etna | firs |
| cusp | disk | dupe | evil | fisc |
| cuss | diva | dyad | ewer | fish |
| cyma | dive | dyer | ewes | flag |

| | | | | |
|---|---|---|---|---|
| flak | funk | girt | hajj | hive |
| flam | furl | gist | hake | hoar |
| flan | | glee | hale | hoax |
| flap | G | glib | hame | hobo |
| flat | Gael | glob | hand | hock |
| flaw | gaff | glum | hank | hold |
| flax | gaga | glut | hark | hole |
| flay | gait | gnat | harm | holm |
| flea | gala | gnaw | harp | holp |
| flee | gale | goad | hart | holt |
| flew | gall | gobo | hash | home |
| flex | gamp | goby | hasp | homo |
| floc | gamy | gold | haul | hone |
| floe | gang | gone | hear | hong |
| flop | gaol | gong | heat | honk |
| flow | garb | gore | Hebe | hoot |
| flue | gasp | gory | heed | hops |
| flux | gaud | Goth | heel | hour |
| foal | gaur | gout | heft | hove |
| foci | gawk | grab | heir | howl |
| foes | gean | grad | helm | hued |
| fogy | geek | gram | help | huge |
| font | geld | grit | hemp | hula |
| fool | gene | guff | herb | hulk |
| foot | gens | gulp | Herr | hull |
| fore | gest | guru | hest | hump |
| fork | geum | gust | hewn | hung |
| foul | ghat | gyre | hick | hunt |
| four | ghee | | hide | hurl |
| fowl | gibe | H | high | hurt |
| frap | gild | hack | hill | hush |
| Frau | gill | Hade | hilt | husk |
| fret | gilt | haem | hind | hymn |
| frit | gimp | haft | hint | hype |
| froe | gink | haik | hire | |
| fumy | gird | hail | hist | |

| I | jink | kirk | lees | loon |
|---|------|------|------|------|
| iamb | jinn | kith | lend | lore |
| ibex | jive | kiwi | leno | lorn |
| ibid | jock | knag | Lent | lory |
| ibis | joey | knap | levy | lose |
| icon | john | knar | lewd | lour |
| idem | josh | knee | liar | luau |
| ides | joss | knit | lido | luce |
| idle | Jove | knop | lief | luff |
| idol | jowl | knot | lien | luge |
| ilex | judo | knur | lieu | lull |
| ilia | juju | kohl | lift | lulu |
| imam | Juno | kook | lilt | lune |
| inly | jury | koto | limb | lung |
| iota | jute | kris | limn | lure |
| iris | | kudu | limo | lurk |
| iron | K | | limy | lute |
| isle | kaka | | line | lynx |
| item | kaki | L | ling | lyre |
| iwis | kale | lade | link | lyse |
| | Kali | laic | lino | |
| J | kame | laky | lint | M |
| jade | kart | lama | lira | mace |
| jamb | kava | lamb | lire | maid |
| jape | keck | lame | lisp | mail |
| jarl | keep | land | loam | maim |
| jazz | kelp | lank | lobe | mall |
| jean | kelt | lard | loch | malm |
| jeep | kent | lash | loci | Manx |
| jell | kerf | lath | lock | many |
| jerk | khan | laud | lode | marc |
| jess | kier | lawn | loge | mare |
| jest | kiln | laze | logo | mark |
| jibe | kina | leal | loin | marl |
| jiff | kine | lean | loll | mash |
| jilt | kink | leek | loom | mask |
| | | leer | | |

| | | | | |
|---|---|---|---|---|
| math | mode | neap | odea | P |
| matt | moil | neat | ogee | paca |
| maul | moke | need | ogle | pact |
| Maya | moki | neep | ogre | pail |
| maze | moko | neon | oily | pall |
| mead | mole | nerd | okay | palm |
| mean | moon | nest | okra | palp |
| meat | moor | neve | olio | paly |
| meed | moot | newt | olla | pane |
| meek | mope | nick | omen | pang |
| melt | more | nigh | omit | para |
| memo | mort | nine | once | pard |
| menu | mote | nisi | onus | pare |
| mere | moth | nock | onyx | parr |
| mesa | moue | node | ooze | pate |
| mewl | moxa | noil | oozy | patu |
| mews | muff | noma | opah | paua |
| mica | mull | nome | opal | pawl |
| mice | murk | nook | open | pawn |
| midi | muse | noon | opus | peak |
| mien | musk | nose | oral | peal |
| miff | muss | nosh | orgy | peat |
| mike | must | note | orle | peek |
| milk | mute | noun | orts | peel |
| mime | mutt | nous | oryx | peen |
| mine | myna | nova | ossa | peer |
| mink | myth | nude | otic | peke |
| minx | myxo | nuke | ouch | pelf |
| mire | | null | oust | pend |
| miso | N | numb | ouzo | pent |
| mist | name | | oval | peon |
| mite | nape | O | ovum | peri |
| mitt | nard | oars | oxen | perk |
| moan | nary | oast | Oxon | perm |
| moat | nave | obit | oyer | pert |
| mock | navy | oboe | oyez | peso |

| | | | | |
|---|---|---|---|---|
| phon | Q | rudd | shad | snip |
| pica | quad | ruff | shag | snub |
| pied | quay | rune | shah | snug |
| pier | quid | ruru | sham | soak |
| pimp | quin | ruse | shea | soar |
| ping | quip | ryot | shed | sock |
| piny | quiz | | shim | soda |
| pipi | | S | shod | soil |
| pish | R | sago | shoo | sole |
| pith | raff | saki | shun | soli |
| pity | raga | sard | sial | solo |
| pleb | ragi | sark | sick | soma |
| plie | raki | sate | sift | song |
| plot | rale | scad | sigh | sorb |
| ploy | rand | scan | Sikh | sore |
| plug | rani | scar | sild | soul |
| plum | rapt | scat | sine | soup |
| pock | raze | scot | site | soya |
| poco | razz | scow | skew | spar |
| poll | ream | scud | skin | spay |
| pome | rear | scut | skit | spec |
| pomp | rein | seal | skol | spit |
| pone | rend | seam | skua | spiv |
| pore | rhea | sear | slag | spot |
| pork | riff | seat | slat | spry |
| posy | rill | sect | slaw | spur |
| pout | rime | seed | slay | stay |
| proa | rite | seel | slew | stet |
| puce | rive | seer | sloe | stoa |
| pule | roan | sell | slow | stop |
| pupa | roil | sept | slub | stow |
| purl | role | sera | slur | sudd |
| purr | roll | sere | smew | suds |
| pyre | roue | serf | smit | suet |
| | roup | seta | smut | Suez |
| | roux | sexy | snag | suit |

| | | | | |
|---|---|---|---|---|
| sumo | tern | trek | urus | vote |
| sump | text | tret | uvea | vugh |
| sunk | Thai | trey | | |
| sunn | that | trig | V | W |
| surd | thaw | trio | vain | wadi |
| swab | thew | trow | vair | waft |
| swap | thug | troy | vale | waif |
| swat | tide | true | vamp | wail |
| swot | tier | tsar | vane | wain |
| sync | tiff | tuba | vang | wale |
| | time | tufa | vase | wall |
| T | tine | tuff | veal | wand |
| tabu | tint | tuft | Veda | wane |
| tack | tire | tuna | veer | ware |
| taco | tiro | turf | veil | warp |
| tact | toby | tush | vein | wart |
| tael | toed | tusk | Vela | wary |
| tahr | tofu | tutu | vena | wash |
| tail | toll | twee | vend | wasp |
| talc | tolu | twin | vent | wast |
| tale | tomb | twit | verb | watt |
| tamp | tome | tyke | vert | waul |
| tang | tone | typo | vest | wave |
| tape | tong | tyro | veto | waxy |
| tare | tope | | vice | weak |
| tarn | topi | U | vide | weal |
| taro | tore | ugly | view | wean |
| tart | torr | ulna | vile | ween |
| task | tort | umbo | vina | weft |
| taut | Tory | undo | viny | weir |
| teak | tosh | upas | viol | well |
| teal | toss | Urdu | visa | welt |
| team | tote | urea | viva | wend |
| tech | tout | urge | void | wept |
| teem | trad | uric | vole | were |
| tend | tree | Ursa | volt | wert |

| | | | | |
|---|---|---|---|---|
| wham | wimp | wren | yelp | zarf |
| whet | wine | writ | yeti | zeal |
| whey | wino | | yoga | zebu |
| whim | winy | **Y** | yogi | zeds |
| whin | wipe | yair | yoke | zein |
| whip | wive | yard | yolk | zest |
| whit | woad | yare | yore | zeta |
| whiz | womb | yawl | yowl | zinc |
| whoa | wont | yawn | yuan | Zion |
| whom | wood | yawp | yuck | zone |
| whop | woof | yaws | yule | zoon |
| wick | wore | yean | yurt | Zulu |
| wide | wort | year | | zyme |
| wile | wove | yegg | **Z** | |
| wily | wrap | yell | zany | |

# FIVE-LETTER WORDS

| | | | | |
|---|---|---|---|---|
| A | aegis | allay | anion | arsis |
| abaca | aerie | allot | anise | arson |
| abaci | affix | alloy | annex | artel |
| aback | afoot | aloes | annul | ascus |
| abaft | afore | aloft | anode | asdic |
| abase | agama | aloof | antra | ashes |
| abash | agape | alpha | anvil | askew |
| abate | agate | altar | Anzac | aspen |
| abbey | agave | alter | aorta | aspic |
| abeam | agent | alula | apery | assai |
| abele | aggro | alway | aphid | assay |
| abhor | agist | amain | aphis | aster |
| abode | aglet | amber | apian | astir |
| abort | agley | ambit | aport | atoll |
| abuse | aglow | amble | appal | atony |
| abuzz | agora | ambry | apple | attar |
| abysm | agree | amend | apses | audio |
| abyss | agued | ament | apsis | audit |
| acorn | aisle | amice | aptly | auger |
| acrid | aitch | amide | arbor | aught |
| acute | alary | amine | areca | augur |
| adage | alate | amiss | arena | aural |
| adapt | alder | amity | arete | auric |
| addax | alert | ammon | argil | avast |
| adder | algae | amour | argol | avian |
| addle | algal | ample | argon | awake |
| adept | algid | amuck | argot | awful |
| adieu | algin | ancon | Argus | awned |
| admix | algor | anent | ariel | axial |
| adobe | alias | angel | aroma | axiom |
| adopt | alibi | angry | arras | azoic |
| adore | alien | angst | array | azote |
| adown | align | anile | arris | azure |

B

| | | | | |
|---|---|---|---|---|
| Babel | beige | bleat | botch | broom |
| babul | belay | bleed | bothy | brose |
| bacon | belie | blini | bough | broth |
| bagel | belle | bliss | bourn | Bruin |
| bairn | bench | blood | bower | bruit |
| baize | benne | blows | bowse | brume |
| baker | beret | blues | boyar | brunt |
| balas | berth | blurb | brach | brush |
| balmy | beryl | blurs | bract | brute |
| balsa | besom | blurt | braid | bucko |
| banal | besot | blush | brail | buffo |
| banjo | betel | board | brain | buggy |
| banns | bevel | boast | brake | bugle |
| barge | bezel | bogey | brave | build |
| baric | bhang | bogie | brawl | built |
| basal | bidct | bogle | brawn | bulgy |
| basil | bifid | bogus | braxy | bulla |
| basis | bight | bolar | braze | bully |
| basso | bigot | bolas | bread | burgh |
| baste | bijou | bolus | break | burin |
| batik | bilbo | bombe | brcam | burly |
| baulk | bilge | boned | breed | burnt |
| bayou | bimbo | bongo | brent | burro |
| beach | binge | bonus | breve | burry |
| beano | biped | bonze | briar | bursa |
| beast | bipod | booth | bribe | burse |
| beaus | birch | booze | brief | burst |
| beaut | birth | boozy | brill | busby |
| beaux | bison | borax | brine | butte |
| bebop | blain | bored | brink | butty |
| bedew | blame | boric | briny | buxom |
| bedim | blank | borne | brisk | bwana |
| beech | blare | boron | brock | byssi |
| beget | blase | bosky | broil | byway |
| begum | blaze | bosom | brome | |
| | blear | bosun | brood | |

| C | caulk | chive | clink | costa |
|---|-------|-------|-------|-------|
| cabal | cause | chock | cloak | cotta |
| caber | cavil | choir | clock | couch |
| cable | cease | choke | clone | cough |
| cabob | cedar | chomp | close | coupe |
| cacao | cello | chord | cloth | coved |
| cache | cense | chuff | cloud | coven |
| cacti | cento | churl | clout | covet |
| cadet | chafe | churn | clove | covey |
| cadge | chaff | chute | coach | cower |
| cadre | chain | chyle | coaly | cowry |
| caeca | chair | chyme | coati | coyly |
| cagey | champ | cider | coble | coypu |
| cairn | chaos | cigar | cobra | cozen |
| Cajun | chape | cilia | cocci | crack |
| calix | chard | cinch | cocoa | crake |
| calla | charr | circa | codex | craps |
| calyx | chary | cirri | colic | crass |
| cameo | chasm | cisco | colon | crate |
| canal | cheap | civet | colza | crawl |
| canna | cheep | civil | combo | crazy |
| canny | chela | civvy | comfy | credo |
| canon | chert | clack | comma | creed |
| canto | chevy | claim | conch | creek |
| caper | chick | clary | condo | creel |
| capon | chief | clasp | conga | creep |
| carat | child | clave | conic | crepe |
| cards | chime | clean | cooee | cress |
| caret | chimp | clear | coomb | crick |
| cargo | china | cleat | copal | crime |
| Carib | chine | cleek | copra | crimp |
| carob | chink | cleft | copse | croak |
| carom | chino | clepe | corgi | crone |
| carte | chirm | cliff | corps | crony |
| caste | chirp | climb | corse | croon |
| cates | chirr | clime | cosec | croup |

| | | | | |
|---|---|---|---|---|
| crowd | D | derma | dopey | ducat |
| crown | dacha | deter | Doric | duchy |
| crude | daddy | deuce | dotal | dulia |
| cruet | daily | devil | doter | dully |
| crumb | dally | dhobi | doubt | dulse |
| crump | daman | dhoti | dough | dummy |
| cruse | datum | diary | douse | dunce |
| crust | daunt | dicer | dowdy | duper |
| crypt | davit | dight | dowel | duple |
| cubic | dealt | digit | dower | durra |
| cubit | debar | dilly | downy | durst |
| cuddy | debit | dinar | dowry | dusky |
| culch | debug | dingo | dowse | duvet |
| cully | debut | dingy | doyen | dwale |
| cumin | decay | dinky | draff | |
| cupel | decor | diode | drain | E |
| Cupid | decoy | dipso | drake | eagre |
| curdy | decry | dirge | drama | earth |
| curia | deify | disci | drave | easel |
| curie | deign | disco | drawl | eaves |
| curio | deism | ditto | dread | ebony |
| curry | deist | ditty | dregs | edict |
| curse | deity | divan | dress | edify |
| curst | dekko | divot | drest | educe |
| cusec | delay | divvy | drink | educt |
| cushy | Delft | dixie | droit | eerie |
| cutch | delta | dizzy | droll | egest |
| cutie | delve | docks | drone | egger |
| cutin | demob | dodgy | drool | egret |
| cutis | demos | dogma | dross | eider |
| cycad | demur | doily | drown | eject |
| cycle | denim | dolce | drunk | eland |
| cynic | dense | donee | drupe | elate |
| Czech | depot | donna | druse | elegy |
| | depth | donor | dryad | elemi |
| | derby | dooly | ducal | elfin |

| | | | | |
|---|---|---|---|---|
| elide | erred | faint | filar | forth |
| elite | error | fairy | filch | forty |
| elope | eruct | faith | filth | forum |
| elude | erupt | fakir | finis | fossa |
| elvan | esker | false | fiord | fosse |
| elver | ester | fancy | firry | found |
| elves | estop | farad | first | fount |
| embay | ether | farce | firth | foyer |
| embed | ethic | farcy | fitch | frail |
| ember | ethos | fatal | flail | franc |
| emend | ethyl | fated | flair | fraud |
| emery | etude | faugh | flame | freak |
| emote | evade | fault | flare | friar |
| empty | evert | fauna | fleam | fried |
| enact | evict | feast | fleer | frill |
| ender | evoke | feign | flirt | frisk |
| endue | exact | feint | flong | frith |
| enema | exalt | felly | flora | frons |
| enemy | excel | felon | flour | froth |
| ennui | exeat | femur | flout | frown |
| ensue | exert | fence | fluid | froze |
| entry | exile | fenny | fluke | fruit |
| eosin | expel | feoff | fluky | frump |
| epact | extol | feral | flume | fryer |
| ephod | extra | fetch | fluor | fucus |
| epoch | exude | feted | flush | fudge |
| epode | exult | fetid | flute | fugal |
| epoxy | eyrie | fetor | focal | fugue |
| equal | | fever | focus | fungi |
| equip | F | fibre | foist | funky |
| erase | fable | fiche | folio | furry |
| erect | facer | fichu | foray | furze |
| ergot | facet | fiend | fordo | furzy |
| erica | facia | fifer | forgo | fusee |
| erode | faddy | fifth | forme | fusel |
| erose | fadge | fight | forte | fusil |

| | | | | |
|---|---|---|---|---|
| fussy | gesso | gourd | gules | heron |
| fusty | ghoul | gouty | gumma | hertz |
| futon | giant | grade | gunny | hewer |
| fuzzy | giber | grail | guppy | hexad |
| | giddy | grain | gusto | Hindu |
| G | gigot | graph | gyrus | hinge |
| gabby | gigue | grapy | | hinny |
| gable | gipsy | grate | H | hitch |
| gaffe | girth | graze | Hades | hoard |
| galea | glair | grebe | hafiz | hoary |
| galop | gland | greed | haiku | hocus |
| gamin | glare | green | hakim | hoist |
| gamma | glass | gride | halal | honey |
| gamut | glaze | grief | hanky | horal |
| garth | gleam | grimy | haply | horis |
| gassy | glean | gripe | happy | hotel |
| gaudy | glebe | grist | hards | hovel |
| gauge | gleet | grits | harem | human |
| gaunt | glide | groan | harpy | humid |
| gauss | glitz | groat | harry | humus |
| gauze | globe | groin | harsh | hunks |
| gauzy | glove | grout | hasty | hurst |
| gavel | gloze | gruel | haunt | husky |
| gawky | gluey | grume | havoc | hussy |
| gazer | glume | guaco | hawse | hydra |
| gecko | glyph | guano | hazel | hydro |
| gelid | gnarl | guard | heard | hyena |
| gemma | gnash | guava | hefty | hymen |
| gemmy | gnome | guess | heist | hyoid |
| gemot | gofer | guest | helix | hyrax |
| genet | gonad | guide | helot | hyson |
| genie | goose | guild | helve | |
| genii | gorge | guile | hence | I |
| genre | gorse | guilt | henna | ichor |
| genus | gorsy | guise | henry | ictus |
| geode | gouge | gulch | herby | idiom |

| | | | | |
|---|---|---|---|---|
| idiot | Japan | knave | lathe | lobar |
| idler | jaunt | knead | lazar | locum |
| idyll | jemmy | kneed | leach | locus |
| ileac | jerky | kneel | least | logic |
| ileum | Jesus | knell | ledge | logos |
| iliac | jetty | knelt | leech | loony |
| ilium | jewel | knoll | leery | loose |
| image | jihad | knout | lemur | lotus |
| imago | jingo | knurl | lento | lough |
| imbue | jinks | koala | Lethe | Louis |
| impel | joist | kopje | levee | louse |
| inane | joule | kraal | level | lousy |
| inapt | joust | krait | lever | lowed |
| incur | julep | krill | Levis | loyal |
| incus | junta | krona | lexis | lucid |
| index | jural | krone | liana | lucre |
| inept | jurat | kudos | licit | lumen |
| inert | juror | kulak | liege | lunar |
| ingle | | kvass | limbo | lupus |
| ingot | **K** | kylie | limit | lurch |
| inkle | kapok | | linen | lurgy |
| inter | kappa | **L** | liner | lurid |
| inure | kaput | labia | links | lycee |
| inurn | karma | laden | lipid | lying |
| iodic | kauri | ladle | lisle | lymph |
| ionic | kayak | lagan | lists | lynch |
| irate | kazoo | laird | lithe | lyric |
| irony | kebab | laity | litho | |
| islet | kedge | lamia | litre | **M** |
| issue | keeve | lance | liver | macaw |
| istle | kevel | lapse | lives | macer |
| ivory | khaki | larch | livid | Mafia |
| | kiang | lardy | llama | magma |
| **J** | kinky | largo | llano | Magus |
| jabot | kiosk | laser | loamy | Mahdi |
| jalap | knack | lasso | loath | maize |

| | | | | |
|---|---|---|---|---|
| major | might | mulch | nitre | ogler |
| mamba | milch | mumps | noble | oiled |
| maned | mimic | mungo | nodal | okapi |
| mange | mingy | mural | noddy | oleic |
| mango | minim | murky | nodus | olive |
| mania | mirth | muses | noils | ombre |
| manna | misty | musky | noise | omega |
| manse | mitre | musth | nomad | onion |
| manus | mocha | myall | nonce | oozed |
| Maori | modal | myrrh | nones | opera |
| maple | model | | nonet | opine |
| marge | modem | **N** | noose | opium |
| marly | mogul | nabob | noria | optic |
| marsh | molar | nacre | Norse | orang |
| mater | monad | nadir | north | orate |
| matin | monte | naive | notch | orbed |
| mauve | month | naked | novel | orbit |
| mavis | mooch | nanny | nudge | oread |
| maxim | moody | nasty | nylon | organ |
| mayor | moped | natal | nymph | oriel |
| media | moper | nates | | orlop |
| medic | moral | navel | **O** | ormer |
| melic | morel | navvy | oakum | ornis |
| melon | mores | nawab | oases | orris |
| mercy | motel | neath | oasis | Oscar |
| merge | motet | Negro | oaten | osier |
| merle | motif | negus | obese | ought |
| merry | motto | neigh | ocean | ounce |
| mesne | mould | newel | ochre | outer |
| meson | moult | nexus | ochry | ouzel |
| metal | mount | niche | octal | ovary |
| meths | mourn | nidus | octet | ovate |
| metol | mouse | niece | odeum | overt |
| metro | movie | nifty | odium | ovine |
| mezzo | mucus | nihil | odour | ovoid |
| midge | mufti | nimbi | offal | ovolo |

| | | | | |
|---|---|---|---|---|
| ovule | payee | pinny | pound | Q |
| owlet | payer | pinto | power | quack |
| oxbow | peace | pious | prate | quaff |
| oxide | peach | pipal | prawn | quail |
| ozone | pearl | piper | preen | quake |
| | pease | pipit | prier | quaky |
| P | pecan | pique | prima | qualm |
| padre | pedal | piste | prime | quark |
| paean | peeve | pitch | primp | quart |
| paeon | pekoe | pithy | prink | quash |
| pagan | penal | pivot | prior | quasi |
| paint | pence | pixie | prise | quean |
| palea | penis | plaid | prism | queen |
| palpi | penna | plait | privy | queer |
| palsy | penny | plank | prize | quell |
| panda | peony | plant | proem | query |
| panel | peppy | plaza | prone | quest |
| panic | perch | plead | proof | queue |
| pansy | perdu | pleat | proud | quiet |
| parch | peril | plumb | prowl | quiff |
| pared | perky | plume | proxy | quill |
| parka | perry | plunk | prude | quilt |
| parry | perse | poach | psalm | quint |
| parse | pesky | podgy | psoas | quire |
| party | petit | poesy | pukka | quirk |
| pasha | petty | poise | pulpy | quirt |
| passe | phase | poker | pulse | quite |
| pasta | phial | pokey | pupae | quoin |
| paste | phlox | polar | pupal | quoit |
| pasty | phyla | polio | puree | quota |
| paten | picot | polka | purge | quote |
| patio | piece | polyp | purse | quoth |
| pause | piety | posit | putty | |
| pavan | piggy | posse | pygmy | R |
| pavid | pilot | pouch | pylon | rabbi |
| pawed | pinna | poult | pyxis | rabid |

| racer | revet | rumba | scant | senza |
|-------|-------|-------|-------|-------|
| radar | revue | rummy | scape | sepal |
| radii | rheum | runic | scare | sepia |
| radix | rhino | rupee | scarf | sepoy |
| radon | rhomb | rusty | scarp | septa |
| raise | rhyme | | scary | serac |
| Rajah | riant | S | scena | serai |
| ramie | rider | sable | scene | serge |
| range | ridge | sabot | scent | serif |
| raphe | rifle | sabre | scion | serin |
| rapid | rigid | sacra | scoff | serum |
| ratch | rinse | sahib | scone | serve |
| ratel | risen | saint | scoop | setae |
| rathe | ritzy | saker | scope | sewer |
| ratio | rivet | salep | score | shade |
| ravel | roach | salmi | scorn | shake |
| raver | roast | salsa | scour | shako |
| rayed | robin | salve | scout | shale |
| rayon | robot | salvo | scowl | shaly |
| razor | roger | samba | scrag | shank |
| react | rogue | sambo | scree | shard |
| realm | Romeo | Santa | scrim | share |
| reave | rondo | sapid | scrip | shawl |
| rebel | roost | sassy | scrum | shawm |
| rebus | rosin | Satan | scuba | sheaf |
| recto | rotor | satay | scull | shear |
| redan | rouge | satin | scurf | sheen |
| reedy | rouse | satyr | scute | sheep |
| reeve | roust | sauce | seamy | sheer |
| reign | route | sauna | sebum | sheik |
| reins | rover | savoy | sedge | shell |
| remix | rowan | savvy | sedgy | shied |
| renal | rowel | sawer | seine | shier |
| resin | royal | sayer | seize | shine |
| retch | ruche | scald | semen | ships |
| revel | ruddy | scalc | senna | shire |

| | | | | |
|---|---|---|---|---|
| shirk | slide | spasm | stars | stupe |
| shirr | slier | spate | start | style |
| shive | slink | spawn | stave | suave |
| shoal | sloop | spear | stead | suede |
| shoer | sloth | spell | steak | suety |
| shoes | smalt | sperm | steal | sugar |
| shook | smash | spice | steam | suint |
| shoon | smear | spiel | steed | suite |
| shred | smell | spile | steer | sully |
| shrew | smile | spiny | stein | super |
| shrub | smirk | splay | stele | surah |
| sibyl | smock | spoil | steps | sural |
| sidle | smolt | spook | stich | surge |
| siege | snack | spoor | sties | surgy |
| sieve | snafu | spore | stile | surly |
| sigma | snake | spout | sting | sushi |
| silly | snarl | sprat | stipe | swain |
| sinew | sneer | spree | stoat | swami |
| sinus | snide | sprig | Stoic | swang |
| siren | snood | sprit | stoke | swank |
| sisal | snook | spume | stoma | sward |
| sitar | snoop | spunk | stone | sware |
| sixty | socks | spurn | stook | swarm |
| skeet | socle | spurt | store | swart |
| skein | solan | sputa | stork | swash |
| skimp | solar | squab | stoup | swath |
| skink | solus | squad | stout | swear |
| skint | sonar | squat | straw | sweat |
| skirl | sonde | squaw | stray | swill |
| skirt | sooth | squib | strep | swink |
| skive | sorry | squid | strew | swipe |
| skulk | sorus | staid | stria | swirl |
| slain | sough | stake | strop | swish |
| sleek | souse | stalk | strum | swoon |
| sleep | spade | stall | strut | sword |
| slept | spank | stark | stupa | sylph |

synod

**T**
tabes
tabid
table
taboo
tabor
tacet
tache
tacit
tafia
taiga
taint
tales
talus
tamed
Tamil
tamis
tanka
tansy
taper
tapir
tapis
tardy
tares
targe
tarot
tarry
tarsi
tasse
tatty
taunt
taupe
tawer
tawny

tawse
taxon
tazza
teens
teeny
telex
telic
tempi
tempo
tempt
tench
tenet
tenon
tenor
tepee
terra
terse
tesla
thane
thaws
theca
thegn
theme
there
therm
theta
thews
thief
thigh
thill
thing
think
third
thole
thorp
throb

throe
thrum
thyme
tiara
tibia
tidal
tiers
tigon
tilde
tilth
times
tinct
tinea
tinge
tired
tires
titan
tithe
titre
tizzy
toady
toddy
toffy
token
tonal
tonic
tonne
tools
tooth
topaz
topee
toper
toque
Torah
torch
torsk

torso
torte
torus
total
totem
touch
tough
towel
toxic
toxin
trace
tract
trait
trash
trass
trave
trawl
tread
trend
trews
triad
tribe
trice
trick
trike
trill
trine
tripe
trite
troll
trope
troth
trout
trove
truce
trunk

truss
truth
tryst
tuber
tufts
tulle
tumid
tunic
tunny
turps
tutor
twain
tweak
tweed
tweet
twerp
twill
twine
twirl
tyros

**U**
udder
ukase
ulcer
ulnar
ultra
umbel
umber
umbra
umiak
unapt
unbar
under
unfit
unify

| | | | | |
|---|---|---|---|---|
| union | verse | vowel | whiff | wrist |
| units | verso | vulva | whine | write |
| untie | verst | vying | whirl | wrong |
| urate | verve | | whirr | wroth |
| urban | vesta | **W** | whisk | wrung |
| urine | vetch | wacke | whist | wryly |
| usage | vexed | waddy | whole | wurst |
| usher | viand | wafts | whoop | |
| usurp | vibes | wager | whore | **X** |
| usury | vicar | wages | whorl | xenon |
| utter | video | wagon | widow | xylem |
| uvula | views | wails | width | |
| | vigil | waist | wield | **Y** |
| **V** | villa | waive | Wigan | yacht |
| vague | villi | wally | wight | yahoo |
| valet | vinic | waltz | wince | yapok |
| valid | vinyl | wanly | windy | yearn |
| valse | viola | wares | wings | years |
| value | viper | watch | winze | yeast |
| valve | viral | water | wired | yield |
| vapid | Virgo | waver | witan | yobbo |
| varec | virtu | waxen | witty | yodel |
| varix | virus | weald | wives | yogis |
| varus | visor | weary | wizen | yokel |
| vatic | vista | wedge | women | youth |
| vault | vital | weeds | works | yucky |
| vaunt | vitta | weepy | worms | yummy |
| Vedic | vivid | weigh | worst | |
| vegan | vixen | weird | worth | **Z** |
| velar | vocal | welsh | wound | zamia |
| veldt | vodka | wench | wrack | zebra |
| velum | vogue | whale | wrapt | zilch |
| venal | voice | wharf | wrath | zloty |
| venom | voile | wheat | wreak | zonal |
| venue | volta | whelk | wrest | zooid |
| Venus | vomit | whelm | wring | zoril |
| verge | vouch | whelp | | |

# FIVE-LETTER MULTIPLE WORDS

**A**
A-bomb
act up
a deux
ad hoc
ad lib
ad rem

**B**
be-all
by-end

**C**
CD-ROM
CS gas
cut up

**D**
dry up

**F**
f-word
f-stop

**G**
get at
get on
get up
go far
go off
G-suit

**H**
H-bomb
he-man
he-men

**I**
in-law

in for
in tow

**L**
leg it
leg up
let up

**M**
mix up
Mr Big

**N**
no joy

**O**
on ice
on tap

**R**
R and R
rat on
re-run
rub in
run-in

**S**
say-so
sci fi
set to
set up
sit in
sit up

**T**
T-cell
tie-in

tie-up
try on

**U**
U-boat
uh-huh
up-end
U-turn

**W**
wag it

**X**
X-axis

**Y**
Y-axis

# SIX-LETTER WORDS

| | | | | |
|---|---|---|---|---|
| A | adduce | agouti | ampere | Apollo |
| abacus | adduct | aguish | amulet | appeal |
| abated | adhere | ailing | analog | appear |
| abbess | adieus | airbus | anchor | append |
| abduct | adieux | akimbo | angina | arable |
| abject | adjoin | alalia | angler | arbour |
| abjure | adjure | alarum | animus | arcade |
| ablate | adjust | albeit | anklet | arcane |
| ablaut | adnate | albino | annals | Arctic |
| ablaze | Adonis | alcove | anneal | ardent |
| abrade | adrift | alexia | annexe | ardour |
| abrupt | adroit | alexin | annual | areola |
| abseil | adsorb | alight | anoint | argent |
| absent | advent | aliped | anonym | argosy |
| absorb | advice | alkali | anorak | armada |
| absurd | advise | allege | ansate | arrant |
| acacia | aerate | allude | anthem | arrear |
| acarid | aerial | allure | anther | artery |
| acarus | aerobe | almond | antiar | artful |
| accede | affair | almost | antler | artist |
| accent | affect | alpaca | antrum | ascend |
| access | affirm | alumna | anyone | ashore |
| accost | afflux | alumni | aorist | ashram |
| accrue | afford | always | aortal | aslant |
| acedia | affray | Amazon | aortic | asleep |
| acetic | Afghan | ambary | aoudad | aspect |
| aching | afraid | ambles | Apache | aspire |
| acquit | agaric | amends | apathy | assail |
| acting | agency | amerce | apiary | assent |
| acuity | agenda | amidst | apiece | assert |
| acumen | aghast | amnion | aplomb | assign |
| adagio | agnail | amoeba | apnoea | assize |
| addict | agnate | amoral | apogee | assort |

| | | | | |
|---|---|---|---|---|
| astern | awning | basset | belong | bisect |
| asthma | axilla | bateau | beluga | bisque |
| astral | azalea | batman | benign | bistro |
| astray | azotic | batten | benumb | bitter |
| astute | | bauble | benzol | blanch |
| asylum | B | bawdry | berate | blazer |
| ataxia | babble | bazaar | bereft | blazon |
| ataxic | baboon | beacon | Berlin | bleach |
| atomic | badger | beadle | bertha | bleary |
| atonal | baffle | beagle | bestow | blench |
| atoned | bagful | beaker | bethel | blenny |
| atrium | bailee | beaten | betide | blight |
| attach | bailey | beauty | betray | blithe |
| attack | bailie | becalm | bettor | blonde |
| attest | ballet | became | bewail | bloody |
| attire | ballot | beckon | beware | blotch |
| attune | bamboo | bedaub | beyond | blouse |
| auburn | banana | bedbug | bezoar | blowzy |
| augury | bandit | bedlam | biased | bluing |
| august | bangle | beeper | biases | blunge |
| aurora | banish | beetle | biceps | bobbin |
| aurous | banker | befall | bicker | bobble |
| Aussie | banner | before | biform | bobcat |
| author | bantam | befoul | bigamy | bobwig |
| autism | banyan | beggar | bijoux | bodega |
| autumn | banzai | begird | billet | bodice |
| avatar | baobab | behalf | billon | bodkin |
| avaunt | barbel | behave | billow | boffin |
| avenge | barbet | behead | binary | boggle |
| avenue | barbie | behest | binate | boiler |
| averse | barium | behoof | bionic | bolero |
| aviary | barley | behove | biopsy | bolide |
| avocet | barque | beldam | biotic | bolter |
| avouch | basalt | belfry | biotin | bonbon |
| avowal | basket | belief | birdie | bonito |
| aweigh | Basque | bellow | bireme | bonnie |

| | | | | |
|---|---|---|---|---|
| bonsai | breath | bunker | Caesar | cantor |
| boodle | breech | bunkum | caftan | cantos |
| boogie | breeze | bunyip | caiman | Canuck |
| bookie | breezy | burble | cajole | canvas |
| boomer | brevet | bureau | calash | canyon |
| borage | brewer | burgee | calcar | capote |
| borate | briary | burger | calces | captor |
| boreal | bridle | burgle | calcic | carafe |
| borsch | bright | burial | calico | carbon |
| borzoi | broach | buried | caliph | careen |
| bosket | brogan | burlap | calkin | career |
| botany | brogue | burrow | callow | caress |
| botchy | bromic | bursar | calves | caries |
| botfly | bronco | burton | camber | carina |
| bother | bronze | bushel | camera | carnal |
| bottle | brooch | busker | camion | carnet |
| bottom | broody | buskin | camlet | carpal |
| bought | browse | bussed | camper | carpel |
| bounce | bruise | bustle | campus | carpet |
| bounty | bryony | butane | Canaan | carpus |
| bovine | bubble | butler | canard | carrel |
| bowery | bubbly | buzzer | canary | cartel |
| bowler | buboes | bygone | cancan | carton |
| bowyer | buckra | bypass | cancel | carvel |
| boxing | Buddha | bypath | cancer | casaba |
| boyish | buddle | byword | candid | casein |
| Brahma | budget | | candle | cashew |
| braise | budgie | C | cangue | casino |
| branch | buffer | cachet | canine | casket |
| branks | buffet | cackle | canker | casque |
| branny | bugler | cacoon | cannel | cassia |
| bravos | bulbul | cactus | cannon | castle |
| brawny | bumble | caddie | canopy | castor |
| brazen | bummer | cadent | canter | casual |
| breach | bumper | cadger | cantle | catena |
| breast | bunion | caecum | canton | catnap |

| | | | | |
|---|---|---|---|---|
| caucus | cheese | cither | codify | conics |
| caudal | chemic | citric | coerce | conium |
| caudex | cheque | citron | coeval | conker |
| caudle | cherry | citrus | coffee | conoid |
| caught | cherub | civics | coffer | consul |
| caulis | chiasm | clammy | coffin | contra |
| causal | childe | claret | cogent | convex |
| caveat | chilli | classy | cognac | convey |
| caviar | chilly | clause | coheir | convoy |
| cavity | chintz | clawed | cohere | cookie |
| cavort | chisel | clayey | cohort | coolie |
| celery | chives | cleave | coifed | copier |
| cellar | choice | clench | coitus | coping |
| Celtic | choker | clergy | coleus | Coptic |
| cement | choler | cleric | collar | copula |
| censer | choose | client | collet | coquet |
| censor | chopin | climax | collie | corbel |
| census | choral | clinch | colony | corbie |
| centos | chorea | clinic | colour | corded |
| centre | choric | clique | column | cordon |
| cerate | chorus | cloche | comate | cornea |
| cereal | chosen | clonic | combat | corned |
| cereus | chrism | closet | comber | corner |
| cerise | chrome | clothe | comedo | cornet |
| cerium | chubby | cloven | comely | corona |
| ceruse | chukka | coarse | comfit | corpse |
| cervix | chunky | coaxer | commie | corpus |
| cestus | church | cobalt | commit | corset |
| chaise | cicada | cobble | commix | cortex |
| chalet | cicely | cobweb | compel | corymb |
| chance | cilice | coccus | comply | coryza |
| chapel | cinder | coccyx | concur | cosine |
| charge | cinema | cockle | condom | cosmic |
| charry | cinque | cocoon | condor | cosmos |
| chasse | cipher | coddle | congee | cosset |
| chaste | cirrus | codger | conger | costly |

| | | | | |
|---|---|---|---|---|
| cottar | cruise | cystic | debris | dengue |
| cotter | crumby | | debtor | denial |
| cougar | crusty | D | decade | denier |
| county | crutch | dabble | decamp | denote |
| couple | cubism | dacoit | decant | dental |
| coupon | cuboid | dactyl | deceit | deodar |
| course | cuckoo | daedal | decent | depart |
| cousin | cuddle | daggle | decide | depict |
| covert | cudgel | dahlia | decker | deploy |
| coward | cuisse | dainty | deckle | deport |
| cowboy | culler | damask | decoct | depute |
| cowpat | culver | dammar | decode | deputy |
| coyote | cumber | damned | decree | derail |
| cradle | cumuli | damper | deduce | deride |
| cranny | cupful | damsel | deduct | derive |
| crater | cupola | damson | deepen | dermal |
| cravat | cupric | dander | defame | dermic |
| craven | cupule | dandle | defeat | dermis |
| crayon | curacy | danger | defect | descry |
| crease | curare | daphne | defend | desert |
| create | curate | dapper | defile | design |
| cresol | curdle | dapple | defray | desire |
| cretin | curfew | daring | deific | desist |
| crewel | curios | darnel | deject | desman |
| cringe | curium | dative | delete | despot |
| crinum | curlew | dawdle | delict | detach |
| crises | cursor | dazzle | delude | detail |
| crisis | curtly | deacon | deluge | detain |
| crispy | curtsy | deadly | deluxe | detect |
| critic | cuspid | deafen | delver | detest |
| croaky | custom | dealer | demand | detour |
| crocus | cutler | dearly | demean | deuced |
| crotch | cyclic | dearth | dement | device |
| croton | cygnet | debark | demise | devise |
| crouch | cymbal | debase | demote | devoid |
| cruces | cymose | debate | demure | devour |

| | | | | |
|---|---|---|---|---|
| devout | distal | drachm | easter | employ |
| dewlap | distil | dragon | echoes | enable |
| dexter | dither | draper | echoic | enamel |
| dharma | divert | drawer | eclair | encase |
| diadem | divest | dreamt | ectype | encore |
| diaper | divine | dreary | eczema | encyst |
| dicing | docent | dredge | edible | endear |
| dicker | docile | drivel | editor | endive |
| dictum | docker | drongo | efface | endure |
| diesel | docket | droopy | effect | energy |
| dieter | doctor | dropsy | effete | enfold |
| differ | dodder | drossy | effigy | engage |
| digest | dollop | drowse | efflux | engulf |
| digger | dolman | drowsy | effuse | enigma |
| diglot | dolmen | drudge | eggnog | enmesh |
| dilate | dolour | dubbin | egoism | enmity |
| dilute | domain | duello | egoist | ennead |
| dimmer | domino | duenna | egress | enough |
| dimple | donjon | duffel | either | enrage |
| dimply | doodad | duffer | ejecta | enrich |
| dinghy | doodah | duffle | elapse | ensign |
| dingle | doodle | dugong | elated | ensile |
| dinkum | dormer | duiker | eldest | entail |
| diplex | dorsal | dulcet | elects | entice |
| dipper | dosage | dupery | elicit | entire |
| direct | dossal | duplex | elixir | entity |
| dirndl | dotage | duress | embalm | entomb |
| disarm | dotard | dyeing | embark | entree |
| disbar | doting | dynamo | emblem | enzyme |
| discal | dottle | dynast | embody | Eocene |
| discus | doubly | | emboss | eparch |
| dishes | douche | E | embryo | eponym |
| dismal | doughy | eaglet | emerge | equate |
| dismay | dowlas | earing | emetic | equine |
| disown | downer | earthy | empery | equity |
| dispel | doyley | earwig | empire | eraser |

| | | | | |
|---|---|---|---|---|
| erbium | excise | family | fervid | flaxen |
| ermine | excite | famine | fescue | fledge |
| erotic | excuse | famish | festal | fleece |
| errand | exempt | famous | fetish | fleecy |
| errant | exeunt | fanged | fetter | flexor |
| errata | exhale | farina | fettle | flimsy |
| ersatz | exhort | farmer | feudal | flinty |
| escarp | exhume | farrow | fiasco | flitch |
| eschew | exodus | fasces | fibril | floozy |
| escort | exotic | fascia | fibrin | floppy |
| escrow | expert | father | fibula | floral |
| escudo | expire | fathom | fickle | florid |
| Eskimo | expiry | fatwah | fidget | florin |
| espial | export | faucal | fierce | fluent |
| espied | expose | fauces | fiesta | flurry |
| esprit | exsert | faucet | filial | fodder |
| estate | extant | faulty | fillet | foetal |
| esteem | extend | faunal | fillip | foetus |
| estray | extort | favour | filose | fogies |
| etcher | extras | fawner | finale | foible |
| ethane | eyeful | fealty | finery | foison |
| ethene | eyelet | fecund | finger | folksy |
| ethics | | fedora | finial | follow |
| ethnic | F | feeble | finite | foment |
| euchre | facade | feebly | firkin | fondle |
| eulogy | facial | feeder | firmly | fondly |
| eunuch | facies | feline | fiscal | fondue |
| eureka | facile | fellah | fistic | footer |
| eutaxy | factor | felony | fixity | foozle |
| evicts | faecal | female | fizgig | forage |
| evince | faeces | fennec | fizzle | forbad |
| evolve | faggot | fennel | flabby | forbid |
| exarch | faille | ferial | flange | forego |
| exceed | falcon | ferret | flashy | forger |
| except | fallow | ferric | flaunt | forget |
| excess | falter | ferule | flavin | forgot |

| | | | | |
|---|---|---|---|---|
| formal | furrow | ganoid | gibber | goitre |
| format | fusion | gantry | gibbet | golfer |
| formic | futile | gaoler | gibbon | gopher |
| fossae | future | garage | giblet | gorget |
| fossil | fylfot | garble | giggle | Gorgon |
| fought | | garcon | gigolo | gospel |
| fracas | G | garden | gilder | Gothic |
| freeze | gabble | gargle | gimlet | gouger |
| frenzy | gabion | garish | ginger | govern |
| fresco | gables | garlic | ginkgo | gradin |
| friary | gablet | garnet | girder | grange |
| Friday | gadget | garret | girdle | granny |
| friend | Gaelic | garter | glairy | gratis |
| frieze | gaffer | gasbag | glaive | gravel |
| fright | gaggle | gasket | glance | graven |
| frigid | gaiety | gateau | glazer | graves |
| frijol | gaited | gather | glibly | gravid |
| fringe | gaiter | gauche | glitch | grease |
| frisky | galaxy | gaucho | global | greasy |
| frizzy | galena | gavial | globin | greave |
| frolic | galley | gazebo | gloomy | greedy |
| frosty | gallon | geezer | Gloria | grieve |
| frothy | gallop | geisha | glower | grille |
| frowzy | galore | Gemini | gluten | gringo |
| frugal | galosh | gender | glycol | grippe |
| fruity | gambit | genera | gnawer | grisly |
| frusta | gamble | genial | gneiss | gritty |
| fulfil | gambol | genius | gnomic | groats |
| fulmar | gamete | gentle | gnosis | grocer |
| fumble | gamine | gentry | goalie | groove |
| fungal | gaming | gerbil | goatee | groovy |
| fungus | gammon | gerent | gobbet | groped |
| funnel | gander | gerund | gobies | grotto |
| furfur | ganger | gewgaw | goblet | grouch |
| furore | gangly | geyser | goblin | ground |
| furred | gannet | ghetto | goggle | grouse |

| | | | | |
|---|---|---|---|---|
| grovel | haptic | heroes | hubris | impart |
| growth | harass | heroic | huddle | impede |
| groyne | harlot | heroin | humane | impish |
| guffaw | harrow | herpes | humble | import |
| guilty | haunch | heyday | humbug | impose |
| guinea | hawker | hiatus | humour | impost |
| guitar | hawser | hiccup | hunger | impugn |
| gullet | hazard | hijack | hunker | impure |
| gunman | header | hippie | hurtle | impute |
| gurgle | healer | hispid | husked | inarch |
| gusset | health | hither | hussar | inbred |
| guttae | hearse | hoarse | hustle | incase |
| gutter | hearth | hockey | hybrid | incest |
| guzzle | hearty | hollow | hymnal | incise |
| gypsum | heater | homage | hyphen | incite |
| gyrate | heaven | hombre | hyssop | income |
| gyrose | heaver | homely | | incubi |
| | Hebrew | homily | **I** | incuse |
| **H** | Hecate | honest | iambic | indeed |
| hacker | heckle | honour | iambus | indent |
| hackle | hectic | hoodoo | ibises | indict |
| haemal | hector | hoofed | icicle | indigo |
| haggis | heehaw | hookah | ideate | indite |
| haggle | Hegira | hooker | idiocy | indoor |
| hairdo | heifer | hooves | ignite | induce |
| halide | height | hopple | ignore | indult |
| halter | helium | hornet | iguana | infamy |
| hamate | helmed | horrid | imbibe | infect |
| hamlet | helmet | hosier | imbrue | infest |
| hammer | hemmer | hostel | immune | influx |
| hamper | hempen | hotdog | immure | infuse |
| handle | heptad | hourly | impact | ingest |
| hangar | herald | howdah | impair | inhale |
| hanker | herbal | howler | impala | inhere |
| hankie | heresy | hoyden | impale | inject |
| hansom | hermit | hubbub | impark | injure |

| | | | | |
|---|---|---|---|---|
| injury | J | joyous | kitsch | lariat |
| inlaid | jabber | juggle | kitten | larvae |
| inmate | jabiru | juicer | kittle | larynx |
| innate | jacana | jujube | klaxon | lascar |
| insane | jackal | jumble | knaggy | lateen |
| insect | jadish | jumper | knight | latent |
| insole | jaguar | jungle | knives | lather |
| instil | jalopy | junior | knobby | latria |
| insult | jangle | junket | knotty | latten |
| intact | jargon | junkie | kopeck | latter |
| intern | jarrah | juries | kosher | launch |
| intone | jasper | jurist | kowtow | laurel |
| intuit | jaunty | | | lavabo |
| invent | jejune | K | L | lavish |
| invert | jennet | kabala | labial | lawyer |
| invest | jerboa | Kaffir | labile | laxity |
| invoke | jerked | karate | labium | laying |
| inward | jerkin | keeled | labour | lazily |
| iodide | jersey | keeper | labret | lazuli |
| iodine | jester | kelpie | labrum | league |
| iodise | jetsam | kennel | laches | leaven |
| ireful | Jewish | kernel | lackey | leaves |
| irenic | jigger | ketone | lactic | lecher |
| iridic | jiggle | kettle | lacuna | lector |
| irises | jigsaw | kibble | lading | ledger |
| iritis | jingle | kibitz | lagoon | leeway |
| ironic | jinnee | kidnap | laical | legacy |
| island | jitter | kidney | lambda | legate |
| isobar | jobber | killer | lamely | legato |
| isogon | jockey | kilter | lament | legend |
| isohel | jocose | kimono | lamina | legion |
| isomer | jocund | kindle | lampas | legist |
| isopod | jogger | kindly | lancet | legume |
| issued | jostle | kipper | landed | lender |
| italic | jovial | kirtle | lappet | length |
| itself | joyful | kismet | lapsed | lenity |

| | | | | |
|---|---|---|---|---|
| lenses | litany | lucent | manque | medico |
| lentil | lithia | lumbar | mantis | medium |
| lepton | litmus | lumber | mantle | medley |
| lesion | litter | lunacy | mantra | medusa |
| lessee | little | lunate | manual | meekly |
| lesser | lively | lunged | manure | meetly |
| lesson | livery | lunula | maraca | mellow |
| lessor | lizard | lupine | maraud | melody |
| lethal | llanos | lustra | margin | memoir |
| levier | loathe | lustre | marina | memory |
| levies | lobate | luxury | marine | menace |
| levity | lobule | lychee | marker | menage |
| lewdly | locale | lyrist | marlin | menial |
| liable | locate | | maroon | menses |
| liaise | loculi | **M** | marque | mentor |
| libido | locust | macron | marrow | mercer |
| lichen | lodger | macula | marten | merger |
| ligate | loggia | madden | martyr | merino |
| lignin | loiter | madras | marvel | merlin |
| lignum | loofah | magnet | mascot | merman |
| ligula | looney | magnum | masque | meteor |
| lilies | loosen | magpie | massif | methyl |
| limber | loquat | mahout | matins | metric |
| limpet | lorica | maigre | matrix | mettle |
| limpid | losing | mainly | matron | miasma |
| linage | lotion | malady | mature | midden |
| linden | louche | malice | maxima | middle |
| lineal | louden | malign | Mayday | midget |
| linear | loudly | mallee | mayhap | midrib |
| linnet | lounge | mallet | mayhem | mighty |
| lintel | louvre | mallow | meadow | mikado |
| lipoid | lovage | mammal | meagre | milady |
| liquid | loving | manage | measly | milden |
| liquor | lowboy | manger | meddle | mildew |
| lissom | lowest | mangle | medial | milieu |
| listen | lowing | maniac | median | millet |

| | | | | |
|---|---|---|---|---|
| mimosa | moreen | muslin | nebula | nought |
| mining | morose | mussel | nectar | novena |
| minion | morris | muster | needle | novice |
| minium | morsel | mutant | nelson | nowise |
| minnow | mortal | mutate | nephew | nozzle |
| minter | mortar | mutely | Nereid | nuance |
| minuet | mosaic | mutiny | nestle | nubile |
| minute | mosque | mutism | nether | nuclei |
| mirage | mother | mutton | nettle | nudely |
| mishap | motion | mutual | neural | nudged |
| mislay | motive | mutule | neuron | nudism |
| missal | motley | muzzle | neuter | nugget |
| misuse | motmot | myopia | newton | nuncio |
| mitral | mottle | myriad | nibble | nutant |
| mitred | mottos | myrtle | nicely | nutmeg |
| mitten | mouldy | myself | niched | nutria |
| mizzen | moulin | mystic | nickel | nuzzle |
| mobile | mouser | | nimble | nympho |
| modern | mousse | N | nimbly | |
| modify | mozzie | namely | nimbus | O |
| module | mucous | napalm | niobic | o'clock |
| moggie | muesli | napery | nipper | oafish |
| mohair | muffin | napkin | nipple | obelus |
| moiety | mugger | napper | nitric | object |
| molest | mulish | narial | nitwit | oblate |
| molten | Mullah | narwal | nobble | oblige |
| moment | mullet | natant | nodule | oblong |
| Monday | murder | nation | noggin | oboist |
| monger | murine | native | nonage | obsess |
| monism | murmur | natron | noodle | obtain |
| monkey | murphy | natter | normal | obtect |
| monody | muscat | nature | notary | obtund |
| mopish | muscle | naught | notice | obtuse |
| moppet | museum | nausea | notify | obvert |
| morale | musing | nearby | notion | occult |
| morass | musket | nearly | nougat | ocelot |

| | | | | |
|---|---|---|---|---|
| octane | otiose | pardon | peeler | physic |
| octave | otitis | pariah | peeved | phyton |
| ocular | ouster | parish | pelage | piaffe |
| odious | outlaw | parity | pellet | pianos |
| oedema | outlay | parley | pelmet | piazza |
| offend | outlet | parody | pelvic | pickle |
| office | outset | parole | pelvis | pidgin |
| offing | ovisac | Parsee | penile | pierce |
| oleate | owlish | parson | pennon | piffle |
| onager | oxalis | pascal | penult | pigeon |
| oodles | oxygen | passim | penury | piglet |
| opaque | oyster | pastel | people | pileus |
| opiate | | pastor | pepsin | pilfer |
| oppose | P | pastry | peptic | pillar |
| oppugn | pacify | patent | period | pilule |
| option | packer | pathos | peruke | pimple |
| oracle | packet | patina | peruse | pineal |
| orator | paella | patois | peseta | pinion |
| orchid | pagoda | patrol | pestle | piping |
| ordain | pakeha | patron | petard | pipkin |
| ordeal | palace | patten | petite | piquet |
| ordure | palate | patter | petrel | piracy |
| orgasm | pallet | paunch | petrol | pirate |
| orgies | pallid | pauper | pewter | pistil |
| Orient | pallor | pawner | pharos | pistol |
| origin | paltry | pawpaw | phases | piston |
| oriole | pampas | paynim | phenol | pitmen |
| orison | pamper | peachy | phenyl | placid |
| ornate | panada | pearly | phlegm | plague |
| ornery | pander | pecten | phloem | plaguy |
| orrery | pandit | pectic | phobia | plaice |
| osmose | pantry | pectin | phoney | plaint |
| osmund | papacy | pedant | phonic | planet |
| osprey | papaya | pedate | photic | plaque |
| ossify | papyri | peddle | phrase | plasma |
| ostler | parcel | pedlar | phylum | platan |

| | | | | |
|---|---|---|---|---|
| platen | portal | pueblo | quarto | ramrod |
| player | porter | puffin | quartz | ramson |
| pledge | poseur | puisne | quasar | rancho |
| plenum | possum | pullet | quaver | rancid |
| pleura | potash | pulley | queasy | random |
| plexus | potato | pulpit | quench | ranger |
| pliant | poteen | pulsar | quiche | rankle |
| pliers | potent | pumice | quince | ransom |
| plight | pother | pummel | quinsy | rapids |
| plinth | potion | pundit | quirky | rapier |
| plough | pounce | punish | quiver | rapine |
| plover | praise | pupate | quorum | rapist |
| plunge | prance | purdah | | rappel |
| plural | praxis | purine | R | raptor |
| pocket | prayer | purism | rabbin | rarefy |
| podium | preach | purist | rabbit | rarely |
| poetic | prefer | purlin | rabble | rarity |
| pogrom | prefix | purple | rabies | rascal |
| poison | presto | purser | raceme | rather |
| police | pretty | pursue | racial | rating |
| policy | priest | purvey | racism | ration |
| polity | primal | putrid | raddle | ratios |
| pollen | primer | putsch | radial | rattan |
| polypi | primus | puttee | radian | rattle |
| pomace | priory | puzzle | radish | ravage |
| pomade | privet | python | radium | ravine |
| pommel | prolix | | radius | ravish |
| Pomona | prompt | Q | radula | realty |
| poncho | pronto | quagga | raffia | reaper |
| ponder | prying | quaggy | raffle | rebuff |
| ponies | pseudo | quahog | rafter | rebuke |
| poodle | psyche | quaint | ragout | recant |
| poplar | ptosis | Quaker | raisin | recede |
| poplin | public | quango | ramble | recess |
| poppet | pucker | quanta | ramose | recipe |
| porous | puddle | quarry | ramous | recite |

| | | | | |
|---|---|---|---|---|
| reckon | remand | revert | rookie | sailor |
| recoil | remedy | review | rosary | salaam |
| record | remind | revile | rostra | salami |
| recoup | remiss | revise | rotary | salary |
| rectal | remora | revive | rotate | salify |
| rector | remote | revoke | rotten | salina |
| rectum | render | reward | rotund | saline |
| redact | renege | rewind | rouble | saliva |
| reddle | rennet | rhesus | rubber | sallow |
| redeem | renown | rheumy | rubble | salmon |
| reduce | reopen | rhinal | rubric | saloon |
| reefer | repand | rhymer | rudely | salter |
| refill | repast | rhythm | rueful | salute |
| refine | repeal | rialto | ruffle | salver |
| reflex | repeat | ribald | rugate | samara |
| reflux | repent | riband | rugose | samite |
| refold | repine | ribose | rumble | sampan |
| refuel | report | riches | rumour | sample |
| refuge | repose | rictus | rumple | sandal |
| refuse | repute | riddle | rumpus | sanity |
| refute | rescue | riffle | runnel | sapper |
| regale | resect | rigour | runner | sarong |
| regard | reside | ringer | rupiah | sashay |
| regent | resign | ripple | russet | sateen |
| reggae | resile | riprap | rustic | satire |
| regime | resorb | risque | rustle | satrap |
| regina | resumé | ritual | | Saturn |
| region | retail | rivage | S | saucer |
| regius | retard | roadie | sachet | savage |
| regnal | retina | rochet | sacral | savant |
| regret | retort | rococo | sacred | savour |
| rehash | retuse | rodent | sacrum | sawpit |
| reject | revamp | roller | sadism | sawyer |
| relict | reverb | Romaic | safari | Saxony |
| relief | revere | Romany | sagely | saying |
| relish | revers | rondel | saggar | scalar |

| | | | | |
|---|---|---|---|---|
| scampi | seated | sestet | shrift | sizing |
| scanty | secant | settee | shrike | sizzle |
| scarab | secede | settle | shrill | sketch |
| scarce | secret | severe | shrimp | skewer |
| scarfs | sector | sewage | shrine | skibob |
| scarry | secund | sewing | shrink | skimpy |
| scenic | secure | sexism | shrive | skinny |
| schema | sedate | sexist | shroud | skiver |
| scheme | seduce | sextet | shrove | skivvy |
| schism | seeker | sexton | shrunk | slaggy |
| schizo | seethe | sexual | sicken | slalom |
| school | seldom | shabby | sickie | slangy |
| scilla | select | shadow | sickle | sleave |
| sclera | selves | shaggy | siding | sleaze |
| sconce | sempre | shaman | sienna | sledge |
| scoria | senate | shandy | sierra | sleeky |
| scotch | senega | shaven | siesta | sleepy |
| scotia | senile | shears | signal | sleeve |
| scrawl | senior | sheath | signet | sleigh |
| scream | sennit | sheave | signor | sleuth |
| screed | sensor | sheikh | silage | slicer |
| screen | sentry | sheila | silica | slight |
| scribe | sepsis | shekel | silvan | slinky |
| scrimp | septet | shelve | simian | sliver |
| script | septic | sherry | simile | slogan |
| scroll | septum | shield | simmer | slouch |
| scruff | sequel | shiest | simony | slough |
| sculpt | sequin | Shiite | simoom | sloven |
| scurry | seraph | shimmy | sinewy | sludge |
| scurvy | serene | Shinto | single | sludgy |
| scutch | serial | shoddy | siphon | sluice |
| scutum | series | shogun | sippet | slurry |
| scythe | sermon | shower | sirdar | smirch |
| seaman | serous | shrank | siskin | smithy |
| search | serval | shrewd | sister | smoker |
| seared | sesame | shriek | sitcom | smooch |

| | | | | |
|---|---|---|---|---|
| smooth | speech | squawk | stingy | stymie |
| smudge | speedy | squeak | stipes | suable |
| smutty | sphere | squeal | stitch | subdue |
| snatch | sphinx | squint | stithy | sublet |
| snazzy | spider | squire | stiver | submit |
| sneeze | spiffy | squirm | stodge | suborn |
| snitch | spigot | squirt | stodgy | subtle |
| snivel | spinal | squish | stolid | suburb |
| snobby | spinet | stable | stolon | subway |
| snooty | spiral | stadia | stones | suckle |
| snooze | spirit | staffs | stooge | sudden |
| snugly | splash | stager | storey | suffix |
| soccer | spleen | stalag | stormy | suitor |
| social | splice | stamen | strain | sulfur |
| sodden | spline | stance | strait | sullen |
| sodium | splint | stanza | strand | sultan |
| soever | spoilt | stapes | strass | sultry |
| solace | spoken | staple | strata | sumach |
| solder | sponge | starch | stream | summit |
| solely | spongy | starry | street | summon |
| solemn | spotty | starve | stress | sundae |
| solute | spouse | states | striae | sundew |
| solver | sprain | static | strict | sundry |
| sombre | sprang | stator | stride | superb |
| sonant | sprawl | statue | strike | supine |
| sonata | spread | status | string | supple |
| sonnet | sprint | stayer | strobe | surety |
| soothe | sprite | steady | stroke | surtax |
| sordid | sprout | steamy | stroll | survey |
| sorely | spruce | steely | stubby | suttee |
| sorrel | spunky | steeve | stucco | suture |
| sortie | spurge | steppe | studio | svelte |
| sought | sputum | stereo | stupor | swathe |
| source | squall | sticky | sturdy | sweaty |
| sparse | square | stifle | stylar | swipes |
| specie | squash | stigma | stylus | switch |

| | | | | |
|---|---|---|---|---|
| swivel | tassel | theory | tinges | toxoid |
| sylvan | tattle | theses | tingle | toyboy |
| symbol | tattoo | thesis | tinker | tracer |
| syndic | taught | thieve | tinsel | trader |
| syntax | Taurus | thirst | tipple | tragic |
| Syriac | tauten | thirty | tiptoe | trance |
| syrupy | tavern | thorax | tiptop | trauma |
| system | tawdry | though | tirade | treaty |
| syzygy | tedder | thrall | tiring | treble |
| | tedium | thread | tissue | tremor |
| T | teeter | threat | tither | trench |
| tabard | teethe | thresh | tmesis | trendy |
| tackle | teledu | thrice | tocsin | trepan |
| tactic | telson | thrift | toddle | triage |
| taipan | temper | thrill | toffee | trifid |
| tallow | temple | thrips | toggle | trifle |
| Talmud | tenant | thrive | tomato | trigon |
| tamper | tender | throat | tomboy | trilby |
| tampon | tendon | throes | tongue | triode |
| tandem | tennis | throne | tonite | tripod |
| tangle | tenure | throng | tonsil | Triton |
| tanist | tenuto | throve | topple | triune |
| tanner | tercet | thrown | torero | trivet |
| tannic | teredo | thrush | torpid | trivia |
| tannin | terete | thrust | torpor | trocar |
| Taoism | terror | thwack | torque | troche |
| tappet | testes | thwart | torrid | trogon |
| tariff | testis | thymus | totter | troika |
| tarsal | tetchy | tibial | touché | Trojan |
| tarsia | tether | ticket | touchy | troops |
| tarsus | thaler | tidbit | toupee | trophy |
| tartan | thanks | tiddly | tousle | tropic |
| tartar | thatch | tierce | touter | trough |
| tarter | theirs | tiffin | towage | troupe |
| tartly | theism | timber | toward | truant |
| tasker | theist | timbre | townie | trudge |

| | | | | |
|---|---|---|---|---|
| truism | ultima | unwrap | valved | vessel |
| tsetse | ultimo | upbeat | vamper | vestal |
| tuffet | umbles | uphill | vandal | vested |
| tufted | umlaut | uphold | vanish | vestry |
| tumble | umpire | upkeep | vanity | viable |
| tumour | unborn | uplift | vapour | victim |
| tumult | uncial | uproar | varied | victor |
| tundra | undies | upshot | varlet | viewer |
| tuning | unduly | upside | vassal | vigour |
| tunnel | unfair | uptake | vastly | Viking |
| turban | unfurl | uranic | vector | vilely |
| turbid | unglue | Uranus | veiled | vilify |
| turbot | unholy | urbane | veined | villus |
| tureen | uniped | urchin | vellum | vinery |
| turgid | unique | ureter | veloce | vinous |
| turkey | unisex | urgent | velour | violas |
| turner | unison | urinal | velure | violet |
| turnip | united | ursine | velvet | violin |
| turret | unjust | usance | vendee | virago |
| tusker | unkind | useful | vendor | virgin |
| tussle | unlade | usurer | vendue | virile |
| tuxedo | unless | uterus | veneer | virtue |
| twelve | unload | utmost | venial | visage |
| twiggy | unlock | utopia | venose | viscid |
| twinge | unmask | uvular | venous | viscus |
| twitch | unmoor | | verbal | vision |
| tycoon | unpack | V | verger | visual |
| tympan | unripe | vacant | verify | vitals |
| typhus | unroll | vacate | verily | vitric |
| typify | unruly | vacuum | verity | vittae |
| typist | unsafe | vagary | vermin | vivace |
| tyrant | unseen | valise | versed | vivify |
| | unsung | valley | versus | vizard |
| U | untrue | valour | vertex | voiced |
| ubiety | unveil | valued | vesica | voided |
| uglily | unwary | valuer | vesper | volant |

| | | | | |
|---|---|---|---|---|
| volley | warden | whiner | wolves | yeoman |
| volume | warily | whinge | wombat | yeomen |
| volute | warped | whinny | wooing | yields |
| voodoo | warper | whiten | woolly | yippee |
| vortex | warren | wholly | worsen | yogurt |
| votary | washer | whoops | worthy | yoicks |
| votive | waylay | whoosh | wowser | yonder |
| voyage | wealth | whydah | wraith | yuppie |
| voyeur | weapon | wicker | wrasse | |
| Vulcan | wearer | wicket | wreath | Z |
| vulgar | weasel | wieldy | wrench | zaffre |
| | weaver | wigged | wrests | zcalot |
| W | weekly | wiggle | wretch | zenith |
| waffle | weepie | wigwam | wriest | zephyr |
| wafter | weever | willow | wright | zigzag |
| waiver | weevil | wimble | writer | zinnia |
| wallah | weight | wimple | writhe | zircon |
| wallet | weirdo | window | wrongs | zither |
| wallop | welkin | winker | | zodiac |
| walnut | wether | winkle | Y | zombic |
| walrus | wharfs | winner | yabber | zonate |
| wanglc | wheeze | winnow | Yahveh | zonked |
| wanker | wheezy | wintry | Yahweh | zonule |
| wanted | whence | withal | Yankee | zounds |
| wanton | wherry | wither | yarrow | zygoma |
| wapiti | whilst | wizard | yearly | zygote |
| warble | whimsy | woeful | yeasty | |

# SIX-LETTER MULTIPLE WORDS

**A**
air-bag
air-gun
all for
all out
all set
at hand
at risk
au fait
au lait
au pair

**B**
back up
bad egg
beat it
beat up
bed-pan
bed-sit
big cat
big top
big-wig
blow up
bon mot
boo-hoo
bow-tie
buy-out
bye-bye

**C**
cat-nap
cat-nip

cha-cha
chi chi
coin op
cop-out
cut off
cut out

**D**
deja vu
dog-day
dog-leg
do time
dry-rot
dry-run
dug-out

**E**
egg-cup
egg-nog
en bloc

**F**
fag-end
fan-tan
far-off
far-out
fat cat

**G**
go bust
go-cart
gun-shy

**H**
hack it
hang up
hard-on
hard-up
harp on
haw-haw
head-on
hob-nob
hold up
hoop-la

**I**
ice age
ice cap
ill-use
in a rut
in hock
in situ
in vivo

**J**
jet-lag
jet-set

**K**
kung fu

**L**
lap-dog
lay low
lean-to

leg-bye
line up
lock up
low-key
lump it

**M**
make do
make up
mark up
May Day
mock-up

**N**
New Age
nod off
no joke

**O**
odds-on
off-key
off-set
of note
oil rig
old hat
on edge
one-off
one-way
on-line

**P**
pen pal

pent-up
pig out
play up
pop-gun

**R**
red-hot
rip-off
rot-gut
run-off

**S**
see red
sewn-up
shoo-in
size up
spot-on

**T**
tag-end
tea-bag
tie-pin
two-ply

**W**
wax-end
wrap up

**Y**
yum-yum

# SEVEN-LETTER WORDS

| | | | |
|---|---|---|---|
| A | achieve | aerobic | allowed |
| abalone | acidify | aerosol | almanac |
| abandon | acidity | affable | almoner |
| abashed | acolyte | affably | almonry |
| abdomen | aconite | afflict | already |
| abiding | acquire | affront | althaea |
| abigail | acreage | against | alumina |
| ability | acrobat | ageless | alumnus |
| abluent | acronym | agendum | alunite |
| abolish | acrylic | aggress | amalgam |
| abreast | actress | agility | amateur |
| abridge | actuary | agitate | amatory |
| abscess | actuate | agonise | amazing |
| abscind | acutely | agraffe | ambient |
| abscond | adamant | aground | amenity |
| absence | adaxial | aileron | amentia |
| absinth | address | ailment | amiable |
| absolve | adducer | aimless | amiably |
| abstain | adenoid | airline | ammeter |
| abusive | adherer | airmail | ammonal |
| abuttal | adipose | airport | ammonia |
| abysmal | adjourn | alameda | amnesia |
| academy | adjudge | albumen | amnesty |
| acclaim | adjunct | alchemy | amongst |
| account | adjurer | alcohol | amorist |
| accused | admiral | alfalfa | amorous |
| accuser | adrenal | algebra | amphora |
| acerbic | adulate | aliform | amplify |
| acerose | advance | aliment | ampoule |
| acetate | adverse | alimony | amusing |
| acetify | adviser | aliquot | anaemia |
| acetone | Aeolian | allegro | anaemic |
| acetose | aerator | allergy | anagoge |

anagram
analogy
analyse
analyst
anarchy
anatomy
anchovy
ancient
andante
andiron
android
anemone
angelic
angelus
angling
angrily
anguish
angular
aniline
animate
animism
aniseed
annelid
annuity
annular
annulus
anodyne
anomaly
another
antacid
antenna
anthrax
antigen
antique
antonym
anxiety

anxious
anybody
anywise
apagoge
aphesis
apocope
apology
apostil
apostle
apparel
appease
applaud
applied
appoint
apprise
approve
apraxia
apricot
apropos
aptness
aquatic
aqueous
arbiter
archaic
archery
archive
archway
arduous
aridity
armhole
armoury
arousal
arraign
arrange
arrears
arrival

arsenal
arsenic
article
artisan
artiste
artless
ascetic
ascribe
asepsis
asexual
ashamed
asinine
askance
asperse
asphalt
aspirer
aspirin
asquint
assault
assegai
assuage
astatic
astound
astride
asunder
atelier
atheism
athlete
athwart
atomise
atrophy
attache
attempt
attract
auction
audible

audibly
auditor
augment
aureole
auricle
auroral
auspice
austere
austral
autopsy
avarice
avenger
average
aviator
avidity
avocado
awesome
awfully
awkward
awnless
axially
axolotl
azurite
azygous

B
babbler
babyish
baccate
bacchic
backlog
baffler
bagasse
baggage
bagpipe
bailiff

| | | | |
|---|---|---|---|
| balance | bassoon | belated | billing |
| balcony | bastard | believe | billion |
| baldric | bastion | bellhop | billowy |
| baleful | bathtub | bellows | biltong |
| ballade | batiste | beloved | bindery |
| ballast | batsman | belting | binding |
| balloon | battery | bemused | biology |
| baloney | bauxite | beneath | biplane |
| bambino | bayonet | benefit | bipolar |
| bandage | bazooka | benison | birchen |
| bandeau | beached | benzene | biretta |
| bandore | beanbag | benzine | biscuit |
| baneful | bearded | benzoin | bismuth |
| banking | beastly | bequest | bittern |
| banksia | beatify | bereave | bitumen |
| bannock | beating | berried | bivalve |
| banquet | because | berserk | bivouac |
| banshee | bedding | beseech | bizarre |
| banting | bedevil | besides | blabber |
| baptise | bedight | besiege | blacken |
| baptism | Bedouin | besmear | bladder |
| barbell | bedrock | bespeak | blarney |
| bargain | bedroom | bespoke | blasted |
| barilla | bedside | bestial | blaster |
| barking | bedsore | betoken | blatant |
| barmaid | bedtick | between | blather |
| baronet | beeftea | betwixt | bleeder |
| baroque | beehive | bewitch | blemish |
| barrack | beeline | biaxial | blender |
| barrage | beeswax | bicycle | blessed |
| barrier | beggary | bidding | blether |
| barring | begonia | bifocal | blewits |
| bashful | begrime | bigoted | blinder |
| basilar | beguile | bigotry | blindly |
| basinet | beguine | biliary | blinker |
| bassist | bejewel | bilious | blister |

| | | | |
|---|---|---|---|
| bloated | boycott | buckish | C |
| blooded | bracken | buckler | cabaret |
| blooper | bradawl | bucolic | cabbala |
| blossom | braille | budding | cabinet |
| blotchy | bramble | buffalo | caboose |
| blotter | bravado | buffoon | cadaver |
| blowdry | bravura | bugbear | cadence |
| blowfly | brazier | buggery | cadenza |
| blubber | breadth | builder | cadmium |
| blueing | breathe | bulbous | caesura |
| boarded | brevier | bulimia | cahoots |
| boarish | brevity | bulldog | caisson |
| boggler | brewery | bullion | calcify |
| boiling | bribery | bullock | calcite |
| boletus | briefly | bulrush | calcium |
| bollard | brigand | bulwark | callous |
| boloney | brindle | bumpkin | caloric |
| bolster | brioche | bungler | calorie |
| bombard | brisket | bunting | calotte |
| bombast | bristle | buoyant | calumny |
| bonanza | brittle | burette | Calvary |
| bondage | broaden | burgess | calypso |
| bonfire | brocade | burgher | cambric |
| bookish | broiler | burglar | camphor |
| boorish | brokage | burnish | campion |
| booster | bromate | bursary | camwood |
| bordure | bromide | bushing | canasta |
| boredom | bromine | bushman | candent |
| borough | bronchi | bussing | candour |
| boscage | bronzed | bustard | cannery |
| botanic | brothel | butcher | cannula |
| boudoir | brother | buttery | canteen |
| boulder | brought | buttock | canvass |
| bouncer | bruiser | buzzard | capable |
| bouquet | brusque | bygones | capital |
| bourbon | brutish | | caprice |

| | | | |
|---|---|---|---|
| capsize | Celsius | chattel | circled |
| capstan | censure | chatter | circuit |
| capsule | centaur | cheapen | cistern |
| caption | centime | cheaply | citable |
| captive | central | cheater | citadel |
| capture | century | checker | cithara |
| caramel | ceramic | cheetah | citizen |
| caravan | certain | chemise | citrate |
| caravel | certify | chemist | clacker |
| carbine | cesspit | chequer | clamant |
| carcase | chablis | cherish | clamber |
| carcass | chagrin | cheroot | clamour |
| cardiac | chalice | chevron | clanger |
| careful | challis | Chianti | clapper |
| caribou | chamber | chicane | clarify |
| carnage | chamfer | chicory | clarion |
| carotid | chamois | chiffon | clarity |
| carping | chancel | chignon | classic |
| carrion | chancre | chimera | clatter |
| cartage | channel | chimney | clavier |
| cartoon | chanson | chintzy | cleaner |
| cascade | chaotic | chinwag | cleanly |
| cashier | chapeau | chloral | cleanse |
| cassava | chaplet | chloric | clearer |
| cassock | chapman | cholera | clearly |
| casuist | chapped | chopper | cleaver |
| catarrh | chapter | chorale | clement |
| caterer | charade | chorizo | clicker |
| cathode | charger | chortle | climate |
| caudate | charily | chowder | climber |
| caustic | chariot | chrisom | clinker |
| caution | charity | chronic | clipper |
| cavalry | charter | chuckle | clobber |
| cedilla | chassis | chunder | closely |
| ceiling | chasten | chutney | closing |
| cellule | chateau | cindery | closure |

| | | | |
|---|---|---|---|
| clothes | combing | conduit | contuse |
| cloying | comfort | confect | convene |
| cluster | comical | confess | convent |
| clutter | command | confide | convert |
| coalman | commend | confine | convict |
| coarsen | comment | confirm | convoke |
| coaster | commode | confuse | cookery |
| coaxial | commune | confute | coolant |
| cobbler | commute | congeal | copilot |
| cocaine | compact | congest | copious |
| cochlea | company | conical | coppery |
| cockney | compare | conifer | coppice |
| cockpit | compass | conjoin | copyist |
| coconut | compere | conjure | coracle |
| codeine | compete | connate | cordage |
| codicil | compile | connect | cordate |
| codling | complex | conning | cordial |
| coeliac | compose | connive | cordite |
| coexist | compost | connote | corkage |
| cogency | compote | conquer | cornice |
| cognate | compute | consent | Cornish |
| coinage | comrade | consign | corolla |
| coition | concave | consist | coronal |
| colicky | conceal | console | coroner |
| colitis | concede | consult | coronet |
| collage | conceit | consume | correct |
| collate | concept | contact | corrode |
| collect | concern | contain | corrupt |
| colleen | concert | contemn | corsage |
| college | concise | contend | corsair |
| collide | concoct | content | cortege |
| collier | concord | contest | costume |
| collude | concuss | context | coterie |
| cologne | condemn | contort | cottage |
| colonel | condone | contour | coulter |
| combine | conduct | control | council |

| | | | |
|---|---|---|---|
| counsel | crisply | cunning | dashpot |
| counter | critter | cupping | dastard |
| country | croaker | cuprite | dauphin |
| coupler | crochet | cuprous | dawdler |
| couplet | crocket | curable | dawning |
| courage | crofter | curator | dazzler |
| courier | crooked | curette | deadpan |
| courser | croquet | curious | dealing |
| courtly | crosier | current | deathly |
| couture | crossed | cursing | debacle |
| cowgirl | crowbar | cursive | debased |
| cowherd | crowded | cursory | debater |
| cowlick | crowned | curtail | debauch |
| cowling | crucify | curtain | debouch |
| cowslip | crudely | cushion | debrief |
| coxcomb | crudity | custard | decagon |
| coyness | cruelly | custody | decease |
| cracked | cruelty | cuticle | deceive |
| cracker | cruiser | cutlass | decency |
| crackle | crumble | cutlery | decibel |
| cranial | crumbly | cutting | decided |
| cranium | crumpet | cyanide | decimal |
| crazily | crumple | cyclone | declare |
| creator | crusade | cynical | decline |
| credits | cryptal | cypress | decoder |
| creeper | cryptic | cystoid | decorum |
| cremate | crystal | | defacto |
| crenate | cubicle | D | defamer |
| creosol | cuckold | dabbler | default |
| crested | cudweed | dallier | defence |
| crevice | cuirass | damning | defiant |
| cricket | cuisine | dangler | deficit |
| cricoid | cullion | danseur | defiler |
| crimson | culprit | dappled | deflate |
| crinkle | culture | darling | deflect |
| cripple | culvert | dashing | defraud |

| | | | |
|---|---|---|---|
| defunct | despond | dilemma | distend |
| degrade | dessert | diluent | distich |
| deicide | destine | dimeter | distort |
| deistic | destiny | dimness | disturb |
| delight | destroy | dimpled | disyoke |
| delouse | detente | dinette | diurnal |
| Delphic | detract | diocese | diverge |
| deltaic | devalue | dioptre | diverse |
| deltoid | develop | diploma | divisor |
| demerit | deviant | dipolar | divorce |
| demesne | deviate | diptych | divulge |
| demonic | devilry | direful | dizzily |
| demotic | devious | disable | dockage |
| denizen | devolve | disavow | doeskin |
| density | devoted | disband | dogdays |
| dentate | devotee | discard | doggish |
| dentine | dextral | discern | doggone |
| dentist | dextrin | discord | dogwood |
| denture | diagram | discuss | doleful |
| deplete | dialect | disdain | dolphin |
| deplore | diamond | disease | domical |
| deposit | diarist | disgust | dominie |
| deprave | dibbler | disjoin | doormat |
| depress | dickens | dislike | doorway |
| deprive | dictate | dismiss | dormant |
| derange | diction | disobey | dossier |
| derrick | dietary | display | doublet |
| dervish | dieting | disport | doubter |
| descant | diffuse | dispose | douceur |
| descend | digamma | dispute | doughty |
| descent | digging | disrobe | dowager |
| deserve | digital | disrupt | drabble |
| despair | dignity | dissect | drachma |
| despise | digraph | dissent | draftee |
| despite | digress | distaff | dragoon |
| despoil | dilator | distain | drapery |

drastic
draught
dreamer
dredger
dresser
dribble
drifter
drinker
drizzle
drizzly
droplet
droshky
drought
druidic
drummer
drunken
dualism
dualist
duality
dubiety
dubious
ducally
duchess
ductile
dudgeon
dulcify
dullard
dungeon
dunnage
durable
durably
durance
durmast
dustbin
duteous
dutiful

duumvir
dweller
dwindle
dynamic
dynasty
dysuria

E
eagerly
earache
eardrum
earldom
earnest
earring
earshot
earthen
earthly
easeful
ebonise
ebonite
ebriety
ecbolic
echelon
echidna
eclipse
ecology
ecstasy
ectopic
ectypal
edifice
edition
educate
effable
effulge
egotism
egotist

eidolon
ejector
elastic
elation
elderly
elector
electro
elegant
elegiac
elegise
elegist
element
elevate
elision
elitism
ellipse
elusion
elusive
Elysian
Elysium
emanate
embargo
embassy
emblaze
embolus
embower
embrace
embroil
embryos
emerald
emersed
eminent
emirate
emotion
emotive
empathy

emperor
empiric
empower
empress
emulate
emulous
enamour
enclave
enclose
encrust
endemic
endless
endorse
enfeoff
engaged
English
engorge
engraft
engrail
engrain
engrave
engross
enhance
enounce
enquire
ensnare
entente
enthral
enthuse
entitle
entomic
entrant
entreat
entropy
entrust
entwine

| | | | |
|---|---|---|---|
| envelop | estuary | extract | fashion |
| envious | etching | extreme | fateful |
| environ | eternal | extrude | fatigue |
| eparchy | ethical | exudate | fatuity |
| epaulet | evacuee | eyeball | fatuous |
| epicarp | evangel | eyebrow | fearful |
| epicene | evasion | eyelash | feather |
| epicure | evening | | feature |
| epigram | evident | F | febrile |
| episode | exactly | faceted | federal |
| epistle | examine | faction | feeding |
| epitaph | example | factory | feeling |
| epithet | excerpt | factual | feigned |
| epitome | excited | faculty | fencing |
| epizoon | exclaim | faddish | feoffer |
| epochal | exclude | failing | feoffor |
| epsilon | excreta | failure | ferment |
| equable | excrete | faintly | fernery |
| equably | execute | fairing | ferrate |
| equally | exhaust | fairway | ferrous |
| equator | exhibit | fallacy | ferrule |
| equerry | exigent | falsify | fertile |
| equinox | exotica | falsity | fervent |
| erasure | expanse | fanatic | fervour |
| erector | expense | fancied | festive |
| eremite | expiate | fancier | festoon |
| eristic | explain | fancies | fetlock |
| erosion | explode | fanfare | fewness |
| erotica | exploit | fantail | fiancée |
| erotism | explore | fantasy | fiascos |
| erratic | exposed | faraway | fibroid |
| erratum | expound | farming | fibrous |
| erudite | express | farrago | fiction |
| escapee | expunge | farrier | fiddler |
| esquire | exscind | farther | fidgety |
| essence | extinct | fascist | fielder |

| | | | |
|---|---|---|---|
| fifteen | flicker | forbore | freebie |
| fighter | flighty | forceps | freedom |
| figment | flipper | forcing | freesia |
| figural | flitter | forearm | freezer |
| filbert | flivver | foreign | freight |
| filcher | floater | foreleg | freshen |
| finally | florist | foreman | fretful |
| finance | flotsam | foremen | fretsaw |
| finding | flounce | forerun | fretted |
| finesse | flowery | foresee | friable |
| finical | flowing | foretop | frigate |
| finicky | fluency | forever | Frisbee |
| firearm | flummox | forfeit | frisket |
| firefly | flunkey | forgave | frisson |
| firemen | fluoric | forgery | fritter |
| firstly | fluster | forging | frizzle |
| fishery | fluting | forgive | frogman |
| fission | flutter | forlorn | frontal |
| fissure | fluvial | Formica | fuchsia |
| fistula | fluxion | formula | fulcrum |
| fitness | flyaway | forsake | fulsome |
| fitting | flyleaf | fortify | fumbler |
| fixable | foliage | fortune | funeral |
| fixated | foliate | forward | fungoid |
| fixture | foliose | fossick | fungous |
| flaccid | fondant | founder | funnily |
| flanker | foolery | foundry | furbish |
| flannel | foolish | fragile | furious |
| flapper | footage | frailty | furlong |
| flaring | footman | framing | furnace |
| flatten | foppery | frankly | furnish |
| flaunty | foppish | frantic | furrier |
| flavour | forager | fraught | further |
| fleapit | foramen | frazzle | furtive |
| flexion | forbade | freckle | |
| flexure | forbear | freckly | |

G
gainful
gainsay
Galilee
galipot
gallant
galleon
gallery
galling
gallows
gambier
gambler
gambrel
gangway
garbage
garfish
garland
garment
garnish
gaseous
gastric
gateway
gavotte
gazelle
gazette
gearing
gelding
general
generic
genesis
genetic
genital
genteel
gentian
gentile
genuine

geology
germane
Gestapo
gestate
gesture
ghastly
gherkin
ghostly
giblets
giggler
gilding
gimmick
gingham
ginseng
gipsies
giraffe
girlish
glacial
glacier
gladden
glamour
glaring
glazier
glazing
gleaner
gleeful
glimmer
glimpse
glisten
glister
glitter
globule
glorify
glottal
glottis
glowing

glucose
gluteal
gluteus
glutton
glyphic
glyptic
gnarled
gnocchi
gnostic
gobbler
goddess
Godhead
godless
godlike
godsend
goliard
gondola
goodbye
gorilla
gosling
gouache
goulash
gourmet
gradate
gradual
grafter
grained
grammar
granary
grandee
grandly
grandma
grandpa
granite
grannie
grantor

granule
graphic
grapnel
grapple
gratify
grating
gravely
gravity
grazier
Grecian
gremlin
grenade
greyish
griddle
griffin
griffon
grimace
grinder
griping
gristle
gristly
grizzle
grizzly
grocery
grommet
grooved
grossly
grottos
grouchy
groupie
grubber
grumble
grunter
guanaco
guarded
gudgeon

| | | | |
|---|---|---|---|
| gumboil | Hansard | hearsay | highboy |
| gunboat | hapless | hearten | highway |
| gunfire | happily | heathen | hillock |
| gunnery | harbour | heather | himself |
| gunshot | hardily | heating | hircine |
| gunwale | haricot | heavily | hirsute |
| gushing | harmful | Hebraic | history |
| gutless | harmony | heckler | hoarder |
| guzzler | harness | hectare | hobnail |
| gymnast | harpist | hedging | hogwash |
| | harpoon | hedonic | holding |
| H | harrier | heedful | holiday |
| habitat | harshly | heinous | holland |
| hackler | harvest | heirdom | holster |
| hackles | hashish | heiress | Homburg |
| hackney | hassock | helical | Homeric |
| haddock | hastily | helipad | hominid |
| haggard | hatband | hellish | homonym |
| haggish | hatchet | helpful | honesty |
| haggler | hateful | helping | honeyed |
| halberd | haughty | hemlock | hoodlum |
| halcyon | haulage | henpeck | hopeful |
| halfway | haulier | herbage | horizon |
| halibut | haunted | heretic | hormone |
| halogen | hautboy | heritor | horrify |
| halyard | hauteur | hernial | hosanna |
| hammock | hawking | heroine | hosiery |
| hamster | haycock | heroism | hospice |
| hanaper | hayrick | heronry | hostage |
| handbag | haywire | herring | hostess |
| handful | heading | hetaera | hostile |
| handler | headway | hexagon | hotfoot |
| handout | healing | hexapod | hothead |
| handsaw | healthy | hickory | housing |
| hanging | hearing | hidalgo | howbeit |
| hangman | hearken | hideous | howling |

hulking
humanly
humdrum
humidly
humidor
hummock
hunting
hurling
hurried
hurtful
husband
huskily
hyaloid
hydrant
hydrate
hydrous
hygiene
hymnody

I
Iberian
iceberg
icepack
iciness
idiotic
idolise
idyllic
igneous
ignoble
ignobly
ikebana
illegal
illicit
illness
imagery
imagine

imbiber
imitate
immense
immerge
immerse
immoral
impasse
impaste
impasto
impeach
imperil
impetus
impiety
impinge
impious
implant
implode
implore
impound
impress
imprest
imprint
improve
impulse
inanity
inboard
inbreed
incense
incisor
incline
include
incubus
indexer
indexes
indices
indoors

inducer
indulge
ineptly
inertia
inexact
infancy
infante
inferno
infidel
inflame
inflate
inflect
inflict
ingoing
ingrain
ingrate
ingress
inhabit
inhaler
inherit
inhibit
inhuman
initial
inkling
inkwell
innards
innings
inquest
inquire
inquiry
inshore
insider
insight
insipid
inspect
inspire

install
instant
instate
instead
instill
insular
insulin
insurer
integer
intense
interim
intrude
inutile
invader
invalid
inveigh
inverse
invoice
involve
iridium
irksome
isohyet
isolate
isonomy
isotope
isthmus
itemise
iterate

J
jackass
jackdaw
jackpot
jacktar
Jacobin
jaconet

Jacuzzi
janitor
jasmine
javelin
jawbone
jaywalk
jealous
Jehovah
jejunum
jittery
jobless
jocular
joinder
joinery
joining
jointed
jointer
jointly
jollify
jollity
jonquil
jotting
journal
journey
jouster
joyless
jubilee
Judaism
juggler
jugular
jujitsu
jumbuck
juniper
Jupiter
juryman
jurymen

justice
justify

K
keelson
keeping
kenosis
keratin
kerbing
kestrel
ketchup
keyhole
keynote
kibbutz
killing
killjoy
kiloton
kindred
kinetic
kingcup
kingdom
kinglet
kinless
kinship
kinsman
kinsmen
kirtled
kitchen
kithara
knacker
knavery
knavish
kneeler
knitter
knobbed
knocker

knotted
knowing
knuckle
Kremlin
Krishna
krypton

L
labarum
labiate
laconic
lacquer
lactate
lacteal
lactone
lactose
lacunae
lacunar
ladybug
laggard
lagging
laicise
lambast
lambent
lambert
lambkin
lamella
lampoon
languid
languor
lanolin
lantern
lanyard
larceny
lateral
lattice

launder
layette
leakage
lechery
lectern
legible
leisure
lemming
leonine
leotard
leprous
leveret
lexicon
lignite
lineage
lingual
linseed
liquefy
liqueur
liturgy
lobelia
lobster
lockage
lockjaw
lockout
locular
lodging
loftily
logging
logical
logwood
longbow
longing
longish
lookout
loosely

| | | | |
|---|---|---|---|
| lopping | maculae | manilla | miniver |
| lorgnon | madding | maniple | miracle |
| lottery | Madeira | mankind | misrule |
| lounger | madness | manlike | missile |
| loutish | Madonna | mannish | mission |
| lovable | maestro | mansard | missive |
| lowbrow | magenta | mansion | mistake |
| lowland | magical | manumit | mistily |
| lowness | magnate | marabou | mistime |
| loyally | magneto | marbled | mixable |
| loyalty | magnify | mariner | mixture |
| lozenge | Mahatma | marital | mobbish |
| lucency | mailman | marquee | mobster |
| lucerne | majesty | martial | mockery |
| lucidly | Malacca | masonry | modally |
| Lucifer | malaise | masseur | modesty |
| luckily | malaria | massive | modicum |
| luggage | Malayan | mastiff | modular |
| lugsail | malefic | matador | mofette |
| lullaby | mallard | matelot | moisten |
| lumbago | malleus | maudlin | mollify |
| lumping | malmsey | mawkish | mollusc |
| lunatic | Maltese | mayoral | momenta |
| lunette | malting | mazurka | monadic |
| lunular | mammary | meander | monarch |
| lurcher | mammoth | mediate | moneyed |
| lustful | manacle | memento | mongrel |
| lustily | manager | menthol | moniker |
| lustral | manakin | mercury | monitor |
| lustrum | manatee | miasmal | monkeys |
| | mandate | midriff | monocle |
| M | mandrel | mileage | monsoon |
| macabre | mangler | militia | monster |
| macadam | manhole | milksop | montage |
| machete | manhood | mimicry | montane |
| machine | manikin | minaret | monthly |

| | | | |
|---|---|---|---|
| moonlit | mummify | niggard | octagon |
| moorage | muncher | nirvana | octopod |
| moorhen | mundane | nitrate | octopus |
| mooring | muriate | nitrous | octuple |
| Moorish | murkily | nodular | oculist |
| moraine | murrain | nogging | oddball |
| morally | muscled | noisome | oddment |
| morceau | musette | nominal | oddness |
| mordant | musical | nominee | odorous |
| mordent | mustang | nonplus | Odyssey |
| morello | mustard | nosegay | oersted |
| morning | mustily | nostrum | oestrus |
| morocco | mutable | nourish | offence |
| morphia | mutably | novella | offhand |
| mortice | mycosis | novelty | officer |
| mortify | myeloid | noxious | offside |
| moselle | mystery | nuclear | ogreish |
| mottled | mystify | nucleus | oilskin |
| mottoes | | nullify | oldness |
| moulder | N | numeral | olivary |
| mounted | naivety | nuptial | olivine |
| Mountie | nankeen | nurture | Olympic |
| mourner | naphtha | nymphet | omicron |
| mousing | napless | | ominous |
| mouthed | narwhal | O | omnibus |
| movable | nascent | oarlock | onanism |
| movably | naughty | oarsman | onanist |
| mudlark | nebulae | oatmeal | oneness |
| muezzin | neglect | obelisk | onerous |
| muffled | neither | obesity | oneself |
| muffler | nemesis | oblique | ongoing |
| muggins | Neptune | obscene | onshore |
| mugwort | nervous | obscure | onwards |
| mullion | neurone | obverse | oolitic |
| mullock | neutral | obviate | ootheca |
| mumbler | niblick | occlude | opacity |

| | | | |
|---|---|---|---|
| opaline | otalgia | package | pattern |
| opening | otolith | paddock | patties |
| operate | otology | padrone | paucity |
| operose | ottoman | pageant | paunchy |
| opinion | ourself | paisley | paviour |
| opossum | outback | paladin | payable |
| opposed | outcast | palaver | payload |
| oppress | outcome | palette | payment |
| optical | outcrop | palfrey | payroll |
| optimal | outdoor | palmist | peacock |
| optimum | outface | palmyra | peafowl |
| opulent | outflow | panacea | peasant |
| oration | outgrow | panache | pebbled |
| oratory | outlast | pannier | peccant |
| orbital | outline | panoply | peckish |
| orchard | outlive | paprika | pedlary |
| ordered | outlook | parable | peerage |
| orderly | outmost | paradox | peeress |
| ordinal | outport | paragon | peevish |
| oregano | outpost | parapet | pelagic |
| organic | outpour | parasol | pelican |
| organum | outrage | parfait | peloria |
| orifice | outrank | parlour | peltate |
| origami | outride | parlous | penalty |
| orology | outward | parquet | penance |
| orotund | ovarian | parsley | pendant |
| Orphean | overawe | partial | pending |
| orphrey | overdue | paschal | penguin |
| osculum | oversee | passive | pennant |
| osmosis | overtly | pastern | pennies |
| osmotic | oviduct | pastime | pensile |
| osseous | ovulate | pasture | pension |
| ossicle | oxidisc | patella | pensive |
| ossuary | | pathway | peonage |
| ostiary | P | patient | peppery |
| ostrich | pacific | patrial | pepsine |

| | | | |
|---|---|---|---|
| peptone | Pharaoh | plaited | pottery |
| percale | pharynx | plateau | poultry |
| percent | philtre | platoon | poverty |
| percept | phoenix | plenary | powdery |
| perdure | phonate | pleural | prairie |
| perfect | phonics | pliable | praline |
| perfidy | phrasal | plugger | prating |
| perform | phrenic | plumage | prattle |
| perfume | physics | plummet | praying |
| perfuse | pianist | plunder | prebend |
| pergola | piastre | plywood | precede |
| perhaps | picador | poleaxe | precept |
| periapt | piccolo | polemic | precise |
| perigee | pickaxe | pollard | predate |
| periwig | picking | pollute | predict |
| perjure | pickled | polygon | preface |
| perjury | picture | polymer | prefect |
| permute | piddock | pompous | prelate |
| perplex | piebald | pontiff | prelude |
| persist | piggery | pontoon | premier |
| persona | piggish | popular | premise |
| pertain | pigment | porcine | premium |
| perturb | pigskin | portage | prepaid |
| perusal | pigtail | portend | prepare |
| pervade | pilgrim | portent | prepuce |
| pervert | pillage | portico | presage |
| pessary | pillion | portion | present |
| petrify | pillory | portray | preside |
| pettish | pincers | possess | presume |
| petunia | pioneer | postage | pretend |
| Pfennig | piquant | postern | pretext |
| phaeton | piranha | posture | pretzel |
| phalanx | pithily | potable | prevail |
| phallic | pivotal | potency | prevent |
| phallus | placate | pothole | preview |
| phantom | placebo | pottage | prickle |

prickly
primacy
primary
primate
priming
primula
printer
prithee
privacy
private
privily
privity
probate
probity
problem
proceed
process
proctor
procure
prodigy
produce
product
profane
profess
proffer
profile
profuse
progeny
program
project
prolate
prolong
promise
promote
pronate
pronged

pronoun
propane
prophet
propose
prosaic
prosody
prosper
protean
protect
protege
protein
protest
proverb
provide
proviso
provoke
provost
prowess
prowler
proximo
prudent
prudery
prudish
prurigo
psalter
psychic
ptyalin
puberty
publish
puckery
puckish
pudding
pudenda
puerile
pulsate
pumpkin

pungent
punster
puritan
purloin
purport
pursuit
putrefy
pygmies
pyjamas
pyramid
Pyrrhic

Q
quantum
quarrel
quartet
queries
quibble
quilled
quinine
quintet

R
raccoon
racquet
radiant
radiate
radical
raiment
ramekin
rampage
rampant
rampart
rancour
rapport
rapture

ratchet
raucous
raunchy
ravioli
reactor
realign
realise
realist
reality
realtor
rebirth
rebound
rebuild
receipt
receive
recital
reciter
reclaim
recline
recluse
recount
recover
recruit
rectify
rectory
recycle
redcoat
redhead
redneck
redoubt
redound
redress
redskin
referee
refined
reflect

| | | | |
|---|---|---|---|
| reforge | reposit | retrace | Riviera |
| refract | repress | retract | rivulet |
| refrain | reprint | retreat | roadway |
| refresh | reprise | retrial | roaring |
| refugee | reproof | reunion | robbery |
| refusal | reprove | reunite | rockery |
| regalia | reptant | revelry | roebuck |
| regatta | reptile | revenge | roguery |
| regency | repulse | revenue | roguish |
| regimen | reputed | reverie | rollbar |
| regnant | request | reverse | rollick |
| regrate | requiem | revisit | rolling |
| regress | require | revival | rollmop |
| regular | requite | revolve | romance |
| regulus | reredos | rewrite | rompers |
| reissue | rescind | rhenium | rondeau |
| rejoice | rescuer | rhizoid | rookery |
| relapse | reserve | rhodium | rooster |
| related | reshape | rhombic | roseate |
| relator | residue | rhombus | rosette |
| release | resolve | rhubarb | rostrum |
| reliant | resound | ribbing | rotator |
| relieve | respect | ribcage | rotunda |
| relievo | respire | rickets | roughly |
| remarry | respite | rickety | rouleau |
| remnant | respond | ricotta | rounded |
| remorse | restart | rifling | routine |
| remount | restful | rigging | rowboat |
| removal | restive | ringent | rowlock |
| removed | restore | ringlet | royally |
| renewal | rethink | riotous | royalty |
| rentier | retiary | riposte | rubbing |
| replace | reticle | risible | rubbish |
| replete | retinal | rissole | rubella |
| replevy | retinue | rivalry | rubeola |
| replica | retired | riveted | ruction |

| | | | |
|---|---|---|---|
| ruffian | sanicle | scamper | scrotal |
| ruffled | sanious | scandal | scrotum |
| ruinous | sapajou | scanner | scruffy |
| rummage | saphead | scantly | scrunch |
| rupture | sapient | scapula | scruple |
| rustler | sapling | scarify | scuffle |
| | Saracen | scarlet | sculler |
| S | sarcasm | scarper | sculpin |
| Sabbath | sarcoma | scarves | scupper |
| saccate | sarcous | scatter | scutate |
| saccule | sardine | scenery | scuttle |
| sackbut | sashimi | scented | scythed |
| sacking | satanic | sceptic | seafood |
| saddler | satchel | sceptre | seagull |
| sadness | satiate | schemer | sealant |
| saffron | satiety | scherzo | sealing |
| sailing | satinet | schmalz | seaport |
| sainted | satiric | schmuck | seasick |
| saintly | satisfy | scholar | seaside |
| salient | satrapy | scholia | seating |
| sallies | satyric | sciatic | seaward |
| salsify | saucily | science | seaweed |
| saltant | saunter | scissor | seclude |
| saltern | saurian | scoffer | secrecy |
| saltier | sausage | scooter | secrete |
| saltire | savanna | scoriae | sectile |
| saltish | saveloy | scorify | section |
| saltpan | saviour | Scorpio | secular |
| salvage | savoury | scotoma | securer |
| samisen | sawbuck | scourer | sedilia |
| samovar | sawdust | scourge | seducer |
| Samoyed | saxhorn | scraggy | seedbed |
| sampler | scabies | scratch | seedily |
| samurai | scalene | scrawny | seeming |
| sanctum | scallop | screech | seepage |
| sangria | scalpel | scribal | segment |

| | | | |
|---|---|---|---|
| seismic | shallot | shrilly | sketchy |
| seizure | shallow | shrivel | skilful |
| selenic | shamble | shudder | skilled |
| selfish | shampoo | shuffle | skillet |
| selvage | shanked | shunter | skimmer |
| sematic | shapely | shuteye | skipper |
| seminal | sharper | shutter | skitter |
| seminar | sharply | shuttle | skulker |
| Semitic | shatter | shyness | skyjack |
| senator | Shavian | shyster | skylark |
| sensory | shaving | sibling | skyline |
| sensual | shearer | sidecar | skyward |
| sequent | sheathe | sideway | slacken |
| sequoia | sheaves | siemens | slacker |
| seriate | shebang | sighted | slammer |
| serious | shellac | sightly | slander |
| serpent | shelled | signify | slashed |
| serpigo | shelter | signora | slasher |
| serrate | shelves | signore | slatted |
| serried | sherbet | silence | slavery |
| servant | sheriff | silicon | slavish |
| service | shifter | siliqua | sleekly |
| servile | shimmer | silvery | sleight |
| serving | shindig | similar | slender |
| session | shingle | simious | slicker |
| setback | shipper | sincere | sliding |
| setting | shivery | sinewed | slimmer |
| settled | shooter | singlet | slinger |
| settler | shopper | sinking | slipper |
| seventh | shorten | sinless | slipway |
| several | shortly | sinuate | slither |
| sexless | shotgun | sinuous | slitter |
| sextant | shotten | sirloin | sloughy |
| shackle | showery | sirocco | slumber |
| shading | showing | sitting | slyness |
| shafted | showman | situate | smacker |

| | | | |
|---|---|---|---|
| smarten | solvent | spinach | staring |
| smartly | somatic | spindle | starlet |
| smashed | soother | spindly | starlit |
| smatter | sophism | spinner | startle |
| smelter | sophist | spittle | stately |
| smidgen | soprano | splashy | statics |
| smidgin | sorcery | splodge | station |
| smiling | sorghum | splotch | statism |
| smitten | sorosis | splurge | statist |
| smoking | soulful | sponger | stature |
| smother | soutane | sponsor | statute |
| smuggle | sozzled | sporran | staunch |
| snaffle | spangle | springe | stealth |
| snapper | spaniel | springy | steamer |
| sneaker | spanner | sputnik | steeple |
| snicker | sparing | squabby | stellar |
| sniffle | sparkle | squalid | stencil |
| snigger | sparrow | squally | stepson |
| snippet | spastic | squalor | sterile |
| snooker | spatial | squamae | sternly |
| snorkel | spatter | squashy | sternum |
| snorter | spatula | squeeze | steroid |
| snowcap | special | squelch | stetson |
| snowman | species | squiffy | steward |
| snuffle | specify | squinch | stibial |
| snuggle | speckle | stabile | stichic |
| soaking | spectra | stacked | sticker |
| soapbox | spectre | staddle | stickle |
| soberly | speller | stadium | stiffen |
| society | spelter | stagger | stiffly |
| sockeye | spencer | staging | stilted |
| sojourn | spender | stalked | stimuli |
| soldier | spheral | stamina | stipend |
| solicit | spheric | stammer | stipple |
| soloist | spicate | stannic | stipule |
| soluble | spidery | stapler | stirrer |

| | | | |
|---|---|---|---|
| stirrup | stylite | sunfish | swindle |
| stoical | styloid | sunlamp | swollen |
| stomach | suavely | sunrise | syllabi |
| stomata | suavity | sunroof | sylphid |
| stopgap | subacid | sunspot | symptom |
| stopper | subdued | sunward | synapse |
| stopple | subject | support | synergy |
| storage | sublime | suppose | synodic |
| stories | subside | supreme | synonym |
| stowage | subsidy | supremo | syringe |
| strange | subsist | surface | systole |
| stratum | subsoil | surfeit | |
| stratus | subsume | surfing | T |
| strayer | subtend | surgeon | tableau |
| streaky | subvert | surgery | tabloid |
| stretch | succeed | surmise | taborer |
| striate | success | surname | taboret |
| strigil | succour | surpass | tabular |
| striker | succumb | surplus | tacitly |
| stringy | sucking | surreal | tactics |
| striped | sucrose | survive | tactile |
| strophe | suction | suspect | taction |
| strudel | suffice | suspend | tactual |
| strumae | suffuse | sustain | tadpole |
| stubbed | suggest | sutured | taffeta |
| stubble | suicide | swagger | takeoff |
| stubbly | sulfate | swallow | talcose |
| student | sulkily | swarthy | talcous |
| studied | sulphur | sweater | taliped |
| stumble | sultana | sweeper | talipes |
| stumper | summary | sweeten | talipot |
| stunner | summons | sweetie | talking |
| stupefy | sunbeam | sweetly | tallage |
| Stygian | sunburn | swelter | tallboy |
| stylish | sundial | swiftly | tallier |
| stylist | sundown | swimmer | tallies |

| | | | |
|---|---|---|---|
| tallith | tequila | thready | tonnage |
| tambour | termini | thrifty | tonsure |
| tampion | termite | through | tontine |
| tanager | ternary | thulium | toothed |
| tanbark | terrace | thunder | topical |
| tangent | terrain | thyroid | topless |
| tangram | terrene | thyrsus | topmost |
| tankage | terrier | thyself | topping |
| tankard | terrify | ticking | topsail |
| tannage | terrine | tickler | topsoil |
| tannery | tersely | tidings | torment |
| tanning | tertian | tiffany | tornado |
| tantrum | testacy | tighten | torpedo |
| tapioca | testate | tightly | torrent |
| tarnish | testify | tigress | torsion |
| tattler | tetanic | tillage | tortile |
| taurine | tetanus | timbrel | torture |
| taxable | textile | timidly | totally |
| teacher | textual | timpani | totemic |
| tearful | texture | tinfoil | tottery |
| teargas | thallus | tinting | touched |
| tearing | theatre | tippler | toughen |
| tedious | theorbo | tipster | tourism |
| teeming | theorem | titanic | tourist |
| tegular | therapy | tithing | tourney |
| telling | thereby | titlark | towards |
| tempest | thermal | titmice | towered |
| tempura | thicken | titular | towrope |
| tenable | thicket | toaster | trachea |
| tenancy | thieves | tobacco | tracing |
| tendril | thimble | toccata | tracker |
| tenfold | thinker | toddler | tractor |
| tensile | thirsty | toehold | trading |
| tension | thistle | toenail | traduce |
| tenuity | thorium | tombola | traffic |
| tenuous | thought | tonight | tragedy |

| | | | |
|---|---|---|---|
| trailer | triplet | turbine | unchain |
| trained | tripper | turmoil | uncivil |
| trainee | trireme | turning | unclean |
| trainer | trisect | turnkey | uncouth |
| traipse | tritium | turnout | uncover |
| traitor | triumph | tussock | unction |
| trammel | trivial | twaddle | undergo |
| trample | trochal | twelfth | undoing |
| tramway | trodden | twibill | undress |
| trannie | trolley | twiddle | undying |
| transit | trollop | twining | unearth |
| transom | trooper | twinkle | unequal |
| trapeze | trophic | twinned | ungodly |
| trapper | tropism | twister | unguent |
| travail | trotter | twitter | unhappy |
| trawler | trouble | twofold | unheard |
| treacle | trounce | twosome | unhinge |
| treadle | trouper | tympana | unhorse |
| treason | truancy | tympani | unicorn |
| trekker | trucker | typeset | uniform |
| trellis | truckle | typhoid | unities |
| tremble | truffle | typhoon | unkempt |
| tremolo | trumpet | typhous | unknown |
| trepang | trundle | typical | unleash |
| trestle | trussed | tyranny | unlucky |
| tribune | trustee | | unmanly |
| tribute | trypsin | U | unmixed |
| triceps | tsarina | ukelele | unmoved |
| trickle | tsunami | ululate | unnamed |
| trident | tubular | umbrage | unnerve |
| triform | Tuesday | umpteen | unnoted |
| trigger | tugboat | unarmed | unquote |
| trilogy | tuition | unaware | unravel |
| trimmer | tumbler | unbound | unready |
| trinity | tumbrel | unbowed | unscrew |
| trinket | tuneful | uncanny | unshorn |

| | | | |
|---|---|---|---|
| unsound | vacuous | verdant | viscous |
| unspent | vacuums | verdict | visible |
| untamed | vaginal | verdure | visibly |
| untruly | vagrant | versify | visitor |
| unusual | valance | version | vitamin |
| upbraid | valency | vertigo | vitiate |
| upgrade | valiant | vesical | vitrify |
| upright | valvate | vesicle | vitriol |
| upsilon | vamoose | vespine | vivaria |
| upstage | vampire | vestige | vividly |
| upstart | vanilla | vesture | volcano |
| upsurge | vantage | veteran | voltage |
| upswing | vapidly | vexilla | voluble |
| uptight | variant | viaduct | voucher |
| upwards | variety | vibrant | voyager |
| uraemia | various | vibrate | vulpine |
| uranium | varmint | vibrato | vulture |
| urethra | varnish | viceroy | |
| urgency | varsity | vicinal | W |
| urinary | Vatican | vicious | wadding |
| urinate | vaulted | victory | waddles |
| urology | vedette | victual | waggish |
| useless | veering | viduity | wagoner |
| usually | vegetal | village | wagtail |
| utensil | vehicle | villain | wailing |
| utilise | velamen | villein | waiting |
| utility | velours | vincula | wakeful |
| Utopian | velvety | vinegar | walkout |
| utricle | venatic | vintage | walkway |
| utterly | venison | vintner | wallaby |
| uxorial | ventage | violate | warbler |
| | ventral | violent | warfare |
| V | venture | violist | warhead |
| vacancy | veranda | virtual | warlike |
| vaccine | verbena | viscera | warlock |
| vacuity | verbose | viscose | warlord |

| | | | |
|---|---|---|---|
| warning | weighty | willing | wrecked |
| warpath | welcome | willowy | wrestle |
| warrant | welfare | windage | wriggle |
| warrior | wellies | windbag | wringer |
| warship | western | winding | wrinkle |
| washing | wetness | winglet | writing |
| waspish | whaling | winsome | written |
| wassail | wharves | wishful | wrongly |
| wastage | wheaten | wistful | wrought |
| wasting | wheedle | withers | wryness |
| wastrel | wheeler | without | |
| watcher | wheelie | witless | X |
| wattage | whereas | witness | xanthic |
| wavelet | whether | wizened | xanthin |
| waverer | whetter | wobbler | |
| waxwork | whimper | wolfish | Y |
| waybill | whippet | womanly | yardage |
| wayside | whisker | woodcut | yashmak |
| wayward | whisper | woodman | yawning |
| wealthy | whistle | woollen | Yiddish |
| wearily | whither | wordily | yoghurt |
| wearing | whiting | wording | younker |
| weather | whitish | workday | |
| weaving | whittle | workshy | Z |
| webbing | whoever | worldly | zealous |
| Website | whoopee | worrier | zeolite |
| wedding | whopper | worship | zillion |
| wedlock | widower | worsted | zincous |
| weekday | wielder | wrangle | zoogamy |
| weekend | wigless | wrapper | zoology |
| weeping | wildcat | wreathe | |

# SEVEN-LETTER MULTIPLE WORDS

## A
air-base
air-lock
also-ran
ant-bear
ant-bird
ant-hill

## B
back pay
bail out
ball boy
bear hug
bee-moth
bell-boy
beta ray
big bang
big-time
bit part
bone-ash
bone-dry
brush up
built-in
built-up
bunk bed
buzz-saw

## C
cat scan
check up
cold war
cue ball

## D
dab hand
drop out
dead-end
dead-eye
deep-sea
dew-claw
dew-drop
die-hard
do proud
drag-net
drip-dry
drive-in

## E
ebb-tide
egg-flip
ego-trip
en masse
en route

## F
fall guy
fall-out
faux pas
flare-up
fox-trot

## G
G-string
gear-box
go Dutch
go-ahead

grown-up
gum tree

## H
hack-saw
hair-net
hair-pin
half-wit
hands-on
hang out
hare-lip
has-been
heel-tap
high-hat
hit list
hot line
hyped up

## I
ice pick
ice-fall
ice-floe
ice-foot
ill-bred
ill-will
ill-wind
in-depth
in-house
in so far
Iron Age

## J
John Doe

juke-box

## K
keep mum
kick-off
king-pin
knee-cap
knees-up
know-all
know-how

## L
log-book
look-see
lose out
low tide
low-bred
low-down
low-life
low-rise
low-tech
luck-out
lump sum
lying-in

## M
make hay
make way
man-hour
man-made
mixed-up
mug-shot
musk-rat

N
nest egg

O
off-line
off-load
oil well
old gold
old hand
old maid
old-time
open air

P
patch up
pay dirt
pen name
pep pill
pep talk
phone-in
pot shot
pre-empt
press-up
pro rata

pro-life

R
re-cover
re-entry
read-out
right on
rip cord
road hog
roe deer

S
sand box
sea lane
sea legs
sea lion
sea wall
sell out
send-off
shake-up
shape up
shot put
ski pole
skid row

sky-blue
sky-high
snarl-up
so and so
stand-by
stand-in
stand-up
stick-up
stir-fry
swear by

T
tail-end
take-out
tally-ho
tax-free
tea cosy
the pits
throw up
tie line
time lag
time off
time-out

top gear
tote bag
trade-in
turn off
twin-tub
two-step

W
wart hog
weigh up
weigh-in
well-off
wet suit
whiz kid
who's who
wild oat
wine bar
wine box
wing nut
wise guy
work-out
would-be
wry-neck

# EIGHT-LETTER WORDS

A
aardvark
abattoir
abdicate
abductor
aberrant
abetment
abeyance
abjectly
ablative
ablution
abnegate
abnormal
abomasum
abortion
abortive
abradant
abrasion
abrasive
abrogate
abruptly
abscissa
absentee
absently
absolute
absolver
abstract
abstruse
absurdly
abundant
abutment
academic
accident

accolade
accoutre
accredit
accuracy
accurate
accursed
accustom
acentric
acerbity
achiever
acidosis
acoustic
acquaint
acridity
acrimony
acrostic
actinism
actinium
actinoid
activate
actively
activist
activity
actually
aculeate
addendum
addition
additive
adenoids
adequacy
adequate
adherent
adhesion

adhesive
adjacent
adjuster
adjutant
admonish
adoption
adoptive
adorable
adorably
adroitly
adscript
adultery
advanced
advancer
advisory
advocaat
advocacy
advocate
aeration
aerially
aerobics
aesthete
affected
affiance
affinity
affluent
afforest
affright
aggrieve
agitated
agitator
agnostic
agrarian

agrimony
agronomy
aigrette
airborne
airbrush
aircraft
airfield
airiness
airshaft
airspace
airstrip
airtight
alacrity
alarming
alarmist
albinism
alderman
aldermen
alehouse
alfresco
alienate
alkaline
alkalise
alkaloid
allegory
alleluia
allergen
alliance
allocate
allspice
alluring
allusion
allusive

| | | | |
|---|---|---|---|
| alluvial | angelica | appetite | arterial |
| alluvion | animated | applause | Artesian |
| alluvium | animator | apposite | articled |
| almighty | annalist | appraise | artifice |
| alphabet | annotate | approach | artistic |
| alpinist | announce | approval | artistry |
| Alsatian | annually | apterous | asbestos |
| alterant | annulate | aptitude | asperity |
| although | anorexia | aqualung | asphyxia |
| altitude | anteater | aquarium | aspirant |
| altruism | antecede | Aquarius | aspirate |
| alveolar | antedate | aquatics | aspiring |
| ambience | antelope | aqueduct | assassin |
| ambition | anterior | aquiline | assaying |
| ambrosia | anteroom | arachnid | assemble |
| ambulant | antibody | arboreal | assembly |
| ambulate | antidote | arborist | assessor |
| amenable | antimony | Arcadian | assignee |
| amenably | antipode | archaism | assonant |
| American | antitype | archduke | assorted |
| amethyst | antlered | archives | asterisk |
| amicable | anything | ardently | asteroid |
| amicably | anywhere | argonaut | astonish |
| ammonite | aperient | arguable | astutely |
| amperage | aperitif | arguably | Athenian |
| amputate | aperture | argument | athletic |
| anaconda | aphorism | aristate | atomiser |
| analects | apiarian | armament | atrocity |
| analogue | apiarist | armature | attacker |
| analysis | apodosis | armchair | attestor |
| anarchic | apologia | armoured | attitude |
| anathema | apoplexy | aromatic | attorney |
| ancestor | apostasy | arpeggio | atypical |
| ancestry | apostate | arrogant | audacity |
| andirons | apparent | arrogate | audience |
| anecdote | appendix | artefact | audition |

auditory
Augustan
Austrian
autobahn
autocrat
automate
autonomy
autotype
autumnal
aversion
aviation
avifauna
avowable
avowedly

B
baccarat
bachelor
bacillus
backbite
backbone
backchat
backdate
backdrop
backfire
backhand
backlash
backpack
backside
backspin
backwash
backyard
bacteria
badinage
badmouth
bagpiper

bailable
balancer
baldness
ballcock
ballyhoo
balmoral
baluster
banality
bandanna
banderol
bandsman
banister
bankable
banknote
bankrupt
banterer
barbaric
barbecue
bareback
barefoot
bareness
baritone
barnacle
barnyard
baronage
baroness
baronial
barracks
basaltic
baseless
baseline
basement
baseness
basilica
basilisk
bathrobe

beamless
bearable
bearskin
beatific
beautify
beavered
bechance
bedstead
bedstraw
beechnut
beefcake
beetling
beetroot
befriend
befuddle
begetter
beggarly
beginner
begotten
begrudge
beguiler
behemoth
beholden
beholder
belabour
believer
belittle
bellyful
bendable
benedick
benedict
benefice
bequeath
berceuse
besmirch
besotted

besought
bestride
betrayal
betrayer
beverage
bewilder
biannual
biblical
biconvex
bicuspid
biennial
bifocals
bigamist
billhook
billycan
bimanous
binaural
binnacle
biparous
birdseed
bisexual
bitterly
bivalent
biweekly
blacking
blackish
blackleg
blackout
blameful
bleacher
bleeding
blessing
blinding
blissful
blistery
blithely

| | | | |
|---|---|---|---|
| blizzard | boundary | brunette | calliope |
| blockade | boutique | brutally | calliper |
| blockage | bouzouki | buckshee | Cambrian |
| blockish | bowsprit | buckshot | cameleer |
| bloomers | bracelet | buckskin | camellia |
| blowhole | brackish | Buddhism | camisole |
| blowlamp | braggart | Buddhist | campaign |
| bludgeon | braiding | building | campfire |
| bluebell | brakeman | bulkhead | campsite |
| bluenose | brandied | bulldoze | camshaft |
| blushing | brandish | bulletin | canaille |
| boarding | brattice | bullfrog | candidly |
| boastful | brawling | bullhead | canister |
| bobbinet | breakage | bullring | cannabis |
| bodywork | breasted | bullwhip | cannibal |
| boggling | breather | bungalow | cannonry |
| Bohemian | breeched | bungling | canonise |
| boldness | breeches | buoyancy | canoodle |
| bollocks | breeding | burglary | canorous |
| bombsite | breviary | Burgundy | canticle |
| bonhomie | brickbat | busybody | capacity |
| bonneted | bridging | butchery | capriole |
| bookcase | brighten | buttress | capsicum |
| bookworm | brimless | buzzword | captious |
| bootjack | brimming | | capuchin |
| bootlace | brindled | C | caracara |
| bootless | brocaded | caboodle | caracole |
| Bordeaux | broccoli | caffeine | carapace |
| bordello | brochure | cajolery | carbolic |
| borrower | bronchia | calabash | carbonic |
| botanist | bronchus | calamine | cardigan |
| bottomed | brooklet | calamity | cardinal |
| botulism | brougham | calculus | carefree |
| bouffant | brouhaha | calendar | careless |
| bouillon | browbeat | calender | carinate |
| bouncing | browning | calfskin | carnival |

| | | | |
|---|---|---|---|
| carousel | cellaret | childbed | cleanser |
| carriage | cellular | childish | clearing |
| cartload | cemetery | chilling | cleavage |
| Casanova | cenotaph | chimaera | cleavers |
| casemate | centrist | chinless | clematis |
| casement | ceramics | chipmunk | clemency |
| casework | Cerberus | chipping | clerical |
| caseworm | cerebral | chivalry | clerihew |
| cashmere | cerebrum | chloride | climatic |
| cassette | cerement | chlorine | clincher |
| castanet | ceremony | choirboy | clinical |
| castaway | cervical | choleric | clippers |
| castrate | cesspool | chrismal | cliquish |
| casually | cetacean | christen | cloddish |
| casualty | chaconne | churlish | cloister |
| catacomb | chairman | chutzpah | clothier |
| catalyse | chancery | ciborium | clothing |
| catalyst | chandler | cicatrix | clownish |
| catapult | chaplain | cicerone | clubfoot |
| cataract | charcoal | cincture | clubhaul |
| catching | charisma | cinerary | clueless |
| category | charming | cinnamon | clumsily |
| catenate | Chartism | circular | coachman |
| catheter | chasseur | citation | coactive |
| Catholic | chastise | citatory | coalesce |
| caudated | chastity | civilian | coarsely |
| cauldron | chasuble | civility | coasting |
| causable | cheating | claimant | cobaltic |
| causally | checkout | clambake | cockatoo |
| causeway | cheerful | clannish | cockcrow |
| cautious | chemical | clansman | cockerel |
| cavalier | chenille | claptrap | cockeyed |
| caviller | cherubic | clarinet | cocksure |
| celerity | chessman | classics | cocktail |
| celibacy | chestnut | classify | codename |
| cellarer | chickpea | clavicle | codeword |

| | | | |
|---|---|---|---|
| coercion | composer | contrive | crannied |
| coercive | compound | convener | crawfish |
| cogently | compress | converge | crayfish |
| cogitate | comprise | converse | creation |
| cognomen | computer | conveyor | creative |
| coherent | conceive | convulse | creature |
| cohesion | concerto | coolness | credence |
| cohesive | conclave | copulate | credible |
| coiffeur | conclude | copybook | creditor |
| coiffure | condense | coquetry | crescent |
| coincide | confetti | coquette | crevasse |
| colander | confined | cordless | cribbage |
| coleslaw | conflict | corduroy | criminal |
| collagen | confound | coregent | crispate |
| collapse | confront | coronary | critical |
| collared | confused | corporal | critique |
| collator | congress | corridor | croaking |
| colliery | conjoint | corselet | crockery |
| colloquy | conjugal | corvette | crossbar |
| colonial | conjunct | cosmetic | crossbow |
| colossal | conjurer | costumed | crosscut |
| colossus | conquest | cotenant | croupier |
| coloured | conserve | cottager | cruciate |
| columnar | consider | coupling | crucible |
| comatose | consoler | courtesy | crucifer |
| comeback | conspire | courtier | crucifix |
| comedian | constant | covenant | crusader |
| commando | construe | coverage | crushing |
| commence | consular | coverall | cryonics |
| commerce | consumer | covering | cubiform |
| commoner | contempt | coverlet | cucumber |
| communal | continue | covetous | cufflink |
| commuter | contract | cowardly | culinary |
| complain | contrary | coxswain | culottes |
| complete | contrast | cracknel | culpable |
| composed | contrite | crackpot | cultural |

cultured
cumbrous
cumulate
cupboard
cupidity
curative
currency
curtness
cyclamen
cyclical
cyclonic
cylinder
cynicism
cystitis

D
dabchick
dactylic
daffodil
daiquiri
dalmatic
damnable
dandruff
danseuse
darkling
darkness
darkroom
database
dateless
dauphine
daybreak
daydream
daylight
dazzling
deadhead
deadline

deadlock
deadness
deafness
dealfish
dealings
deathbed
debility
debonair
debutant
decadent
decanter
deceased
decimate
decipher
decision
decisive
deckhand
decorate
decorous
decrease
decrepit
dedicate
defecate
defender
defiance
definite
deflower
deformed
defrayal
deftness
delegate
deletion
delicacy
delicate
delirium
delivery

delusion
delusory
demagogy
demarche
demented
dementia
democrat
demolish
demoniac
demonism
demurely
denarius
deniable
denounce
depilate
deportee
depraved
deprived
deputise
deranged
derelict
derision
derisive
derisory
derogate
describe
descrier
deserter
deserved
designer
desirous
desolate
despotic
destruct
detached
detailed

detainee
detector
dethrone
detonate
detoxify
detrital
detritus
devilish
devotion
devoutly
dewpoint
dextrose
diabetes
diabetic
diabolic
diaconal
diagnose
diagonal
dialling
dialogue
dialysis
diameter
dianthus
diapason
Diaspora
diastase
diastole
diatomic
diatonic
diatribe
dictator
didactic
didymous
dietetic
diffract
digitate

digitise
dihedral
dilation
dilative
dilatory
diligent
dilution
diluvial
diminish
dinosaur
diocesan
diplomat
dipstick
dipteral
directly
director
disabled
disagree
disallow
disarray
disaster
disburse
disciple
disclaim
disclose
discount
discover
discreet
diseased
disgorge
disgrace
disguise
dishevel
disinter
disjoint
dislodge

disloyal
dismount
disorder
dispatch
dispense
disperse
dispirit
displace
disposal
disposed
disprove
disquiet
dissolve
dissuade
distance
distaste
distinct
distract
distress
district
distrust
diuretic
dividend
divinity
division
divisive
divorcee
docility
dockyard
doctoral
doctrine
document
doddered
dogfight
doggedly
doggerel

dogmatic
dogsbody
doldrums
dolomite
dolorous
domestic
domicile
dominant
dominate
domineer
dominion
donation
doomsday
doorjamb
doornail
doorstop
dormouse
doubloon
doubtful
dovetail
downcast
downfall
downpour
downsize
downtown
downturn
downward
downwind
doxology
dragoman
drainage
dramatic
draughty
drawback
dreadful
dressage

dripping
driveway
dropping
drudgery
duckbill
duckling
dulcimer
dullness
dumpling
dungaree
dunghill
duodenum
duration
dwelling
dynamics
dynamite
dynastic
dyslexia
dyspnoea

E
earnings
easement
easterly
eastward
eclectic
ecliptic
economic
ecstatic
Edentate
edgeways
edgewise
edifying
educator
eeriness
efficacy

| | | | |
|---|---|---|---|
| effluent | employee | entrepot | ethereal |
| effusion | employer | enuresis | ethology |
| effusive | emporium | envelope | ethylene |
| eggplant | emulsify | enviable | etiolate |
| eggshell | encircle | environs | eucalypt |
| egoistic | encroach | envisage | eugenics |
| eighteen | encumber | epidemic | eulogise |
| ejection | endanger | epidural | euphoria |
| election | endoderm | epilepsy | Eurasian |
| elective | enduring | epilogue | evacuate |
| electric | energise | Epiphany | evaluate |
| electron | enervate | episodic | evanesce |
| elegance | enfeeble | equalise | evenness |
| elenchus | enfilade | equality | eventful |
| elevator | engaging | equation | eventide |
| eleventh | engender | equipage | eventual |
| eligible | engineer | erection | evermore |
| ellipsis | engorged | eruption | eversion |
| elongate | engraver | eruptive | everyday |
| eloquent | enkindle | escalade | everyone |
| emaciate | enormity | escalate | eviction |
| embalmer | enquirer | escapade | evidence |
| embattle | ensconce | escapism | evildoer |
| embezzle | ensemble | escapist | examinee |
| embitter | enshrine | escargot | examiner |
| emblazon | enshroud | esculent | excavate |
| embolden | ensilage | esoteric | exchange |
| embolism | entangle | espalier | excision |
| emergent | entellus | especial | exciting |
| emeritus | enthrone | espousal | execrate |
| emersion | enticing | espresso | executes |
| emigrant | entirety | essayist | executor |
| eminence | entrails | estimate | exegesis |
| emissary | entrance | estrange | exemplar |
| emission | entreaty | etcetera | exercise |
| emphatic | entrench | eternity | exertion |

exhalant
exigency
exiguous
existent
exorcise
exorcism
expedite
expertly
explicit
explorer
exponent
exporter
exposure
extender
exterior
external
exultant
exuviate
eyeglass
eyepiece
eyesight
eyeteeth

F
fabulous
faceless
facility
factotum
fadeless
fainting
faithful
falconer
falconry
falderal
fallible
falsetto

familiar
fandango
fantasia
farcical
farewell
farinose
farmyard
farriery
farthest
farthing
fastback
fatalism
fatalist
fatality
fatherly
faubourg
favoured
fearless
fearsome
feasible
feathery
featured
February
feckless
feculent
federate
feedback
felicity
feminine
feminism
ferocity
ferreter
ferryman
festival
feverfew
feverish

fibrosis
fiddling
fidelity
fiendish
figurine
filament
filature
filigree
filtrate
finalist
finality
fineness
finespun
fingered
fireball
fireplug
fireside
firmness
fitfully
fixation
flagella
flagging
flagpole
flagrant
flagship
flambeau
flamenco
flamingo
flapjack
flashing
flatfoot
flatiron
flatness
flattery
flautist
flawless

flaxseed
flection
fleeting
fletcher
flexible
flinders
flippant
floccose
flooding
floorage
flooring
flotilla
flounder
flourish
flowered
fluently
fluidity
fluoride
flypaper
fogbound
foldaway
foliated
folklore
folktale
follicle
fondling
fondness
foolscap
footfall
foothill
foothold
footnote
footpath
footslog
footwork
forceful

| | | | |
|---|---|---|---|
| forcible | fountain | fugleman | garrison |
| forebear | fourfold | fulcrums | garrotte |
| forebode | foursome | fullback | gaslight |
| forecast | fourteen | fumarole | gasoline |
| forefoot | foxglove | fumeless | gauntlet |
| foregone | foxhound | fumigate | gelatine |
| forehand | fraction | function | gelidity |
| forehead | fracture | funereal | geminate |
| forelock | fragment | furfural | gemstone |
| foremast | fragrant | furlough | gendarme |
| foremost | Fraulein | furmenty | generate |
| forenoon | freakish | fuselage | generous |
| forensic | freckled | fusilier | genetics |
| forepart | freeborn | futility | genitals |
| foreplay | freehand | futurity | genitive |
| foresail | freehold | | genocide |
| foreskin | freewill | G | geometry |
| forestay | frenetic | gadabout | Georgian |
| forester | frenzied | gadgetry | geranium |
| forestry | frequent | galactic | ghoulish |
| foretell | frescoed | Galilean | gigantic |
| foretime | freshman | galleass | giggling |
| forewarn | fretwork | galliard | gimcrack |
| foreword | Freudian | galloper | girlhood |
| formalin | friction | galvanic | giveaway |
| formally | friendly | gameness | glabrous |
| formerly | frighten | gamester | glaciate |
| formless | frontage | gangland | gladioli |
| formulae | frontier | gangling | gladness |
| forsooth | frosting | ganglion | glanders |
| forswear | fructify | gangrene | glandule |
| fortieth | fructose | gangster | glasnost |
| fortress | fruition | gaolbird | glaucoma |
| fortuity | frumenty | garboard | glibness |
| forzando | frumpish | gardenia | glissade |
| foulness | fugitive | gargoyle | gloaming |

| | | | |
|---|---|---|---|
| globular | greeting | hallmark | hedgerow |
| globulin | gridiron | handbill | hedonism |
| gloomily | grievous | handbook | heedless |
| glorious | grimness | handcuff | hegemony |
| glossary | grizzled | handgrip | heighten |
| glumness | groining | handicap | heirloom |
| gluttony | grosbeak | handmaid | heliacal |
| glycerin | grottoes | handsome | heliport |
| glycerol | grouping | hangnail | hellbent |
| glycogen | growling | hangover | Hellenic |
| goatherd | grudging | harangue | helminth |
| Godspeed | gruesome | hardback | helmsmen |
| goitrous | grumpish | hardness | helotism |
| Golgotha | guaranty | hardship | helpmate |
| golliwog | guardian | hardware | Helvetia |
| goodwill | guerilla | hardwood | henchman |
| gorgeous | Guernsey | harmless | henequen |
| gossamer | guidance | harmonic | heptagon |
| gourmand | guileful | harridan | heraldic |
| governor | gulfweed | hatchery | heraldry |
| graceful | gullible | hatchway | herbaria |
| gracious | gumption | Hawaiian | herdsmen |
| gradient | gunmetal | hawthorn | heredity |
| graduate | gunpoint | haymaker | heritage |
| graffiti | gunsmith | haziness | hermetic |
| gramercy | guttural | headache | herpetic |
| grandeur | gymkhana | headband | hesitate |
| granular | gyration | headgear | Hesperus |
| graphics | gyratory | headland | hibernal |
| graphite | gyrostat | headline | hibiscus |
| grasping | | headlong | hiccough |
| grateful | H | headwind | hidrosis |
| gratuity | habitual | heavenly | hieratic |
| gravelly | hacienda | hebetate | highball |
| grayling | haematic | hecatomb | highborn |
| greenery | hairline | hedgehog | highbrow |

highland
highlife
highness
hightail
hilarity
hindmost
Hinduism
hireling
Hispanic
historic
hoarsely
Hogmanay
hogshead
holiness
hologram
homeless
homesick
homespun
homework
homicide
homilies
hominoid
homology
homonymy
honestly
honeybee
honeydew
honorary
hoodwink
hooligan
hoosegow
hopeless
hornbill
hornpipe
horologe
horology

horrific
horsemen
hostelry
hotchpot
hotelier
hothouse
hotplate
howitzer
huckster
Huguenot
humanism
humanist
humanity
humanoid
humidify
humidity
humility
humorist
humorous
humpback
hustings
hyacinth
hydrogen
hydropic
hygienic
hymenium
hypnosis
hypnotic
hysteria

I

iatrical
icebound
idealism
identify
ideogram

ideology
idocrase
idolater
ignition
ignominy
illation
illumine
illusion
illusory
imbecile
imitator
immanent
immature
imminent
immobile
immodest
immolate
immortal
immunise
immunity
imparity
imperial
impetigo
implicit
impolite
importer
imposing
imposter
impotent
imprison
improper
impudent
impunity
impurity
inaction
inactive

inasmuch
inchoate
incident
incision
incisive
increase
incubate
indebted
indecent
indented
indicant
indicate
indigene
indigent
indirect
indolent
industry
inequity
inertial
infamous
infantry
inferior
infernal
infinite
infinity
inflated
informal
informer
infringe
infusion
infusive
inhalant
inherent
inhumane
inimical
iniquity

| | | | |
|---|---|---|---|
| initiate | intubate | jocosity | **L** |
| injector | inundate | jocundly | labourer |
| innately | invasion | jodhpurs | lacerate |
| innocent | invasive | jubilant | lacrimal |
| innovate | inveigle | jubilate | lacrosse |
| innuendo | inventor | judgment | lacunose |
| insanity | inverted | judicial | ladybird |
| inscribe | investor | jumpsuit | ladylike |
| insecure | inviting | junction | ladylove |
| insignia | involute | juncture | laically |
| insolent | inwardly | Jurassic | lamasery |
| insomnia | ironbark | juristic | lambaste |
| inspired | ironclad | juvenile | lambskin |
| inspirer | ironwood | | lamented |
| inspirit | ironwork | **K** | laminate |
| instance | irrigate | keelhaul | lancelet |
| instinct | irritant | keenness | landfall |
| instruct | isolated | keepsake | landlady |
| insulate | isotherm | kerchief | landlord |
| integral | issuable | kerosene | landmark |
| intended | Isthmian | keyboard | landmass |
| intently | | keystone | langlauf |
| interact | **J** | kibitzer | language |
| intercom | jackeroo | kickshaw | languish |
| interior | jailbird | kilobyte | lankness |
| intermix | jalousie | kilogram | lanneret |
| internal | jamboree | kilowatt | lanoline |
| Internet | jaundice | kindling | lapidary |
| Interpol | jealousy | kinetics | lapidate |
| interval | jeopardy | kingship | larboard |
| intimacy | Jeremiah | kinsfolk | larkspur |
| intimate | jeroboam | knapsack | larrikin |
| intonate | jettison | knapweed | larynges |
| intrepid | jeweller | knickers | latchkey |
| intrigue | jingoism | kohlrabi | latitude |
| intruder | jocosely | | latterly |

laudable
laudanum
laughter
laureate
lavation
lavatory
lavender
lawgiver
laxative
layabout
laziness
lazulite
leafless
leanness
leapfrog
leathery
lecithin
lecturer
legalese
legalise
legality
legatine
legation
leggings
leisured
lemonade
lemuroid
lengthen
lenience
leniency
lenitive
leporine
lethargy
lettered
leucosis
levanter

leveller
leverage
levigate
levirate
levitate
lewdness
libation
libeller
liberate
libretto
licensee
lifebuoy
lifelike
lifeline
lifelong
lifetime
ligament
ligation
lighting
ligneous
limerick
linchpin
lineally
linesman
lingerer
lingerie
linguist
liniment
linoleum
lipstick
listless
literacy
literary
literate
literati
litigant

litigate
liveried
liverish
loathing
lobbyist
lobotomy
localise
localism
locality
location
locative
lodestar
lodgment
logician
loiterer
lollipop
lonesome
longboat
longhand
loophole
lordship
lorikeet
lovebird
lovesick
loyalist
lucidity
luckless
lukewarm
luminary
luminous
lunation
luncheon
lungwort
luscious
lustrous
lustrums

lutenist
lutetium
lymphoid
lymphoma
lyrebird
lyricism
lyricist

M
macaroni
macaroon
maccaboy
machismo
mackerel
madhouse
madrigal
magazine
magnesia
magnetic
magnolia
maharaja
maharani
mahogany
mainland
mainmast
mainsail
mainstay
maintain
majestic
majority
malarial
malinger
maltreat
maltster
Mammalia
mandarin

| | | | |
|---|---|---|---|
| mandible | matelote | meringue | misogyny |
| mandolin | material | mesdames | misplace |
| mandrake | maternal | mesmeric | misprint |
| mandrill | matrices | messmate | misquote |
| manfully | matronal | metallic | misshape |
| mangrove | matronly | metaphor | misspell |
| maniacal | maturate | meteoric | misspent |
| manicure | maturity | methinks | mistaken |
| manifest | maverick | metrical | mistreat |
| manifold | maximise | miasmata | mistress |
| manorial | mayoress | midnight | mistrust |
| manpower | meagrely | midships | mitigate |
| mantelet | meanness | migraine | mnemonic |
| mantissa | meantime | mildness | mobility |
| manually | measured | militant | moccasin |
| marathon | mechanic | military | moderate |
| marauder | mediator | militate | moderato |
| marbling | medicate | milkweed | modestly |
| marginal | medicine | milkwort | modifier |
| marigold | medieval | milliner | modulate |
| marinade | mediocre | millpond | moisture |
| maritime | meditate | minatory | molasses |
| marjoram | meekness | mindless | molecule |
| markedly | megabyte | minimise | molehill |
| marksman | megastar | minister | moleskin |
| marquess | megawatt | minority | momentum |
| marquise | mclamine | minstrel | monadism |
| marriage | melanoma | minutely | monarchy |
| martinet | meltdown | minutiae | monastic |
| marzipan | membrane | mirthful | monetary |
| massacre | memorial | mischief | mongoose |
| masseuse | memorise | miscount | monogamy |
| masterly | meninges | mishmash | monogram |
| masthead | merchant | misjudge | monolith |
| mastitis | merciful | misnomer | monopoly |
| matchbox | meridian | misogamy | monorail |

monotony
monoxide
monsieur
monument
moonbeam
moralise
morality
moreover
moribund
morosely
morphine
mortally
mortgage
mortuary
mosquito
mothball
motherly
motivate
motorise
motorist
motorway
moulding
mountain
mounting
mournful
moussaka
mouthful
moveable
movement
movingly
muchness
mudguard
multiple
multiply
mumbling
munition

murderer
muscular
mushroom
musician
musingly
musketry
mutation
mutilate
mutineer
mutinous
mutually
myelitis
Myrmidon
mystical
mythical

N
nameless
namesake
Napoleon
narcosis
narcotic
narrator
narrowly
natation
natatory
national
nativity
nauseate
nauseous
nautical
nautilus
navigate
nearness
neatness
nebulous

necklace
neckline
necropsy
necrosis
needless
negation
negative
nematode
neophyte
nepotism
neuritis
neurosis
newlywed
newscast
newshawk
newsreel
newsroom
nickname
nicotine
niggling
nightcap
nihilism
nihilist
ninepins
nineteen
nitrogen
nobility
nobleman
noblesse
nodulous
nominate
nonesuch
nonsense
nonstick
noontide
noontime

normally
Norseman
northern
notation
notching
notebook
notional
noumenon
novelist
nowadays
nuisance
numbness
numerary
numerate
numerous
nuptials
nutrient
nutshell

O
obduracy
obedient
obituary
objector
oblation
obligate
obliging
oblivion
observer
obsidian
obsolete
obstacle
obstruct
obtruder
obtusely
occasion

| | | | |
|---|---|---|---|
| occupant | opulence | outstrip | overtime |
| occupier | oratorio | outwards | overtone |
| odiously | ordinand | outweigh | overture |
| odometer | ordinary | overalls | overview |
| oenology | ordinate | overbear | overwind |
| offender | ordnance | overcame | overwork |
| offering | organise | overcast | oxymoron |
| official | organism | overcoat | |
| offshoot | organist | overcome | P |
| offshore | oriental | overdose | pacifier |
| offstage | original | overdraw | pacifist |
| ohmmeter | ornament | overflow | paganism |
| oilcloth | orthodox | overhang | painless |
| oiliness | osculant | overhaul | painting |
| ointment | otiosity | overhead | palatial |
| oleander | outboard | overhear | palatine |
| oligarch | outbreak | overheat | paleface |
| Olympiad | outburst | overhung | paleness |
| omelette | outcaste | overkill | palimony |
| omission | outclass | overland | palisade |
| oncology | outdated | overleaf | palomino |
| oncoming | outdoors | overleap | palpable |
| onlooker | outfield | overload | palpably |
| ontology | outflank | overlong | pamphlet |
| oologist | outgoing | overlook | pancreas |
| openness | outhouse | overlord | pandanus |
| operable | outlying | overmuch | pandemic |
| operatic | outmatch | overpass | panorama |
| operator | outmoded | overrate | pantheon |
| operetta | outpoint | override | parabola |
| opponent | outreach | overripe | paradigm |
| opposite | outrider | overrule | paradise |
| optician | outright | overseer | paraffin |
| optimise | outshine | oversize | parakeet |
| optimism | outsider | overstay | parallel |
| optional | outsmart | overtake | paralyse |

| | | | |
|---|---|---|---|
| paramour | pedestal | Pharisee | platypus |
| paranoia | pedicure | pharmacy | playback |
| paranoid | pedigree | pheasant | playmate |
| parasite | peekaboo | phonetic | playtime |
| paravane | peephole | phrasing | pleading |
| parental | peepshow | phthisis | pleasant |
| parergon | peerless | physique | pleasing |
| Parisian | peignoir | pickings | pleasure |
| parlance | Pekinese | piddling | plebeian |
| Parmesan | pellagra | piercing | plectrum |
| paroxysm | pellucid | pilchard | Pleiades |
| partaker | penalise | pileated | plethora |
| particle | penchant | pilferer | pleurisy |
| partisan | pendulum | pillager | pliantly |
| passable | penitent | pimiento | pluckily |
| passably | penknife | pinafore | plumbing |
| Passover | pentagon | pinnacle | pluvious |
| passport | penumbra | pinpoint | poetical |
| password | perceive | pinprick | poignant |
| pastiche | perforce | pipeline | polarise |
| pastille | pericarp | piquancy | polarity |
| pastoral | perilous | pitiable | polemics |
| pastrami | perineum | pitiless | policies |
| patently | periodic | pittance | polished |
| paternal | perjurer | placable | politely |
| pathetic | permeate | placemat | politics |
| patience | perorate | placenta | poltroon |
| pavilion | peroxide | placidly | polygamy |
| pawnshop | personal | planking | polyglot |
| payphone | perspire | plankton | pomander |
| peaceful | persuade | plantain | ponytail |
| pectoral | perverse | plateaus | popinjay |
| peculiar | petition | plateaux | populace |
| pedagogy | petulant | platform | populate |
| pedantic | phalange | platinum | populism |
| pedantry | phantasm | Platonic | populist |

| | | | |
|---|---|---|---|
| populous | presence | pronator | purulent |
| porphyry | preserve | properly | purveyor |
| porpoise | presidio | property | pushover |
| porridge | pressing | prophecy | pussycat |
| portable | pressure | prophesy | pustular |
| porthole | prestige | proposal | puzzling |
| porticos | pretence | propound | pyroxene |
| portrait | previous | prospect | |
| positive | pricking | prostate | Q |
| possible | priestly | protocol | quackery |
| postcard | priggish | protract | quadrant |
| postcode | primeval | protrude | quagmire |
| postdate | primness | provided | quaintly |
| postmark | primrose | provider | quandary |
| postpone | princely | province | quantify |
| posturer | princess | proximal | quantity |
| potbelly | printing | prudence | quarters |
| potently | printout | prurient | quatrain |
| potsherd | priority | psalmist | queerish |
| poultice | prisoner | psalmody | quencher |
| poundage | pristine | psaltery | question |
| powdered | probable | ptomaine | quibbler |
| powerful | probably | publican | quiddity |
| practice | proceeds | puffball | quidnunc |
| practise | proclaim | pugilism | quietude |
| prandial | prodigal | puissant | quilting |
| prankish | producer | pullover | quisling |
| prattler | profound | punctual | quivered |
| preacher | progress | puncture | quixotic |
| preamble | prohibit | pungency | quotable |
| precinct | prolapse | punitive | quotient |
| precious | prolific | puppetry | |
| preclude | prologue | purchase | R |
| predator | promoter | purifier | radially |
| prenatal | prompter | purplish | radiance |
| prepared | promptly | pursuant | radiator |

| | | | |
|---|---|---|---|
| raillery | referral | rephrase | reverend |
| railroad | refinery | reporter | reverent |
| raincoat | reformed | reprieve | reversal |
| raindrop | reformer | reprisal | reviewer |
| rainfall | regality | reproach | revision |
| rambling | regicide | reproval | revivify |
| rapacity | regiment | republic | revolver |
| rapidity | regional | research | rhapsody |
| rashness | register | resemble | rhetoric |
| rational | registry | reserved | rhomboid |
| rattling | regrowth | resident | rhythmic |
| ravenous | regulate | residual | ribaldry |
| reaction | rehearse | resigned | richness |
| reactive | reindeer | resinous | rickshaw |
| readjust | rekindle | resister | ricochet |
| reaffirm | relation | resistor | riddance |
| reappear | relative | resolute | ridicule |
| reasoned | relaxant | resolved | riffraff |
| reassert | relegate | resonant | rightful |
| reassign | relevant | resource | rigidity |
| rebuttal | reliable | response | rigorous |
| receding | reliance | restless | ringworm |
| received | relieved | restrain | ripeness |
| recently | religion | restrict | riverine |
| recessed | relocate | restroom | riveting |
| recharge | remedial | retailer | roadside |
| reckless | remember | retainer | roadster |
| reckoner | remittal | retarded | robotics |
| recorder | remotely | reticent | rocketry |
| recourse | renegade | reticule | romancer |
| recovery | renounce | retiring | romantic |
| recreate | renovate | retrench | rosemary |
| redeemer | renowned | retrieve | rosewood |
| redirect | repairer | retrorse | rosiness |
| redolent | repartee | reusable | rotative |
| redouble | repeated | reveller | rotatory |

| | | | |
|---|---|---|---|
| roughage | sanguine | sciatica | sectoral |
| roulette | sanitary | scimitar | securely |
| royalist | sanitise | scirrhus | security |
| rubicund | Sanskrit | scissors | sedately |
| rubrical | sapidity | scolding | sedation |
| rucksack | sapience | scorcher | sedative |
| rudeness | sapphire | scornful | sediment |
| rudiment | saraband | scorpion | sedition |
| ruefully | sardonic | scouting | sedulity |
| ruffling | sardonyx | scowling | sedulous |
| ruggedly | Satanism | scrabble | seedless |
| ruminant | satirise | scraggly | seedling |
| ruminate | satirist | scramble | seigneur |
| ruthless | saturate | scrannel | selector |
| | saucepan | scraping | selenite |
| S | savagely | scratchy | selfless |
| sabotage | savagery | scrawler | selfsame |
| saboteur | scabbard | screamer | semantic |
| sacristy | scabious | screechy | semester |
| saddlery | scabrous | scribble | seminary |
| sagacity | scaffold | scrounge | Semitism |
| sailboat | scantily | scrubber | semitone |
| salaried | scapular | scrutiny | semolina |
| salaries | scarcely | scullery | senility |
| salesman | scarcity | sculptor | senorita |
| salience | scathing | seafarer | sensible |
| salivate | scavenge | seamless | sensuous |
| saltbush | scenario | seaplane | sentence |
| salutary | sceptred | searcher | sentient |
| sameness | schedule | seascape | sentinel |
| sampling | scheming | seashore | sentries |
| sanctify | schizoid | seasonal | separate |
| sanction | schmaltz | seatbelt | sequelae |
| sanctity | schnapps | secluded | sequence |
| sandwich | scholium | seconder | seraglio |
| saneness | schooner | secondly | seraphic |

| | | | |
|---|---|---|---|
| seraphim | shipping | siliquae | slovenly |
| serenade | shipyard | sillabub | slowness |
| serenely | shirring | simplify | sluggard |
| serenity | shocking | simulate | sluggish |
| sergeant | shopping | sinecure | smacking |
| serrated | shoptalk | singsong | smallpox |
| sesterce | shortage | singular | smashing |
| settling | shortcut | sinister | smelling |
| severely | shoulder | sinkhole | smeltery |
| severity | showcase | sisterly | smocking |
| sewerage | showdown | situated | smoothly |
| sextuple | showroom | sixpence | smoulder |
| sexually | shrapnel | sixpenny | smuggler |
| shabbily | shrewdly | sixtieth | smugness |
| shaddock | shrewish | sizeable | snapshot |
| shafting | shrimper | skeletal | snarling |
| shamanic | shrunken | skeleton | snatcher |
| shambles | sibilant | sketcher | sneaking |
| shameful | sickness | skinhead | sneezing |
| shamrock | sidekick | skiplane | snobbery |
| shanghai | sideline | skipping | snobbish |
| shantung | sidelong | skirmish | snowball |
| shearing | sidereal | skirting | snowdrop |
| sheathed | siderite | skittish | snowfall |
| sheepdog | sideshow | skittles | snuffbox |
| sheepish | sidestep | skylight | snuffler |
| sheeting | sidewalk | slapdash | snugness |
| shelving | sidewall | slashing | sobriety |
| shepherd | sideways | sleepily | sociable |
| shilling | signally | sleeping | socially |
| shinbone | signpost | slightly | Socratic |
| shingled | silencer | slipknot | softball |
| shingles | silently | slippage | softener |
| shipload | silicate | slippery | software |
| shipmate | silicium | slipshod | softwood |
| shipment | silicule | slothful | solarium |

| | | | |
|---|---|---|---|
| solecism | sparsely | squarely | stockpot |
| solemnly | speaking | squatter | stomatic |
| solenoid | specific | squeegee | stopcock |
| solidify | specimen | squiggle | stoppage |
| solidity | specious | squirrel | storeman |
| solitary | speckled | staccato | stowaway |
| solitude | spectral | stagnant | straddle |
| solstice | spectrum | stagnate | straggle |
| solution | speedily | stairway | straight |
| solvable | spelling | stalking | strained |
| solvency | sphygmic | stallion | strainer |
| sombrely | spicular | stalwart | strangle |
| sombrero | spillway | stampede | strapper |
| somebody | spinifex | standard | strategy |
| sometime | spinster | standing | stratify |
| somewhat | spirally | stanhope | streamer |
| songbird | spirited | starched | strength |
| songster | spiteful | stardust | striated |
| sonorous | spitfire | starfish | stricken |
| soothing | spittoon | starkers | strictly |
| sorcerer | splatter | starling | strident |
| sordidly | splendid | statuary | striking |
| sorority | splinter | steadily | stringed |
| soulless | splutter | stealthy | stripper |
| soundbox | spoliate | steaming | struggle |
| sounding | spoonful | steerage | strummer |
| sourness | sporadic | sterling | strumpet |
| sourpuss | sporting | stickler | stubbled |
| southern | sportive | stifling | stubborn |
| southpaw | sprigged | stiletto | studious |
| souvenir | sprinkle | stimulus | stuffing |
| spaceman | sprocket | stinging | stultify |
| spacious | spyglass | stirring | stunning |
| spangled | squabble | stockade | stuntman |
| spanking | squadron | stocking | sturgeon |
| sparkler | squander | stockman | subgenus |

subhuman
sublunar
submerge
subpoena
subpolar
subsonic
subtitle
subtlety
subtotal
subtract
suburban
succinct
suchlike
suckling
suddenly
sufferer
suffrage
suicidal
suitably
suitcase
sukiyaki
sulphate
sunbaked
sunbathe
sunlight
sunshade
sunshine
superbly
superego
superior
superman
supinely
supplant
supplier
supposed
suppress

surcease
surgical
surmount
surplice
surprise
surround
surveyor
survival
survivor
suspense
swelling
swindler
sycamore
syllabic
syllable
syllabus
symbolic
symmetry
sympathy
symphony
symposia
syndrome
synopsis
synoptic
syphilis
systemic
syzygies

T
tableaux
tabulate
taciturn
tackling
tactical
tactless
taffrail

tailgate
tailpipe
tailspin
tailwind
talisman
tamarind
tamarisk
tameable
tameless
tameness
tandoori
tangible
tanistry
tapestry
tapeworm
tarboosh
targeted
tartaric
tartness
tasteful
tattered
taunting
taverner
taxation
taxonomy
taxpayer
teaching
teamster
teaspoon
technics
tectonic
teenager
teetotal
tegument
telecast
telefilm

telegram
telethon
teletype
televise
telltale
telluric
temerity
tempered
template
temporal
tempting
tenacity
tendency
tenderly
tenement
tentacle
terebene
terminal
terminus
terrazzo
terrible
terrific
tertiary
testator
testicle
tetragon
tetrarch
textbook
thalamus
thankful
thatcher
theistic
thematic
theocrat
theology
theories

| | | | |
|---|---|---|---|
| theorise | tiresome | transmit | truffled |
| thespian | titanium | trapdoor | truncate |
| theurgic | titivate | trapezia | trunnion |
| thiamine | titmouse | trapping | trustful |
| thickset | titulary | travails | truthful |
| thievery | toboggan | traverse | tsaritsa |
| thinking | toiletry | travesty | tuberous |
| thinness | toilsome | trawling | tubiform |
| thoracic | tokenism | treasure | tubulous |
| thorough | tolerant | treasury | tumbling |
| thousand | tolerate | treating | tumidity |
| thraldom | tomahawk | treatise | tungsten |
| threaten | tommyrot | trecento | tuppence |
| thresher | topnotch | treenail | turbaned |
| thriller | topology | trembler | turgidly |
| thriving | toreador | trespass | turncoat |
| thrombus | tortilla | triangle | turnover |
| throttle | tortoise | trickery | turnpike |
| thuggery | tortuous | tricycle | turnspit |
| thumping | torturer | trifling | turreted |
| thundery | totality | trillion | tutelage |
| thurible | touching | trimaran | tutorage |
| thurifer | towering | trimming | tutorial |
| Thursday | township | triplane | twaddler |
| ticklish | toxaemia | tripping | tweezers |
| tigerish | toxicant | triptych | twilight |
| tillable | tracheal | trivalve | twopence |
| timbered | trachoma | trochoid | twopenny |
| timeless | traction | trolling | tympanum |
| timeworn | traducer | trombone | typecast |
| timidity | training | trophies | typeface |
| timorous | tranquil | tropical | typology |
| tincture | transact | trousers | tyrannic |
| tinkling | transept | truckage | Tyrolean |
| tinnitus | transfer | trucker | |
| tireless | transfix | truckler | |

U
ubiquity
ugliness
ulcerate
ulcerous
ulterior
ultimate
umbrella
unabated
unallied
unatoned
unawares
unbeaten
unbelief
unbiased
unbidden
unbolted
unbroken
unbuckle
unburden
unbutton
uncommon
unctuous
underarm
undercut
underdog
underlay
underpin
undersea
undertow
undreamt
undulate
uneasily
unending
unenvied
unerring

unevenly
unfading
unfairly
unfasten
unfetter
unformed
unfunded
ungainly
unglazed
ungulate
unharmed
unheeded
uniaxial
unicycle
unionise
unipolar
uniquely
univalve
universe
univocal
unjustly
unkindly
unlawful
unleaded
unlikely
unlisted
unlovely
unmanned
unmuzzle
unpitied
unplaced
unpoetic
unproved
unrepaid
unsaddle
unsafely

unsealed
unseemly
unshaken
unsocial
unsoiled
unspoken
unstable
unsteady
unsuited
untangle
untaught
untidily
untimely
untinged
untiring
untitled
untoward
unvalued
unvaried
unversed
unvoiced
unwanted
unwarily
unwashed
unwieldy
unwisely
unwished
unworthy
upgrowth
upheaval
upholder
upmarket
uppercut
uprising
upstairs
upstream

upstroke
urbanity
urethral
urgently
uroscopy
usefully
uxorious

V
vacation
vaccinal
vagabond
vagrancy
vainness
valerian
validate
validity
valorous
valuable
valuator
valvular
vanadium
vanguard
vanquish
vaporise
vaporous
variable
variance
varicose
varietal
variform
variolar
varletry
vascular
vasculum
vastness

| | | | |
|---|---|---|---|
| vaulting | vicinity | vocalise | wasteful |
| vegetate | Victoria | vocalist | watchful |
| vehement | vigilant | vocation | watering |
| velocity | vigneron | vocative | waterway |
| venality | vignette | voidable | waveless |
| vendetta | vigorous | volatile | waxiness |
| vendible | vileness | volcanic | wayfarer |
| venerate | vilifier | volition | weakness |
| venereal | villager | voltaism | weanling |
| vengeful | villainy | volution | weaponry |
| venially | vincible | vomiting | wearable |
| venomous | vinculum | voracity | weeklies |
| venosity | vinegary | vortices | werewolf |
| venturer | vineyard | votaries | westerly |
| veracity | violable | votively | westward |
| verandah | violator | voussoir | whacking |
| verbally | violence | vulgarly | wharfage |
| verbatim | viperine | | whatever |
| verbiage | viperish | W | wheedler |
| verdancy | virginal | wainscot | whenever |
| verifier | viridity | waitress | wherever |
| vermouth | virtuoso | walkover | whimbrel |
| veronica | virtuous | wallaroo | whimsies |
| versicle | virulent | wanderer | whipcord |
| vertebra | visceral | wantonly | whiplash |
| vertexes | viscount | wardrobe | whirring |
| vertical | visiting | wardroom | whistler |
| vesicate | vitalise | wardship | whitener |
| vespiary | vitality | warhorse | whodunit |
| vestment | vitellin | wariness | wickedly |
| vestured | vitellus | warplane | wigmaker |
| vexation | vitiator | warranty | wildfowl |
| viaticum | vitreous | warrener | wildlife |
| vicarage | vivacity | washable | wilfully |
| vicarial | vivisect | washbowl | wiliness |
| vicinage | vixenish | washroom | windburn |

windfall
windlass
windless
windpipe
windsail
windsock
windward
wineskin
wingspan
winnower
wireless
wiriness
wiseacre
wishbone
witchery
withdraw
withhold

woefully
womanise
wondrous
woodbine
woodcock
woodenly
woodland
woodruff
woodsman
woodwind
woodworm
woolfell
wordplay
workable
workaday
workbook
workload

workmate
workshop
wormwood
worrying
worthily
wrangler
wrapping
wrathful
wreckage
wrestler
wretched
wriggler
wrinkled
wrongful

**Y**
yachting

yarmulke
yearbook
yearling
yearning
yeomanry
yielding
yokemate
yourself
youthful
yuletide

**Z**
Zeppelin
zodiacal
zoophile
zucchini

# EIGHT-LETTER MULTIPLE WORDS

**A**
a la carte
acid rain
acid test
act of God
act of war
air brake
air-to-air
alarm-gun
all at sea
all clear
all fours
all-hours
all-in-all
alley cat
alpha ray
alter ego
alum root
apple-pie
arc light
at a pinch
at random
Ave Maria

**B**
baby boom
bad blood
badly off
band-fish
bank rate
base rate
bass clef
beam-ends

bee-eater
bell buoy
bell rope
below par
beta wave
betel nut
Big Apple
Big Smoke
big mouth
big of you
big stick
bill fold
bird's-eye
bird-call
black eye
black-tie
blow hard
blue chip
bobby pin
bolt-head
bona fide
bone-idle
book club
boom town
boot camp
Boy Scout
brand new
break-out
brick-red
brine-pit
brush-off
bull bars
bull's-eye

bull-calf
bust a gut
butter up
by chance
by rights
by the bye
by the way

**C**
cabin-boy
cable car
call girl
cane-mill
cap it off
card case
card file
cash crop
cash flow
cash-book
cast down
cast iron
chain saw
chill out
chop suey
civet cat
clean-cut
clear-cut
cloak-bag
club moss
co-author
coal mine
cold call
cold feet

cold sore
con amore
coq au vin
Corn Laws
cot death
crew neck
cross-eye
cube root
cul-de-sac
cut glass

**D**
data bank
date line
date palm
date rape
day by day
day-to-day
dead heat
dead meat
dead wood
death row
death tax
dewy-eyed
doggy bag
dog's life
dog-eared
down line
drop kick
dry-clean
dry-nurse
dust bowl
dust coat

duty-free

**E**
easy meat
eau de vie
El Dorado
end paper
epic poet
ex gratia
ex libris
eye-liner

**F**
face lift
fail-safe
fair game
fair play
far flung
fast food
fast lane
feed-pipe
film buff
fine-tune
fish-hook
flake out
flesh-pot
flip-flop
folk song
follow-up
free fall
free port

**G**
gang bang
get a grip
get a life

glad rags
glow-worm
go places
go-getter
goings-on
gold card
golf ball
golf club
grey area

**H**
Hail Mary
half moon
hanger-on
hard copy
hard disk
hard line
hard-core
hard sell
hat trick
head rest
high tide
high wire
high-five
high-rise
higher up
home loan
home-made
hot flush
hula-hula
hung-over
hush-hush
hymn book

**I**
ill-fated

in view of
info-tech
iron lung

**J**
jail bait
jerry can
John Dory
joy-rider
junk food
junk mail

**K**
knee jerk

**L**
Lady Muck
laid-back
lame duck
land mine
last word
lay waste
lead-free
leap year
left-hand
left-wing
legal aid
lie doggo
life-belt
life-size
live-wire
looker-on
lop-eared
Lord Muck
lucky dip
lynx-eyed

**M**
make over
man to man
man-eater
man-of-war
manta-ray
meat-loaf
milch cow
Milky Way
mind's eye
mixed bag
mug's game
musk duck

**N**
near miss
nerve gas
new blood
night owl
non-toxic
nose dive

**O**
off-piste
off-white
oil slick
oil-field
old guard
old-timer
olive oil
on record
on the air
on the dot
one-liner
one-sided
one-track

open-eyed

**P**
pall-mall
pea-green
per annum
pin money
polka dot
port-wine
pot-roast
pre-exist
pro forma
pump-room
put-up job

**R**
rap music
red cedar
red dwarf
red earth
reed-pipe
reef knot
rest home
right off
ring-true
river-bed
road-rage
road-test
role-play
roll call
roly-poly
romp-home
root beer
root crop
rose-pink
rough-cut

round-arm
runner-up
rush hour
rye-bread
rye-grass

**S**
sack race
salt lick
salt-mine
salt-wort
sand trap
sand-hill
sand-bank
sash cord
sea eagle
sea horse
sea level
sea snake
sea-grass
sea-rover
self-love
self-made
self-pity
self-rule
self-sown
sheep-dip
short-rib
sick list
side dish
sit tight
skim milk
skin-deep
sloe-eyed
small fry
smart set

smart-ass
smash-hit
snow line
snow-boot
snub-nose
so-called
sob story
solar day
some such
souped-up
soy sauce
soya bean
space bar
span-roof
spar deck
spell-out
sperm oil
split pea
spun silk
spur gear
Star Wars
star-sign
stock car
strung-up
sun-dried
sweet pea

**T**
tabby-cat
tall ship
tally-man
tap-dance
tape deck
taste bud
tax haven
tea chest

team-mate
tear-drop
tee-shirt
tenon saw
test tube
thole-pin
thumbs up
time zone
tommy gun
tone-deaf
top brass
trade-off
trash can
tree fern
tree frog
trial run
true love
true-blue
true-bred
twin-born
two-edged
two-faced

**U**
Uncle Sam
Uncle Tom
up-in-arms
up-to-date
uric acid

**V**
via media

**W**
wall-eyed
war dance

war paint
war-whoop
washed-up
water bed
water ice
water-hen
water-pot
water-ram
wave-worn
wax paper
wax-cloth
wax-light

waxed-end
well born
well-bred
well-done
well-knit
well-read
well-to-do
well-worn
wet nurse
wheat-fly
wheel-man
whey-face

white ant
white lie
white tie
white-hot
white-out
whole hog
wide-eyed
wild card
wild oats
wild-eyed
wire-rope

wood pulp
wood-lark
wool-dyer
write-off

Y
Yale lock

Z
zero hour
zoom lens

# NINE-LETTER WORDS

**A**
abatement
abdominal
abhorrent
abhorring
abolition
aborigine
absorbing
abstinent
absurdity
abundance
accession
accipiter
accompany
accordion
accretion
acetylene
acoustics
acquiesce
acquittal
acrobatic
acropolis
actualise
actuality
acuteness
adaptable
addiction
addressee
adduction
adherence
adjacency
adjective
admirable

admirably
admission
adoptable
adoration
adornment
adulation
adumbrate
adventure
adverbial
adversary
adversely
adversity
advertise
advisable
aerialist
aerodrome
aerometer
aerospace
aesthetic
affection
affidavit
affiliate
affluence
aforesaid
Afrikaans
afterglow
afterlife
aftermath
aggravate
aggressor
agitation
agreeable
agreement

alabaster
albatross
alcoholic
alertness
algebraic
alienable
alignment
alimental
allegedly
allegoric
allemande
allotment
allowable
alongside
altercate
alternate
altimeter
altissimo
aluminium
aluminous
alveolate
amazement
ambiguity
ambiguous
ambitious
amblyopia
ambrosial
amendment
amidships
amphibian
ampleness
amplified
amusement

anabolism
anabranch
analgesic
analogous
anandrous
anarchism
anatomise
ancestral
anchorage
anchorman
ancillary
anecdotal
animation
animosity
announcer
annulment
anonymity
anonymous
anthology
antipathy
antipodes
antiquity
anxiously
apartheid
apartment
apathetic
apologise
appalling
appendage
appertain
appetiser
appliance
applicant

appointee
apportion
appraisal
apprehend
arabesque
arbitrary
archangel
arduously
armadillo
armistice
arrogance
artillery
ascendant
ascension
ascertain
asparagus
aspersion
assertion
assertive
assiduous
associate
assonance
assurance
assuredly
asthmatic
astrodome
astrology
astronaut
astronomy
athletics
atonement
atrocious
attention
attentive
attribute
audacious

austerity
authentic
authority
autoclave
autocracy
autograph
automatic
autopilot
auxiliary
available
avalanche
avocation
avoidance
awakening
awestruck
axiomatic

B
backslide
backtrack
backwater
backwoods
bagatelle
bakehouse
balaclava
balalaika
balefully
ballerina
ballistic
bamboozle
bandicoot
bandwagon
baptismal
barbarian
barnstorm
barometer

barracuda
barricade
barrister
battalion
bawdiness
beauteous
beautiful
bedfellow
bedspread
beefeater
beestings
befitting
behaviour
beleaguer
belemnite
bellicose
beryllium
besetting
bespatter
betrothal
bicameral
billabong
billiards
bilocular
binocular
biography
biologist
biorhythm
birdbrain
birthmark
bisection
blackjack
blackmail
blandness
blaspheme
bleakness

blindfold
blindness
bloodshed
bloodshot
blossomed
blowtorch
boatswain
bobsleigh
bodyguard
boldfaced
bombastic
bombshell
bookmaker
boomerang
botanical
boulevard
boundless
brasserie
breakable
breakdown
breastpin
breeching
briefcase
brigadier
brilliant
brimstone
briquette
broadcast
broadloom
broadness
broadside
brotherly
brushwork
brutalise
brutality
brutishly

buccaneer
bucketful
buckthorn
buckwheat
buffeting
bulkiness
bulldozer
bumblebee
bumptious
burliness
bushiness
bushwhack
buttercup
butterfly
butternut
bystander

C
cacophony
Caesarean
cafeteria
cairngorm
calaboose
calcaneum
calculate
calenture
calibrate
caliphate
callosity
calmative
Calvinism
calvities
camarilla
camelhair
camembert
cameraman

campanula
camphoric
campstool
cancerous
candidate
Candlemas
cankerous
capacious
capillary
capitular
Capricorn
capsaicin
capsulate
captaincy
captivate
captivity
carbonado
carbonise
carbuncle
carcinoma
cardboard
cardsharp
caretaker
carnivore
carpenter
carpentry
carpetbag
carpeting
cartilage
cartogram
cartridge
cartwheel
caryopsis
casemated
Cassandra
casserole

casuarina
casuistic
cataclysm
catalepsy
catalogue
catalysis
cataplexy
catatonia
catchment
catchpole
catchword
cathedral
catoptric
cattlemen
Caucasian
causality
causation
causeless
cauterise
cavalcade
cavernous
ceaseless
celebrate
celestial
celestite
cellarman
centipede
centurion
cerecloth
certainty
certifier
certitude
cessation
cetaceous
chafferer
challenge

chambered
chameleon
champagne
chandlery
changeful
chaparral
character
chartered
charwoman
chauffeur
cheapness
checklist
checkmate
cheerless
chelonian
chemistry
chequered
cherisher
chicanery
chickweed
chidingly
chieftain
chilblain
childless
Chinatown
chipboard
chiselled
chivalric
chlorotic
chocolate
chokebore
chokedamp
choleraic
chorology
Christian
Christmas

| | | | |
|---|---|---|---|
| chromatic | cognisant | commendam | conferrer |
| chronicle | coheiress | commensal | confessed |
| chrysalid | coherence | commenter | confessor |
| chrysalis | colcannon | comminute | confidant |
| chuckling | collation | commissar | confluent |
| churchman | collative | committal | conformer |
| cigarette | colleague | committee | confusion |
| circuitry | collected | commodity | congenial |
| cirrhosis | collector | commodore | congested |
| civilised | colligate | commonage | congruity |
| claimable | collision | commotion | congruous |
| clapboard | collocate | communard | conically |
| clarifier | collodion | communism | conjugate |
| classical | collotype | communist | connector |
| classmate | collusion | compactly | connivent |
| cleanness | collusive | companion | conqueror |
| clearance | colocynth | compeller | conscious |
| cleavable | colonelcy | competent | conscript |
| clerkship | coloniser | complaint | conserver |
| cleverish | colonnade | compliant | consignee |
| clientele | colosseum | component | consonant |
| clockwise | colostomy | composite | conspirer |
| clockwork | colostrum | concavely | constrain |
| cloisonne | colouring | concealer | constrict |
| cloistral | colourist | conceited | consulate |
| closeness | coltishly | concentre | consulter |
| cloudless | colubrine | concierge | consuming |
| clubhouse | columbine | concisely | contagion |
| coalfield | columbium | concision | contender |
| coalition | columella | concordat | contented |
| coastline | columnist | concourse | continent |
| coastwise | combatant | concubine | continual |
| cocainise | combative | condiment | continued |
| cockroach | comforter | condition | continuum |
| cockscomb | comically | conducive | contralto |
| coemption | commander | conductor | contriver |

contumely
contusion
conundrum
convector
convexity
convivial
cookhouse
copyright
coralline
coralloid
cordately
cordelier
cordially
cordiform
coreopsis
coriander
corkscrew
cornelian
cornfield
cornflour
cornstalk
corollary
corporate
corporeal
corpulent
corpuscle
correctly
corrector
correlate
corrosion
corrosive
corrupted
corticate
cortisone
coruscate
corymbose

coseismal
cosmonaut
costively
costumier
countdown
countless
courteous
courtship
courtyard
couturier
coverture
covetable
cowardice
crackdown
crackhead
craftsman
cranberry
crankcase
crapulous
crassness
cravingly
craziness
credulity
credulous
cremation
crematory
crenature
crenulate
crescendo
crestless
crimeless
criminate
crippling
crispness
criterion
criticise

crocodile
crookedly
croquette
crossbred
crossness
crossover
crosswind
crosswise
crossword
crotchety
crowberry
crudeness
cryometer
cubically
cubiculum
cuckoldry
cucullate
cudgeller
culminate
cultivate
cunningly
curiosity
curiously
curliness
currently
currycomb
curtailer
curtilage
curvature
cushioned
custodial
custodian
customary
cuttingly
cyclorama
cyclotron

cylindric
cymbalist
cynically
cyprinoid
cystotomy
cytoplast

D
dachshund
dalliance
Dalmatian
damascene
damnation
damnatory
dandelion
dangerous
daredevil
dartboard
Darwinian
dashboard
dastardly
dauntless
davenport
deaconess
deadening
deadlight
deafening
deathless
deathlike
deathsman
deathtrap
debatable
debauched
debenture
debutante
decadence

| | | | |
|---|---|---|---|
| decagonal | deflation | departure | deterrent |
| decalcify | deflector | depasture | detonator |
| deceitful | defluxion | depicture | detractor |
| decennial | defoliant | depletion | detriment |
| decennium | deformity | depletory | devaluate |
| deception | defrauder | deposable | devastate |
| deceptive | degrading | depositor | developer |
| decidedly | dehydrate | deprecate | deviation |
| deciduous | dejection | depredate | devilment |
| decilitre | delicious | depressed | deviously |
| decimally | delighted | depressor | devisable |
| decimator | delineate | depurator | devitrify |
| declaimer | delirious | derisible | devotedly |
| declinate | deliverer | derivable | dexterity |
| declining | demagogic | derringer | diablerie |
| declivous | demandant | descanter | diabolise |
| decoction | demanding | descender | diabolism |
| decollate | demeanour | describer | diachylon |
| decompose | demisable | desecrate | diaconate |
| decorator | demission | deserving | diacritic |
| dedicated | demiurgic | designate | diactinic |
| dedicatee | democracy | designing | dialectal |
| dedicator | demulcent | desirable | dialogism |
| deduction | demurrage | desolated | diametral |
| deductive | demystify | desolater | diamonded |
| defalcate | dendritic | desolator | dianoetic |
| defeatist | denotable | desperado | diaphragm |
| defection | denouncer | desperate | diarrhoea |
| defective | denseness | despotism | diastolic |
| defendant | dentately | destroyer | diathermy |
| defensive | dentiform | desuetude | diathesis |
| deference | dentistry | desultory | diathetic |
| deferment | dentition | detective | dichogamy |
| deficient | deodorant | detention | dichotomy |
| definable | deodorise | detergent | dictation |
| definably | deoxidise | determine | dictatrix |

didactics
dietarian
different
difficult
diffident
diffluent
diffusion
diffusive
digastric
digenesis
digestive
digitalin
digitalis
dignified
dilatable
diligence
dimension
dimidiate
dinothere
Dionysian
dioptrics
diphthong
dipterous
directive
disaffect
disaffirm
disappear
disarming
disavowal
disbelief
disburden
discerner
discharge
discoidal
discolour
discomfit

discourse
discovery
discredit
discusser
disembark
disengage
disfigure
dishonest
dishwater
disinfect
dislocate
dismantle
dismissal
disorient
disparage
disparate
dispeller
dispenser
dispersal
displayer
displease
disposed
dispraise
disproval
disregard
disrelish
disrepair
disrepute
disseisor
dissemble
dissenter
dissident
dissipate
dissolute
dissolver
dissonant

distemper
distiller
distorted
disturbed
disturber
divergent
diversify
diversion
diversity
diverting
dividable
divisible
divulsion
divulsive
dizziness
doctorate
doctrinal
dodecagon
dogmatise
dolefully
dominator
doorplate
dormitory
dosshouse
doubtless
doughtily
dowerless
downgrade
downiness
downright
downstage
downwards
draconian
draftsman
dragonfly
drainable

drainpipe
dramatist
draperied
dreamland
driftwood
drinkable
driveller
dromedary
drugstore
drumstick
dualistic
dubiously
duckboard
dumbfound
duodenary
duplicate
duskiness
dutifully
dysentery
dyspepsia
dyspeptic
dysphoria

E
eagerness
eaglewood
earliness
earnestly
earthward
earthwork
earthworm
easterner
eavesdrop
ebullient
eccentric
economise

| | | | |
|---|---|---|---|
| economist | embrasure | endurance | erudition |
| ecosphere | embrocate | energetic | erythrite |
| ectoblast | embroider | engineman | escalator |
| ectomorph | embryonic | engrailed | esplanade |
| edelweiss | emendator | engraving | essential |
| edibility | emergency | enjoyable | establish |
| editorial | eminently | enjoyment | estaminet |
| education | Emmenthal | enlighten | estimable |
| educative | emollient | enrapture | estimator |
| Edwardian | emolument | enrolment | estuarial |
| effectual | emotional | entelechy | estuarine |
| efficient | empathise | enteritis | esurience |
| effluence | emphasise | entertain | esuriency |
| effluvium | empirical | entoblast | Ethiopian |
| effulgent | emptiness | entophyte | ethmoidal |
| egression | emulation | entourage | ethnology |
| ejaculate | emulative | enunciate | etiquette |
| elaborate | emunctory | ephemeral | euphemism |
| elbowroom | enactment | epidermis | euphonium |
| eldership | enchanted | epigraphy | evergreen |
| electoral | enchanter | epileptic | everybody |
| electrode | enclosure | epitomise | evocation |
| electuary | encompass | epizootic | evocative |
| elegantly | encounter | eponymous | evolution |
| elemental | encourage | equipment | examining |
| elevation | encrinite | equipoise | exanimate |
| eliminate | endearing | Equisetum | exanthema |
| ellipsoid | endeavour | equitable | exarchate |
| eloquence | endlessly | equivocal | excavator |
| elsewhere | endoblast | equivoque | exceeding |
| elucidate | endocrine | eradicate | excellent |
| emanation | endomorph | erectness | exception |
| embarrass | endoplasm | erogenous | excessive |
| embattled | endoscope | eroticism | exchanger |
| embellish | endowment | erroneous | exchequer |
| embracery | endurable | erstwhile | excitable |

| | | | |
|---|---|---|---|
| exclaimer | expressly | fascicled | fireproof |
| exclusion | expulsion | fascinate | firmament |
| exclusive | expurgate | fashioner | fisherman |
| excrement | extension | faultless | fishiness |
| excretion | extensity | faveolate | fistulous |
| excurrent | extensive | favourite | fixedness |
| excursion | externals | febricula | flaccidly |
| excursive | extortion | febrifuge | flagellum |
| execrable | extradite | feculence | flagrancy |
| execution | extremist | fecundate | flagstaff |
| executive | extricate | fecundity | flagstone |
| executory | extrinsic | fellowman | flammable |
| executrix | extrovert | felonious | flashback |
| exegetics | extrusion | ferocious | flatterer |
| exemplary | exuberant | ferrotype | flatulent |
| exemption | exuberate | fertilise | flaunting |
| exerciser | exudation | fertility | flavoured |
| exfoliate | | festivity | fleckless |
| exhalable | F | fetidness | fledgling |
| exhausted | fabricate | fetishism | fleetness |
| exhibitor | facetious | feudalism | flexitime |
| existence | facsimile | feudalist | flightily |
| expansion | factorial | feudality | flippancy |
| expatiate | faithless | fibrinous | flocculus |
| expectant | faldstool | fictional | floodgate |
| expedient | falsehood | figurante | flotation |
| expertise | falseness | filiation | flouncing |
| expiation | falsifier | filigreed | flowering |
| expiatory | faltering | filleting | fluctuant |
| explainer | fanciless | fillister | fluctuate |
| expletive | fancywork | filminess | flyweight |
| explicate | fantasise | filoplume | foliation |
| exploiter | fantastic | fimbriate | following |
| explosive | farandole | financial | foodstuff |
| expositor | farmhouse | firebreak | foolhardy |
| expounder | farmstead | fireplace | foolproof |

| | | | |
|---|---|---|---|
| footloose | franchise | G | geniality |
| footprint | francolin | gaberdine | genitival |
| footstool | frankness | gabionade | gentleman |
| forasmuch | fraternal | gainsayer | gentlemen |
| forbidden | freelance | galantine | genuflect |
| forceless | Freemason | galingale | geodesist |
| foreclose | freestyle | galleries | geologise |
| forecourt | freighter | Gallicise | geologist |
| forefront | Frenchify | Gallicism | geomancer |
| foregoing | Frenchman | gallinule | geomantic |
| foreigner | frequency | gallivant | geometric |
| foreshore | freshness | gallowses | georgette |
| foresight | fricassee | gallstone | geriatric |
| forestall | frightful | galvanise | germander |
| foretaste | frogmarch | galvanism | germanium |
| formalise | frontless | gardening | germicide |
| formalism | frontward | garibaldi | germinate |
| formalist | frostbite | garmented | gerundive |
| formative | fructuous | garreteer | gestation |
| formulary | frugality | garrotter | gibberish |
| formulate | fruiterer | garrulity | girandole |
| fornicate | fruitless | gasconade | gladiator |
| forsythia | frustrate | gasholder | gladiolus |
| forthwith | fruticose | gastritis | glamorise |
| fortifier | fulgurate | gastropod | glandered |
| fortitude | fulminate | gatehouse | glandular |
| fortnight | fulsomely | gaucherie | glassware |
| fortunate | fundament | gaudiness | glengarry |
| fossilise | fungicide | gaugeable | glissando |
| fosterage | funicular | gazetteer | glomerate |
| foundling | funiculus | gearshift | glomerule |
| foundries | funnelled | gearwheel | glueyness |
| foveolate | furiously | geminated | glutinous |
| fractions | furnished | gemmation | glyceride |
| fractious | furnisher | genealogy | godmother |
| framework | fustigate | generator | godparent |

goffering
gogglebox
goldenrod
goldfield
goldsmith
gondolier
gonophore
goosander
gorgonian
gospeller
gossipped
Gothicism
goutiness
graceless
gracility
gradation
graduator
grandness
grandpapa
grandsire
granulate
granulite
granulose
grapevine
graphical
grassland
gratifier
gratulate
graveness
gravitate
greatness
greenback
greenhorn
greenness
greenroom
greenwood

grenadier
grenadine
greybeard
greywacke
grievance
grillroom
grimalkin
griminess
groceries
groomsman
grosgrain
grossness
grotesque
grounding
groundsel
gruffness
guardsman
guerrilla
guesswork
guestroom
guidepost
guileless
guillemot
guilloche
guiltless
guncotton
gunpowder
gustatory
guttering
gynoecium
gynophore
gyrfalcon
gyroscope

H
habergeon

habitable
hackberry
hackneyed
haematoid
hagiology
hailstone
hailstorm
hairiness
hairpiece
hairstyle
halfpence
halfpenny
halitosis
Halloween
Hallowmas
halophyte
hamstring
handiness
handiwork
handlebar
handshake
handspike
handstand
haphazard
happening
haranguer
harbinger
hardboard
hardihood
harlequin
harmfully
harmonica
harmonise
harpooner
harquebus
harshness

harvester
hastiness
hatchback
hatchment
hatefully
haversack
hazardous
headlight
headphone
headpiece
headstall
headstone
healthful
heartache
heartburn
heartfelt
heartless
heartsick
heartsore
heartwood
heaviness
hegemonic
heinously
hellebore
hemicycle
hemistich
herbalist
herbarium
herbivore
hereabout
hereafter
heretical
hereunder
hermitage
hetaerism
heterodox

hexachord
hexagonal
Hibernian
hidebound
hierarchy
hierogram
hierology
hilarious
hilliness
hindsight
hippocras
hirundine
hispidity
histogram
histology
historian
hoarfrost
hoariness
hobgoblin
hobnailed
hodometer
hollyhock
homestead
homewards
homicidal
homiletic
homograph
homophone
homunculi
honeymoon
hopefully
hopscotch
horologer
horseback
horsehair
horseplay

horseshoe
horsetail
horsewhip
hortative
hostility
hourglass
housemaid
housewife
howsoever
hoydenish
huckaback
huffiness
humankind
humdinger
humectant
humiliate
Hungarian
hunkydory
hurricane
husbandry
huskiness
hybridise
hybridism
hydrangea
hydraulic
hydrocele
hydrofoil
hydrology
hydrolyse
hydrozoan
hylozoism
hymnology
hyperbola
hyperbole
hypnotise
hypnotism

hypocrisy
hypocrite
hypogeous
hyponasty
hypostyle

I
ichthyoid
iconology
ideograph
idiomatic
idiopathy
ignitable
ignoramus
ignorance
iguanodon
illegally
illegible
illiberal
illogical
imaginary
imbricate
imbroglio
imbuement
imitative
immanence
immanency
immediacy
immensity
immersion
immigrant
immigrate
immodesty
immovable
immutable
impartial

impassion
impatiens
impeacher
impedance
impellent
impendent
imperator
imperfect
imperious
impetrate
impetuous
impingent
implement
impliedly
important
importune
imposture
impotence
impounder
imprecise
improbity
improving
improvise
imprudent
impudence
impulsion
impulsive
inability
inamorata
inamorato
inanimate
inaudible
inbreathe
incapable
incarnate
inception

| | | | |
|---|---|---|---|
| inceptive | infantile | inquiring | interline |
| incidence | infantine | insatiate | interlink |
| incipient | infection | insectary | interlock |
| inclement | infective | insertion | interlope |
| inclusive | inferable | insincere | interplay |
| incognito | infertile | insinuate | interpose |
| incorrect | infirmary | insistent | interpret |
| incubator | infirmity | insolence | intersect |
| incubuses | inflation | insolvent | intervene |
| inculcate | influence | inspector | intestacy |
| inculpate | influenza | instanter | intestate |
| incumbent | informant | instantly | intestine |
| incurable | infuriate | instigate | intorsion |
| incursion | infusible | insularly | intricacy |
| incurvate | ingenious | insulator | intricate |
| indecency | ingenuity | insulting | intriguer |
| indecorum | inglenook | insurable | intrinsic |
| indelible | ingrained | insurance | introduce |
| indelibly | inherence | insurgent | introvert |
| indemnify | inherency | integrant | intrusion |
| indenture | inheritor | integrate | intuition |
| indexical | inhibiter | integrity | intuitive |
| indigence | inhumanly | intellect | inunction |
| indignity | injurious | intendant | inurement |
| indispose | injustice | intensely | inutility |
| inducible | innermost | intensify | invention |
| inductile | innervate | intensity | inventive |
| inductive | innkeeper | intention | inventory |
| indulgent | innocence | intercept | inversion |
| indweller | innocuous | interface | invidious |
| inebriant | innovator | interfere | inviolate |
| inebriate | innuendos | interfuse | invisible |
| ineffable | inoculate | interject | invisibly |
| ineffably | inodorous | interlace | involucel |
| inelastic | inorganic | interlard | involucre |
| inelegant | inquiline | interleaf | inwrought |

irascible
irascibly
irksomely
ironbound
ironstone
ironworks
irradiant
irradiate
irregular
irritable
irritably
irruption
irruptive
isinglass
isoclinal
isolation
isomerism
isosceles
isotheral
Israelite
italicise
Italicism
itchiness
iteration
iterative
itinerary
itinerate

**J**
jaborandi
jacaranda
jargonise
jealously
jeeringly
jellyfish
jequirity

jewellery
jitterbug
jockstrap
jocularly
jocundity
joviality
joylessly
joyriding
judgeship
judicable
judicator
judicious
juiceless
juiciness
juridical
jurywoman
justifier
juvenilia
juxtapose

**K**
kalsomine
karabiner
kentledge
keratosis
keystroke
kidnapper
killingly
kilohertz
kilolitre
kilometre
kinematic
kinswoman
kinswomen
kitchener
kittiwake

knavishly
knockdown
knowingly
knowledge
kymograph

**L**
laborious
labouring
labyrinth
lacerable
lacertian
laciniate
lactation
laevulose
laminated
lampblack
lancewood
landgrave
landowner
landscape
landslide
lanthanum
larghetto
lassitude
lastingly
latecomer
laterally
laudatory
laughable
laughably
laundress
lawgiving
lazaretto
lazybones
leafiness

leakiness
leasehold
leastways
lecherous
leftovers
legendary
legionary
legislate
leitmotif
leniently
lethargic
letterbox
leucocyte
leucotomy
levelling
levelness
lexically
liability
libellous
liberally
liberator
librarian
libration
libratory
lickerish
lifeblood
ligatured
lightness
lightning
lightship
lightsome
limestone
limitable
limitless
limpidity
lineament

lineation
lineolate
lingering
lingulate
lintwhite
liquation
liquefier
liquidate
liquidise
liquorice
literally
litigable
litigious
litterbug
liturgies
liturgist
liverwort
liveryman
liverymen
livestock
lixiviate
locksmith
locomotor
lodestone
loftiness
logarithm
logically
logistics
logograph
logogriph
logomachy
loincloth
longcloth
longevous
longitude
longshore

loopholed
looseness
loquacity
lowermost
Lowlander
lowliness
lubricant
lubricate
lubricity
lucidness
luckiness
lucrative
lucubrate
ludicrous
lumbrical
lumpishly
lunisolar
lustfully
lustiness
luxuriate
luxurious
lymphatic
lyonnaise

M
macadamia
macaronic
macaronis
macedoine
machinate
machinery
macrocosm
macrurous
madrepore
maelstrom
magically

magistral
magnesian
magnesium
magnetise
magnifier
magnitude
mainframe
mainsheet
majuscule
malachite
maladroit
malanders
malicious
malignant
malignity
mallemuck
malleolar
malleolus
mammalian
mammalogy
mammogram
mammonism
mammonist
mammonite
mandatory
manducate
manganate
manganite
manhandle
Manichean
manifesto
manipular
mannequin
mannerism
mannerist
manoeuvre

manometer
manyplies
margarite
marginate
marijuana
marketing
marmalade
marmoreal
marquetry
marrowfat
marsupial
marsupium
martially
martyrdom
masculine
masochism
massagist
massively
masterful
matchable
matchless
matchwood
maternity
matriarch
matricide
matrimony
matronage
matutinal
maulstick
mausoleum
mawkishly
maxillary
meaningly
meanwhile
meatiness
mechanise

| | | | |
|---|---|---|---|
| mechanism | merriment | midsummer | modernism |
| mechanist | mescaline | midwinter | modernist |
| medallion | mesmerise | migration | modulator |
| medallist | mesmerist | migratory | moistness |
| mediately | mesoblast | milestone | molecular |
| mediation | mesophyte | milkiness | momentary |
| mediatise | messenger | millboard | momentous |
| mediative | messianic | millenary | monadical |
| medically | messieurs | millepore | monarchal |
| medicinal | messiness | milligram | monastery |
| megabucks | metalline | millipede | monatomic |
| megahertz | metallise | millstone | monobasic |
| megaspore | metameric | mincemeat | monochord |
| megathere | metaplasm | minefield | monocline |
| meliorate | meteorite | miniature | monocular |
| meliorism | meteoroid | mirthless | monodrama |
| melodrama | methaglyn | misbehave | monologue |
| meltingly | methodise | misbelief | monoplane |
| meltwater | Methodist | mischance | monostich |
| memorable | methought | miscreant | monotreme |
| memoranda | metonymic | misdirect | monticule |
| memoriser | metrology | misemploy | moodiness |
| menagerie | metronome | miserable | moonlight |
| mendacity | mezzotint | misgiving | moonraker |
| Mendelism | miasmatic | misguided | moonshine |
| mendicant | micaceous | misinform | moonshiny |
| meniscoid | microbial | mismanage | moonstone |
| Menshevik | microchip | misreport | moraliser |
| menstrual | microcosm | missioner | morbidity |
| mentality | microfilm | mistiness | mordacity |
| mercenary | micrology | mistletoe | mortality |
| mercerise | micropyle | mobocracy | mortgagor |
| merciless | microtome | mockingly | mortician |
| mercurial | microwave | modelling | mosaicist |
| mercurous | micturate | moderator | motorbike |
| merganser | middleman | modernise | motorboat |

motorcade
moustache
mucronate
muddiness
mullioned
multifoil
multiform
multiplex
multitude
mundanely
murderess
murderous
murmuring
muscovado
musically
mustiness
mutilator
muttering
mydriasis
mydriatic
myography
myrobalan
mysticism
mythicise
mythology

N
nameplate
Narcissus
narcotise
narration
narrative
naseberry
nastiness
natrolite
nattiness

naumachia
navigable
navigably
necessary
necessity
necrology
nectarial
needfully
neediness
nefarious
negligent
negotiate
neighbour
Neolithic
neologise
neologism
neoplasty
nephology
nephritic
Neptunian
neptunium
nervation
nervously
nescience
Nestorian
neuralgia
neuralgic
neurology
neurotomy
neutrally
newspaper
newsprint
Newtonian
nictation
nightclub
nightfall

nightmare
nightspot
nighttime
nigritude
ninetieth
nobleness
noctiluca
nocturnal
noiseless
nominally
nominator
nonentity
nonillion
nonpareil
northerly
northward
northwest
Norwegian
nostalgia
nostalgic
nostology
notabilia
notochord
notoriety
nourisher
novelette
novitiate
noxiously
nucleolus
nullipara
nullipore
numerable
numerical
nummulite
nunneries
nursemaid

nutritive
nystagmus

O
obbligato
obcordate
obedience
objectify
objection
objective
obliquity
oblivious
obscenity
obscurely
obsecrate
observant
observing
obstinate
obtrusion
obturator
obviously
occipital
occultism
octagonal
octastyle
octillion
octopuses
odourless
offensive
officiate
officious
offspring
olecranon
oleograph
olfactory
ombudsman

omissible
onomastic
onslaught
oogenesis
operative
operculum
ophiology
opportune
oppressor
oppugnant
optometer
opulently
orangeade
orbicular
orchestra
organised
orgiastic
orientate
originate
orphanage
orthodoxy
orthoepic
oscitancy
osteology
osteotome
ostracise
ostracism
otherwise
oubliette
ourselves
outermost
outgrowth
outnumber
outskirts
outspoken
outspread

outwardly
overblown
overboard
overcloud
overcrowd
overdress
overdrive
overjoyed
overmatch
overpower
overreach
overreact
oversleep
overstate
overstock
overtrade
overtrain
overvalue
overwhelm
oviferous
oviparous
ownership
oxidation
oxygenate
oxygenise
ozocerite

P

pacemaker
pachyderm
packaging
pademelon
pageantry
painfully
palatable
palatably

Palladian
palladium
palletise
palliasse
palmately
palmistry
palpebral
palpitate
pandurate
panegyric
panelling
panhandle
panoplied
pantalets
pantheism
pantheist
pantomime
paparazzo
paperback
papeterie
papillary
parachute
paragraph
paralytic
paramedic
parameter
paramount
parapeted
parataxis
parchment
paregoric
parentage
pargeting
parhelion
parotitis
parquetry

parricide
parsimony
partially
partitive
partridge
passenger
passional
passively
passivity
pastorale
pastorate
pasturage
patchwork
paternity
patiently
patriarch
patrician
patrimony
patriotic
patrolman
patroness
patronise
peaceable
peaceably
peasantry
peccaries
pectinate
pecuniary
pedagogic
pedagogue
pederasty
pedicular
pedometer
peevishly
pellitory
pencilled

pendently
pendragon
peneplain
peneplane
penetrate
peninsula
penitence
penniless
pennywort
pensioner
pentagram
pentangle
pentarchy
Pentecost
penthouse
penurious
perceiver
percolate
perdition
peregrine
perfecter
perfectly
perfervid
performer
perfumery
perimeter
periphery
perispore
peristome
peristyle
permanent
permeable
persecute
persevere
persimmon
personate

personify
personnel
persuader
pervasive
perverted
perverter
pessimism
pestilent
petiolate
petrology
petticoat
pettiness
pettishly
petulance
petulancy
phagocyte
phalanger
phalanges
phalarope
pharisaic
pharyngal
pheromone
philately
philippic
philology
phlebitis
phonetics
phonogram
phonology
phosphate
phosphene
phosphide
phosphite
photocell
photocopy
phototype

phrenetic
phycology
phyllopod
physicist
pickthank
piecemeal
piecework
pietistic
piggybank
pikestaff
pimpernel
pineapple
pinnately
pinstripe
pipsqueak
piratical
pirouette
piscatory
pisolitic
pistillate
pitchfork
piteously
pithiness
pituitary
pityingly
pixilated
placement
placental
placidity
plainness
plainsong
plaintiff
plaintive
planarian
planetoid
plasmatic

plasterer
platinise
platinous
platitude
Platonism
plausibly
playfully
plaything
plenarily
plenitude
plentiful
pleuritic
ploughboy
ploughman
plumpness
plunderer
pluralise
pluralism
pluralist
plurality
Plutonian
plutonium
pneumonia
pneumonic
poignancy
pointedly
pointsman
poisonous
policeman
politesse
political
politicly
pollution
polonaise
polybasic
polygonal

| | | | |
|---|---|---|---|
| polymorph | precision | primitive | propriety |
| polyphone | precocity | princedom | proptosis |
| polystyle | predatory | prismatic | proscribe |
| polythene | predicant | privateer | prosector |
| pompadour | predicate | privately | prosecute |
| pomposity | predictor | privation | proselyte |
| pompously | prefatory | privatise | prosiness |
| poorhouse | preferrer | privilege | prostrate |
| porcelain | prefigure | probation | protester |
| porcupine | pregnable | probative | prototype |
| porterage | prejudice | proboscis | protozoan |
| portfolio | prelatist | processor | providing |
| portrayal | prelusive | proclitic | provision |
| possessed | premature | proconsul | provisory |
| posterior | preoccupy | prodigies | provoking |
| posterity | prepotent | profanity | proximity |
| posthaste | preputial | professed | prudently |
| postnatal | prerecord | professor | prurience |
| postulate | preschool | profiteer | pruriency |
| potassium | prescient | profusely | psoriasis |
| potentate | prescribe | profusion | psychotic |
| potential | prescript | prognosis | ptarmigan |
| potpourri | presentee | projector | pubescent |
| poussette | presenter | prolepsis | publicise |
| powerless | preserver | proleptic | publicity |
| practical | pretended | prolixity | publisher |
| practised | pretender | promenade | puerilism |
| practiser | preterite | prominent | puerility |
| pragmatic | pretermit | promising | puerperal |
| preachify | prettyish | promotion | pugnacity |
| prebendal | preventer | promotive | puissance |
| precatory | priceless | pronation | pullulate |
| precedent | priestess | pronounce | pulpiness |
| preceding | primarily | proofread | pulpiteer |
| preceptor | primatial | propeller | pulsatile |
| precisely | primipara | proponent | pulverise |

| | | | |
|---|---|---|---|
| pumiceous | quarterly | ravishing | redoubted |
| punchball | quartzite | razorbill | reducible |
| punctuate | queerness | readdress | reduction |
| pungently | querulous | readiness | redundant |
| punishing | quickener | realistic | refectory |
| pupillary | quicklime | realities | reference |
| puppeteer | quickness | reanimate | reflation |
| purchaser | quiescent | reappoint | reflector |
| purgative | quietness | rearguard | reflexive |
| purgatory | quittance | reasoning | reforming |
| puritanic | quixotism | reattempt | refractor |
| purloiner | quizzical | rebaptism | refresher |
| purposive | quodlibet | rebellion | refurbish |
| pursuance | quotidian | recapture | refurnish |
| pushchair | | receiving | refutable |
| pussyfoot | R | receptive | regardant |
| putative | rabbinate | recession | regardful |
| putridity | rabidness | recipient | regarding |
| pyramidal | racehorse | reckoning | registrar |
| pyrethrum | racialism | reclusive | regretful |
| pyritical | racketeer | recognise | regularly |
| pyrogenic | raconteur | recollect | regulated |
| pyrolysis | radiantly | reconcile | rehearsal |
| pyromania | radiogram | recoverer | rehearser |
| pyrometer | radiology | recreancy | reimprint |
| | raininess | recrement | reinforce |
| Q | rainproof | recruiter | reinspire |
| quadratic | rampantly | rectangle | reinstall |
| quadrille | rancidity | rectifier | reinstate |
| quadruped | rancorous | rectitude | reiterate |
| quadruple | randomise | rectorate | rejection |
| Quakerism | rapacious | rectorial | rejoinder |
| qualified | rapturous | recurring | relevance |
| qualities | raspberry | recurvate | relieving |
| quarryman | ratepayer | recusancy | religious |
| quartered | rauwolfia | recycling | remainder |

remigrate
remindful
remission
remittent
removable
renascent
renitency
renovator
reparable
reparably
repeating
repellent
repentant
replenish
reportage
reposeful
repossess
represent
reprimand
reprobate
reptilian
republish
repugnant
repulsive
reputable
resentful
reservist
residence
residuary
resilient
resistant
resonance
resonator
restfully
restively
resultant

resurgent
resurrect
retaining
retaliate
retention
retentive
reticence
retractor
retrieval
retriever
retrocede
reversely
reversion
revocable
revolting
revulsion
revulsive
rewarding
rheometer
rhinology
rhythmics
rightness
rigidness
ringleted
riotously
ritualism
ritualist
riverside
roadblock
rockiness
roisterer
roominess
Roquefort
rosaceous
rosewater
rostellum

rotundity
roughness
roundelay
roundworm
rubberise
ruffianly
ruination
ruinously
runcinate
rusticity
rustiness

S
sabadilla
sackcloth
sacrament
sacrifice
safeguard
safflower
sagacious
sailboard
sailcloth
sainthood
salacious
salesroom
salmonoid
saltation
saltwater
salubrity
salvation
sanctuary
sandiness
sandpaper
sandpiper
sandstone
sandstorm

sapiently
sarcastic
sargassum
sartorius
satanical
satellite
saturable
saturated
saturnine
saunterer
saxophone
scalloped
scantling
scapegoat
scapolite
scarfskin
scarifier
scatology
scatterer
scavenger
scentless
sceptical
scheelite
schistose
schlemiel
schnauzer
schnozzle
schoolboy
sciential
scintilla
scirrhoid
sclerosis
sclerotic
scoliosis
scorbutic
scorecard

| | | | |
|---|---|---|---|
| scraggily | sensorium | sheldrake | sinuosity |
| scrapbook | sentencer | shellfish | siphonage |
| scratcher | separable | shiftless | skyrocket |
| screaming | separably | shingling | slackness |
| screwball | separator | shipboard | slanderer |
| scrimmage | September | shipshape | slapstick |
| scrimshaw | septenary | shipwreck | slavishly |
| sculpture | sepulchre | shoreline | sleekness |
| scumbling | sepulture | shortfall | slenderly |
| scutcheon | sequester | shorthand | slighting |
| searching | serenader | shortwave | slivovitz |
| seaworthy | serialise | shoveltul | slouching |
| sebaceous | scriccous | shoveller | slumberer |
| secateurs | seriously | showiness | smilingly |
| seclusion | sermonise | showpiece | smokeless |
| secretion | serviette | showplace | smokiness |
| secretory | servilely | shuffling | sniveller |
| sectarian | servitude | sibilance | snowberry |
| secularly | sessional | sibylline | snowstorm |
| securable | sevenfold | sidelight | soapstone |
| seditious | seventeen | siderosis | soberness |
| seduction | severable | sidetrack | sobriquet |
| seductive | severance | sidewards | socialise |
| segmental | sexuality | sightless | socialism |
| seigneury | shadiness | signalman | socialist |
| selective | shakiness | signatory | socialite |
| selenious | shallowly | signorina | societies |
| semibreve | shambling | silicosis | sociology |
| semicolon | shameless | siliquose | sociopath |
| semiology | shapeless | similarly | softcover |
| semisolid | sharpener | simpatico | softening |
| seneschal | sharpness | simpleton | solfeggio |
| sensation | shaveling | simulator | solidness |
| senseless | sheepcote | sincerely | soliloquy |
| sensitise | sheepfold | sincerity | solitaire |
| sensitive | sheepskin | singleton | sometimes |

| | | | |
|---|---|---|---|
| somnolent | speedwell | stagnancy | stolidity |
| sonneteer | spelunker | stainless | stomacher |
| sootiness | spermatic | staircase | stomachic |
| sophistry | sphincter | stairwell | stonewall |
| sophomore | spiciness | stalemate | stoniness |
| sopranino | spiculate | staleness | stoplight |
| sorceress | spindrift | staminate | stoutness |
| sorriness | spininess | stanchion | straggler |
| sortilege | spinnaker | standpipe | strangely |
| sottishly | spinosity | starboard | strangles |
| soundless | spirillum | starchily | strangury |
| soundness | spiritual | statement | stratagem |
| sourdough | spleenful | stateroom | strategic |
| southeast | spleenish | statesmen | streamlet |
| southerly | splendour | stationer | strenuous |
| southmost | splenetic | statistic | stretcher |
| southward | splintery | statuette | stricture |
| southwest | spokesman | statutory | stringent |
| sovereign | spoliator | steamboat | stripling |
| sovietism | spoonbill | steepness | strobilus |
| spacewalk | sporangia | steersman | strongbox |
| spadework | sporozoan | stellular | strontium |
| spaghetti | sportsman | stepchild | struggler |
| spareness | spotlight | sterilise | studiedly |
| sparingly | spoutless | sterility | stupefier |
| sparteine | springbok | sternmost | stupidity |
| spasmodic | springing | stiffener | stylishly |
| spatulate | springlet | stiffness | suability |
| speakable | sprinkler | stigmatic | subalpine |
| spearmint | sputterer | stimulant | subarctic |
| specially | squalidly | stimulate | subdeacon |
| spectacle | squeamish | stinkweed | subduable |
| speculate | stabilise | stipitate | subereous |
| speculums | stability | stitching | sublessee |
| speechify | stableboy | stockpile | sublimate |
| speedball | stableman | stockyard | sublimely |

| | | | |
|---|---|---|---|
| sublunary | suppurate | symbolist | tectonics |
| submarine | supremely | symmetric | telegraph |
| subnormal | surcharge | symposium | telemeter |
| subscript | surfboard | synagogue | teleology |
| substance | surgeoncy | syncopate | telepathy |
| subtenant | surmising | syndicate | telephone |
| subtitles | surmullet | syneresis | telltales |
| subverter | surpliced | synizesis | tellurian |
| successor | surprised | synonymic | tellurium |
| succotash | surrender | syntactic | temporary |
| succulent | surveying | synthesis | temptable |
| sudorific | suspender | synthetic | tenacious |
| suffering | suspensor | | tenaculum |
| suffocate | sustainer | T | tenderise |
| suffragan | swaggerer | tablature | tendinous |
| suffusion | swallower | tableware | tenebrous |
| suggester | swansdown | tabularly | tenseness |
| sulkiness | swarthily | tacamahac | tensility |
| sulphuret | sweatband | tactician | tentative |
| sulphuric | sweatshop | tailboard | tepidness |
| sultanate | sweetener | tailoring | termagant |
| summarily | sweetmeat | tailplane | terminate |
| summarise | sweptwing | talkative | terrorise |
| summation | swiftness | tangerine | terrorism |
| summonses | swimmeret | tantalise | terseness |
| sumptuous | swindling | tarantula | tessitura |
| sunniness | swinishly | tarnisher | testament |
| sunstroke | swordplay | tarpaulin | testatrix |
| superfine | swordsman | tartarise | testimony |
| superglue | sycophant | tautology | tetralogy |
| supernova | syllogise | tawniness | thatching |
| superpose | syllogism | taxidermy | theatrics |
| supersede | symbiosis | taximeter | theocrasy |
| superstar | symbiotic | taxonomic | theogonic |
| supervise | symbolise | teachable | theomachy |
| suppliant | symbolism | technique | theoriser |

thickhead
thighbone
thinkable
thirstily
thirtieth
thrashing
threefold
threshold
thrilling
throttler
throwaway
throwback
thumbless
thumbnail
thumbtack
thyroxine
tidewater
tightknit
tightrope
timbering
timeshare
timidness
timocracy
tiredness
titillate
titularly
toadstool
tolerance
tolerator
tollbooth
tomentose
tonometer
tonsillar
toolmaker
toothache
toothpick

topically
tormentil
tormentor
tornadoes
torpidity
torridity
touchline
touchmark
touchwood
toughness
townsfolk
trabecula
traceably
tracksuit
tractably
tradesmen
tradition
trainable
traitress
transcend
transform
transient
transmute
transpire
transport
transpose
trappings
trattoria
traveller
traverser
treadmill
treasurer
trebuchet
trembling
tremulous
triatomic

tribalism
tribesman
tribology
tribunate
tributary
triclinic
triennial
triforium
trigonous
trilinear
trilobate
trimester
trinomial
triumphal
trivially
troopship
troubling
trousseau
truculent
trumpeter
truncheon
tubulated
tulipwood
tumidness
turbidity
turbinate
turbulent
turgidity
turnabout
turnround
turnstone
turntable
turquoise
tutorship
tyrannise
tyrannous

U
ultimatum
umbellate
unadorned
unadvised
unamiable
unanimous
unassured
unavenged
unbeknown
unblessed
unbounded
unceasing
uncertain
uncivilly
unclouded
unconcern
uncovered
uncrowned
undaunted
undecided
underbred
underdone
underfoot
undermine
underpass
underplay
undersell
undershot
underside
undertone
underwear
underwood
undesired
undivided
undoubted

| | | | |
|---|---|---|---|
| undreamed | unquietly | vaccinate | veracious |
| undulated | unreality | vacillate | veratrine |
| undutiful | unrelated | vagueness | verbalise |
| unearthly | unscathed | vainglory | verbalist |
| unendowed | unsettled | valentine | verdigris |
| unengaged | unsheathe | vallation | veridical |
| unequable | unsightly | vallecula | veritable |
| unequally | unskilled | valuation | vermicide |
| unexpired | unsoundly | valueless | vermiform |
| unexposed | unsparing | vandalism | vermilion |
| unfeeling | unspotted | vapidness | verminous |
| unfeigned | unstained | vaporific | verrucose |
| unfitness | unstamped | vapourish | versatile |
| unfitting | unstudied | variation | versifier |
| ungallant | untainted | variegate | vertebral |
| unguarded | untenable | varieties | vesicular |
| unhappily | untrained | variolate | vestibule |
| unheedful | unwelcome | variolous | vestigial |
| unheeding | unwilling | variously | vexatious |
| uniformly | unwitting | varnisher | vibratile |
| uninjured | unwounded | vasectomy | vibration |
| uniparous | unwritten | vasomotor | vibrative |
| unisexual | unwrought | vassalage | vibratory |
| Unitarian | updraught | veeringly | vicariate |
| univalent | upholster | vegetable | vicarious |
| unjointed | uppermost | vehemence | vicarship |
| unknowing | uprightly | vehicular | vicennial |
| unlearned | urceolate | vellicate | vicereine |
| unluckily | usherette | velveteen | viciously |
| unmatched | utilities | veneering | victimise |
| unmeaning | utterable | venerable | Victorian |
| unmerited | utterance | vengeance | victories |
| unmixedly | uttermost | veniality | videlicet |
| unmusical | | ventilate | videotape |
| unnoticed | V | ventricle | viewpoint |
| unopposed | vacancies | venturous | vigesimal |

vigilance
vigilante
villiform
villosity
violently
violinist
virescent
virginity
virgulate
virtually
virtuosos
viscosity
viscounty
visionary
visualise
vitelline
vitiation
vitriolic
vivacious
vividness
vocalness
voiceless
volcanoes
voltmeter
volunteer
voodooism
voracious
vorticism
vouchsafe
vulcanian
vulcanism
vulcanite
vulgarise
vulnerary
vulturine

W

wailingly
waistband
waistcoat
waistline
wallabies
walloping
wallpaper
wandering
warehouse
warranter
warrantor
washiness
waspishly
wassailer
wasteland
wasteness
wastepipe
watchband
watchword
waterbuck
waterfall
waterfowl
waterless
watermark
watershed
waterside
wayfaring
waywardly
weariness
wearisome
weathered
weeknight
weighable
weirdness
westwards
whalebone

wheatmeal
wheedling
wheelbase
wherefore
whereupon
wherewith
wherryman
whetstone
whichever
whimperer
whimsical
whirlwind
whiskered
whisperer
wholemeal
wholeness
wholesale
wholesome
widowhood
wieldable
willpower
windblown
windbreak
windiness
windswept
wineglass
winepress
wisecrack
withdrawn
withering
withstand
witnesser
woebegone
wolfhound
wolfishly
wolverine

womenfolk
wonderful
woodcraft
woodlouse
wordiness
workbench
workhorse
workhouse
worldling
worldwide
worthless
wrestling
wristband
wrongdoer

X

xenophile
xylograph
xylophone

Y

yachtsman
yardstick
yellowish
yesterday
youngster

Z

zealously
zeugmatic
zoography
zoologist
zootomist
zucchetto
zygomatic
zymometer

# NINE-LETTER MULTIPLE WORDS

**A**
about face
ad interim
ad nauseam
air-cooled
alma mater
amino acid
angel dust
angle-iron
arctic fox

**B**
baby grand
bald-faced
ballot box
battle cry
bay window
bell tower
belly-flop
black hole
blind date
blood bank
bomb-proof
bon voyage
booby trap
bore stiff
boric acid
bottoms up
brain dead
brain wave
brand-iron
brazil nut
bread line

break away
bride-cake
broad bean
Bronze Age
brown coal
buffet car
bugle horn
bush-metal
by the book

**C**
Canada Day
candle-nut
cane sugar
cap in hand
carpet-rod
cart-horse
case study
cashew nut
cast-steel
castor oil
casual sex
cat litter
cat-silver
cease fire
chain gang
chain mail
cheek-bone
cherry-pit
chop-house
clay-slate
clog-dance
close call

close-time
cloth hall
cloth-yard
cloud nine
co-trustee
coach-hire
coal-black
coal-plant
coffee bar
cold cream
colour bar
come clean
come of age
comic book
common law
coral reef
coral tree
coral-wood
cost a bomb
cost price
cotton-gin
cough drop
court hand
court-roll
cow-feeder
crab louse
crab-apple
cramp-iron
crash dive
crash-land
cream cake
cross-eyed
crow's-feet

crow's-nest
crow-quill
crush room
cut it fine

**D**
damp squib
dapple-bay
dark horse
dead-drunk
death duty
death mask
death rate
death wish
death-bell
deck chair
Deep South
deep space
delta wing
dining car
disc brake
disk drive
dog eat dog
dog-collar
down train
down under
drag queen
drum-major
dumb cluck
dura mater
dust-brand
Dutch oven

**E**
eagle-eyed
early bird
early days
eel-basket
elder-wine
en passant
estate car
et ceteras

**F**
fairy tale
fancy fair
fancy-free
fast track
filter tip
fire power
first-rate
flag-waver
flap-carcd
flay-flint
flesh-hook
flesh-meat
flood tide
flood-mark
flow chart
folic acid
folk music
food chain
force pump
force-feed
free trade
free verse
free-range
freeze-dry
front door

funny-bone

**G**
gamma rays
gang-plank
get down to
giant ship
gilt-edged
ginger ale
go bananas
go down big
go haywire
go sky high
go-between
going-over
gold plate
golden boy
golf links
goose-step
grace note
grand jury
grand slam
grand tour
gravy boat
great-aunt
Greek fire
Greek gift
green belt
green-eyed
gross-beak
ground hog
ground ivy
guinea pig

**H**
half-baked

half-truth
halo scope
hansom cab
hard facts
hard stuff
hats off to
head first
head start
heavy duty
heroic age
high jinks
high water
high-class
high-flier
high-flown
high-flyer
high-power
hit the hay
hold out on
hold water
home truth
home-grown
honky-tonk
hot potato
hue and cry
humble pie
hush money

**I**
ice hockey
ill at ease
ill-gotten
in so far as
income tax
inner city
inner tube

inside job
inside out
Irish moss
Irish stew
iron horse

**J**
jam-packed
jet engine
jet stream
job-seeker
jobs worth
joss stick

**K**
king-craft
king-sized
kiwi fruit
knight age
knock back

**L**
ladies' man
laid paper
land of Nod
last rites
last-ditch
latter-day
launch pad
lawn mower
lay reader
lay to rest
leave cold
lend a hand
lie in wait
life cycle

life event
light-year
lights out
lily-white
live in sin
live rough
logo mania
long johns
long-range
look sharp
look small
look smart
look-alike
loose-leaf
Lord Mayor
lose heart
lost cause
love child
lower-case

**M**
make a pass
make merry
make use of
mare's-tail
match play
milk teeth
monk's hood
Morse code
moth-eaten

**N**
name names
near thing
no worries
North Pole

north star
Number Ten

**O**
Odd Fellow
odd man out
of no avail
off-limits
Old Bailey
old master
old school
on balance
on the mend
on the trot
open doors
orlop deck
out of date
out of hand
out of turn

**P**
packed out
party line
peace camp
peace pipe
penny-wise
per capita
petit four
phone call
pick clean
pier table
pillar box
piping hot
poison gas
poker-face
pole vault

polo shirt
press-gang
prime time
punch card
put paid to

**R**
radial ply
radio wave
raise Cain
rare earth
razor clam
re-educate
re-present
ready-made
red mullet
red pepper
red-handed
red-letter
relay race
relief map
right-wing
ring a bell
rock 'n' roll
role model
round trip
royal blue
run across
run around

**S**
safe house
safety net
safety pin
saint's day
salad days

sales talk
saloon bar
sand wedge
screw pine
sea anchor
sea breeze
seamy side
see things
seed coral
self-drive
self-image
sell short
set theory
set-square
shake a leg
sheet bend
shell suit
shell-duck
shirt-tail
shock-jock
short time
short-term
sickle-man
silver fox
sky-diving
slave ship
sleep with
sloppy joe
slouch hat
small talk
small-time
smart card
snare drum
snow-blind
soap opera
soda water

soft drink
soft touch
soft-focus
soft-pedal
solar wind
solo whist
sore point
sotto voce
soul music
sound bite
sour cream
spaced-out
spark plug
spin a yam
sponge bag
stage door
stag party
steel wool
sticky end
stink bomb
stone-cold
stone-deaf
stop press
store card
straw poll
strike oil

strike pay
string tie
sugar cane
sun lotion
sure thing
sweet-talk
swing-wing
Swiss roll

T

take a part
take heart
take sides
take steps
talking to
tall order
teddy bear
test pilot
theme song
thin on top
think-tank
ticked off
tidal wave
tiger moth
tiger's eye
time flies

tip one off
title deed
to speak of
to the fore
to the life
top drawer
top secret
torch song
totem pole
town house
track shoe
trade wind
trans fats
trunk line
trunk road
tsetse fly
two-stroke

U

under fire
unheard-of
Union Jack
unit trust
up the ante
up the wall
up-country

V

vice versa
visual aid
voice-over
volte-face
vox populi

W

warm front
washed-out
washing-up
wasp waist
water bird
water down
water polo
weak-kneed
well out of
wide-angle
wing chair
wood smoke
work of art
worse luck
worst-case

Y

yester-eve

# TEN-LETTER WORDS

A
abbreviate
abdication
aberration
abhorrence
abjectness
abjuration
abnegation
abnormally
abominable
aboriginal
aborigines
abortively
aboveboard
abridgment
abrogation
abruptness
absolutely
absolution
absolutism
absorbable
absorption
abstemious
abstention
abstinence
abstracted
abstractly
abstrusely
absurdness
abundantly
accelerate
accentuate
acceptable

acceptance
accessible
accidental
accomplice
accomplish
accordance
accountant
accounting
accredited
accumulate
accurately
accusation
accustomed
acquainted
acrobatics
actionable
activeness
adamantine
adaptation
additional
adequately
adjacently
adjectival
adjudicate
adjustable
adjustment
administer
admiration
admiringly
admissible
admittance
admittedly
admonition

adolescent
adroitness
adsorption
adulterate
adulterous
adventurer
advertiser
aerobatics
aeronautic
aerostatic
aesthetics
affability
affectedly
afflicting
affliction
affronting
aficionado
aforenamed
afterbirth
aftershave
aftertaste
afterwards
agapanthus
aggrandise
aggravated
aggression
alarmingly
alcoholism
alexanders
algebraist
alienation
alimentary
allegation

allegiance
allegorise
allegretto
allergenic
alleviator
alliterate
allocation
allurement
alluringly
allusively
alpenstock
alphabetic
alteration
alterative
alternator
altogether
altruistic
amalgamate
amateurish
ambassador
ambidexter
ambivalent
ambulation
ambulatory
ameliorate
amerceable
Amerindian
amiability
ammunition
amphibious
amputation
anagogical
analysable

analytical
anaplastic
anastomose
anatomical
angiosperm
Anglophile
Anglophobe
angularity
annexation
annihilate
annotation
anointment
answerable
antagonise
antagonism
antagonist
antecedent
antepenult
anteriorly
anthracite
anthropoid
antibiotic
anticipate
anticlimax
antifreeze
antiquated
antiseptic
antisocial
antistatic
antithesis
aphoristic
apocalypse
apocryphal
apolitical
apologetic
apoplectic

apostatise
apostolate
apostrophe
apothecary
apotheosis
apparently
apparition
appearance
appeasable
appetising
appetitive
applicable
applicator
appositely
apposition
appreciate
apprentice
approvable
aquamarine
arachnidan
arbitrator
archbishop
archdeacon
archetypal
architrave
aristocrat
arithmetic
Armageddon
arrogantly
arrogation
artfulness
articulate
artificial
asbestosis
ascendancy
asceticism

ascribable
aspersions
asphyxiate
aspidistra
aspiration
aspiringly
assailable
assemblage
assessable
assessment
asseverate
assignment
assimilate
assistance
assortment
assumption
astonished
astounding
astringent
astrologer
astronomer
astronomic
astuteness
asymmetric
atmosphere
attachment
attainable
attainment
attendance
attraction
attractive
auctioneer
audibility
audiometer
auditorium
auscultate

auspicious
Australian
authorship
autocratic
automation
automotive
autonomous
autoplasty
autoteller
avaricious
aviculture

B
Babylonian
backgammon
background
backhanded
backhander
backstroke
bafflingly
balderdash
ballistics
ballooning
balustrade
bandmaster
banishment
bankruptcy
barcarolle
barebacked
barefooted
bargeboard
barleycorn
barometric
barrenness
bastardise
battlement

| | | | |
|---|---|---|---|
| Beaujolais | blackboard | bridesmaid | camouflage |
| beautician | blackguard | bridgehead | campaigner |
| becomingly | Blackshirt | brigantine | candescent |
| bedchamber | blacksmith | brightness | candidness |
| bedclothes | blancmange | brilliance | candyfloss |
| beforehand | blasphemer | brilliancy | canonicals |
| believable | blissfully | broadsheet | canonicity |
| believably | blistering | broadsword | cantaloupe |
| belladonna | blitzkrieg | brokenness | cantatrice |
| belongings | blockhouse | bronchitis | cantilever |
| benefactor | bloodhound | buckjumper | capability |
| beneficent | bloodstain | buckpasser | capacitate |
| beneficial | bloodstock | budgerigar | capitalise |
| benevolent | bloodstone | buffoonery | capitalism |
| besprinkle | blustering | bullheaded | capitalist |
| bestialise | boastfully | bumfreezer | capitulate |
| bestiality | boilersuit | burdensome | cappuccino |
| bestseller | boisterous | bureaucrat | capricious |
| bewitching | bombardier | burglarise | captiously |
| biblically | bookmarker | bushranger | carabineer |
| bibliology | bookseller | buttermilk | carbonated |
| bibliopegy | borderline | buttonhole | carbuncled |
| bibliophil | bothersome | | carcinogen |
| biennially | bottleneck | C | cardiogram |
| billposter | bottlenose | cadaverous | cardiology |
| binoculars | bottomless | calamander | carelessly |
| biogenetic | bowdlerise | calamitous | caricature |
| biographer | boyishness | calcareous | carpellary |
| biometrics | Brahmanism | calceiform | carpellate |
| biophysics | brainchild | calculable | cartwright |
| bipartisan | brainstorm | calculated | castigator |
| birthplace | brazenness | calculator | castration |
| birthright | breadfruit | Caledonian | catabolism |
| birthstone | breakwater | calumniate | catafalque |
| bitterness | breathless | calumnious | catalectic |
| bituminous | bridegroom | camelopard | cataleptic |

| | | | |
|---|---|---|---|
| catchpenny | Chaucerian | clangorous | commonness |
| catechetic | chauvinism | classicism | commonweal |
| catechumen | chauvinist | classicist | communique |
| categorise | cheapskate | classified | commutable |
| catholicon | checkpoint | clavichord | comparable |
| cautionary | cheerfully | clavicular | comparison |
| cautiously | cheeriness | cleverness | compassion |
| celebrated | Chekhovian | clinically | compatible |
| censorious | chemically | clodhopper | compatriot |
| censorship | chessboard | cloistered | compelling |
| censurable | chickenpox | codswallop | compendium |
| centennial | childbirth | cogitation | compensate |
| centralise | childishly | coherently | competence |
| centrefold | chilliness | cohesively | competitor |
| centrifuge | chimerical | collarless | complacent |
| cerebellum | chimneypot | collateral | complement |
| ceremonial | chimpanzee | collection | completely |
| chalcedony | chinchilla | collective | completion |
| chalkiness | chiselling | collegiate | complexion |
| challenger | chivalrous | collocutor | complexity |
| champignon | chlorinate | colloquial | compliance |
| chancellor | chloroform | coloratura | complicacy |
| chandelier | chopsticks | combustion | complicate |
| changeable | Christlike | comeliness | complicity |
| changeless | chromosome | comestible | compliment |
| changeover | chronicler | commandant | compositor |
| channelled | chronology | commandeer | compounder |
| chaplaincy | chubbiness | commanding | comprehend |
| chargeable | churchgoer | commentary | compressed |
| charioteer | churlishly | commentate | compressor |
| charitable | cinerarium | commercial | compromise |
| Charleston | circuitous | commissary | compulsion |
| charmingly | circularly | commission | compulsive |
| chartreuse | circumcise | commitment | compulsory |
| chatelaine | circumflex | commixture | computable |
| chatterbox | circumvent | commonalty | concentric |

conception
conceptual
concertina
concession
conciliate
concluding
conclusion
concoction
concordant
concretely
concretion
concurrent
concussion
condescend
condolence
conduction
conductive
confection
conference
confession
confidante
confidence
confiscate
confluence
conformist
conformity
confounded
congenital
congestion
congregate
congruence
conjecture
conjointly
connection
connivance
conquering

conscience
consecrate
consequent
considered
consistent
consolable
consortium
conspiracy
constantly
constipate
constitute
constraint
consultant
consumable
consummate
contagious
contention
contestant
contiguous
continence
contingent
continuity
continuous
contortion
contraband
contracted
contractor
contradict
contravene
contribute
contrition
controvert
convalesce
convenient
convention
convergent

conversant
conversely
conversion
conveyance
conviction
convincing
convoluted
convulsion
coordinate
copperhead
copulation
copywriter
coquettish
cornucopia
coronation
corpulence
correction
corrective
correspond
corroboree
corrugated
corruption
corticated
costliness
cottontail
councillor
counsellor
counteract
countryman
courageous
covetously
cowpuncher
craftiness
cragginess
crankshaft
credential

creditable
criminally
criosphinx
crisscross
critically
crossbreed
crosscheck
crosspatch
crosspiece
crosstrees
crustacean
crustiness
cryogenics
cryptogram
cryptology
cuckoopint
cuddlesome
cuirassier
cultivable
cultivator
cumbersome
cumbrously
cummerbund
cumulative
curability
curmudgeon
curriculum
curvaceous
cussedness
cuttlebone
cuttlefish
cyberspace
cystoscope

D
daintiness

| daisywheel | definition | denunciate | desiccator |
|---|---|---|---|
| daydreamer | definitive | deodoriser | designator |
| deactivate | deflection | department | designedly |
| deadliness | defrayment | dependably | desolation |
| deathwatch | degeneracy | dependence | despairing |
| debasement | degenerate | dependency | despicable |
| debauchery | degradable | depilation | despondent |
| debentured | dehumanise | depilatory | detachable |
| debilitate | dejectedly | deplorable | detachment |
| debouchure | delectable | deployment | detainment |
| decahedral | delectably | depolarise | detectable |
| decampment | delegation | depopulate | detestable |
| decapitate | deliberate | deportment | detonation |
| decelerate | delicately | deposition | detraction |
| decimation | delightful | depository | detractive |
| decisively | delineator | deprecator | devilishly |
| declassify | delinquent | depreciate | devitalise |
| declension | delocalise | depressant | devolution |
| declinable | delphinium | depression | devotional |
| decolonise | demobilise | depressive | diabolical |
| decompress | democratic | deputation | diagnostic |
| decoration | demography | deracinate | diagonally |
| decorative | demoiselle | deregulate | dialectics |
| decorously | demolisher | deridingly | diaphanous |
| dedication | demolition | derisively | dictionary |
| deductible | demoniacal | derivation | dielectric |
| deepfreeze | demonology | derivative | difference |
| defacement | demoralise | dermatitis | difficulty |
| defamation | demureness | derogation | diffidence |
| defamatory | dendriform | derogatory | diffusible |
| defecation | denominate | desalinate | digestible |
| defendable | denotation | descendant | digitation |
| defensible | denotative | descendent | digitiform |
| deficiency | denouement | descending | digression |
| defilement | densimeter | deservedly | dilapidate |
| definitely | denudation | deshabille | dilatation |

| | | | |
|---|---|---|---|
| dilatorily | disgusting | dissuasion | E |
| dilettante | disharmony | dissuasive | earthbound |
| diligently | dishearten | distension | earthiness |
| dillydally | dishonesty | distillate | earthquake |
| diminuendo | disincline | distillery | earthwards |
| diminution | disinherit | distinctly | ebullience |
| diminutive | disjointed | distortion | echinoderm |
| dimorphous | disloyally | distracted | economical |
| diphtheria | disloyalty | distraught | ecumenical |
| diplomatic | dismissive | distressed | eczematous |
| directness | disordered | distribute | edifyingly |
| disability | disorderly | divaricate | editorship |
| disappoint | dispassion | divergence | effeminate |
| disapprove | dispensary | divination | effervesce |
| disastrous | dispersion | divisional | efficiency |
| disbelieve | dispirited | doggedness | effloresce |
| discerning | displeased | dogmatiser | effortless |
| discipline | disposable | dolorously | effrontery |
| disclaimer | dispossess | domination | effulgence |
| disclosure | disputable | doorkeeper | egocentric |
| discomfort | disqualify | doubtfully | Egyptology |
| disconnect | disrespect | downstairs | eisteddfod |
| discontent | disruption | drawbridge | elasticity |
| discordant | dissatisfy | drawstring | electorate |
| discourage | dissecting | dreadfully | electrical |
| discoverer | dissection | dreadlocks | electronic |
| discreetly | dissembler | dreariness | elementary |
| discretion | dissension | dressmaker | elliptical |
| discursive | dissertate | drossiness | elongation |
| discussion | disservice | drowsiness | eloquently |
| discussive | dissidence | drudgingly | emaciation |
| disdainful | dissimilar | dunderhead | emancipate |
| disembowel | dissipated | durability | emasculate |
| disembroil | dissociate | dysenteric | embankment |
| disenchant | dissoluble | | emblematic |
| disengaged | dissonance | | embodiment |

embroidery
embryology
emendation
emigration
empiricism
employable
employment
enamellist
encampment
encephalic
enchanting
encourager
encroacher
encyclical
endearment
endogamous
endogenous
enervation
engagement
engagingly
enlistment
enormously
enrichment
entailment
enterprise
enthusiasm
enthusiast
enticement
enticingly
entireness
entombment
entomology
enumerator
enunciable
epiglottis
episcopate

epistolary
equability
equanimity
equatorial
equestrian
equivalent
equivocate
eradicable
eradicator
erectility
eremitical
ergonomics
erotomania
eructation
eruptional
erysipelas
escarpment
escritoire
escutcheon
especially
estimation
esuriently
eternalise
ethereally
ethnically
etiolation
etymologic
eucalyptol
eucalyptus
euhemerism
eulogistic
eurythmics
euthanasia
evacuation
evaluation
evanescent

evangelise
evangelism
evangelist
eventually
evidential
eviscerate
exacerbate
exactitude
exaggerate
exaltation
examinable
exasperate
excavation
excellence
excellency
excerption
excitation
excitement
excogitate
excrescent
excruciate
execration
execrative
exhalation
exhausting
exhaustion
exhaustive
exhibition
exhilarate
exhumation
exorbitant
expansible
expatiator
expatriate
expectancy
expedience

expediency
expedition
expellable
expendable
experience
experiment
expertness
expiratory
explicable
explicitly
exportable
exposition
expository
expression
expressive
expressway
expurgator
exsanguine
extendable
extendible
extensible
extenuator
exteriorly
externally
extinction
extinguish
extirpator
extraction
extractive
extraneous
extricable
exuberance
exultation
exuviation
eyeglasses
eyewitness

# F

fabricator
fabulously
facileness
facilitate
factitious
Fahrenheit
fairground
faithfully
fallacious
fanaticism
fancifully
farcically
fastidious
fatalistic
fatherhood
fatherland
fatherless
fathomable
fathomless
faultiness
favourable
favourably
fearlessly
fearnaught
featherbed
federalise
federalism
federation
federative
feebleness
felicitous
fellowship
femininity
fenestrate
fertiliser

fervidness
fetterless
fettuccine
feverishly
fibreglass
fibrillose
fibrositis
fictitious
fieldmouse
figuration
figurative
figurehead
filibuster
firescreen
fishmonger
fisticuffs
flagellate
flamboyant
flashlight
flatulence
flavouring
fleabitten
flightless
floatation
floodlight
fluoridate
fontanelle
footbridge
footlights
forbidding
foreboding
forecastle
forefather
forefinger
foreground
foreordain

forerunner
foreshadow
forfeiture
forgivable
formidable
forthright
fortissimo
fortuitous
foundation
fractional
fragrantly
frangipani
fraternise
fraternity
fratricide
fraudulent
freakishly
freebooter
freeholder
freemartin
freightage
frequenter
freshwater
frictional
friendless
friendship
friskiness
frolicsome
frothiness
fruitfully
fulfilment
fumigation
functional
futuristic
futurology

# G

galvaniser
gamekeeper
gangrenous
gargantuan
garishness
garnishing
gastrology
gastronome
gelatinous
gemination
generalise
generality
generation
generative
generosity
generously
gentlefolk
gentleness
geographer
geological
geophysics
geotropism
geriatrics
ghostwrite
gingivitis
girlfriend
glandulous
glassiness
glimmering
glitterati
globularly
gloriously
glossarial
glossiness
Gnosticism

goalkeeper
goldilocks
gooseberry
gopherwood
gorgeously
Gorgonzola
gormandise
governance
government
gracefully
graciously
graduation
grammarian
gramophone
grandstand
graphology
grassiness
gratefully
gratifying
gratuitous
gravestone
greasiness
greenhouse
Greenpeace
greensward
gregarious
grievously
grindstone
grittiness
grogginess
groundless
groundsman
groundwork
grovelling
grudgingly
guardhouse

guesthouse
guillotine
guiltiness
gunrunning
gunslinger
gymnastics

H
habiliment
habitation
habitually
handicraft
harassment
harmlessly
harmonious
hartebeest
headmaster
headstrong
headwaters
heartbreak
heartiness
heathenish
heavenward
hectically
hectograph
heedlessly
heliograph
heliotrope
hemisphere
henceforth
heptagonal
herbaceous
hereabouts
hereditary
hermetical
hesitation

heterodoxy
hexahedral
Highlander
highwayman
highwaymen
hindermost
Hindustani
hinterland
hippodrome
historical
histrionic
hoarseness
homeliness
homeopathy
homiletics
homogenise
honorarium
honourable
hopelessly
horizontal
horologist
horrendous
horseflesh
horsepower
hospitable
hotchpotch
housebound
houseproud
hovercraft
hullabaloo
humoresque
humorously
humourless
humpbacked
hydraulics
hydrolysis

hydromania
hydroplane
hypodermic
hypostatic
hypotenuse
hypothesis
hysterical

I
icebreaker
iconoclasm
iconoclast
ideologist
idiopathic
idolatrous
ignorantly
illegality
illiterate
illuminate
illuminati
illustrate
imaginable
imbecility
imbibition
imbricated
immaculate
immaterial
immaturely
immaturity
immemorial
immobilise
immobility
immoderate
immodestly
immolation
immorality

| | | | |
|---|---|---|---|
| immunology | incandesce | inebriated | initiative |
| impalpable | incapacity | ineducable | injunction |
| impanation | incautious | inelegance | innocently |
| impartible | incendiary | ineligible | innovation |
| impassable | incestuous | ineloquent | innuendoes |
| impassible | inchoately | inequality | innumerate |
| impatience | incidental | inevitable | inoperable |
| impeccable | incinerate | inexorable | inordinate |
| impediment | incivility | infallible | inquisitor |
| impenitent | inclinable | infamously | insanitary |
| imperative | incoherent | infatuated | insatiable |
| impersonal | incomplete | infectious | insecurely |
| impervious | inconstant | infidelity | insecurity |
| implacable | incredible | infighting | inseminate |
| implicitly | incubation | infiltratc | insensible |
| importance | incumbency | infinitely | insobriety |
| imposingly | indecently | infinitive | insolently |
| imposition | indecision | infinitude | insolvency |
| impossible | indefinite | inflatable | insouciant |
| impoverish | indication | inflection | inspection |
| impregnate | indicative | inflexible | instalment |
| impresario | indictable | informally | instigator |
| impression | indictment | infraction | instructor |
| impressive | indigenous | infrequent | instrument |
| imprimatur | indirectly | inglorious | insularity |
| improbable | indiscreet | ingratiate | insulation |
| improperly | indiscrete | ingredient | intangible |
| imprudence | indisposed | inhabitant | interested |
| impudently | indistinct | inhalation | interloper |
| impugnable | inditement | inherently | intermezzo |
| impuissant | individual | inhibition | internally |
| imputation | indocility | inhumanity | interplead |
| inaccuracy | inducement | inimically | interstate |
| inadequate | indulgence | inimitable | intertwine |
| inapposite | industrial | iniquitous | interweave |
| inaugurate | indwelling | initiation | intestinal |

intimately
intimation
intimidate
intonation
intoxicant
intoxicate
intrepidly
inundation
invalidate
invalidity
invaluable
invariable
investment
inveterate
invigorate
invincible
inviolable
invitation
invitingly
invocation
involution
ionosphere
iridescent
ironmonger
irrational
irrelevant
irresolute
irreverent
irrigation
irritating
irritation
isometrics

**J**
jackanapes
jaggedness

jawbreaker
jeopardise
jocularity
journalese
journalism
journeyman
joyfulness
jubilation
judgmental
judicially
juggernaut

**K**
kettledrum
kindliness
kingfisher
knighthood
knockabout
kookaburra

**L**
laboratory
laceration
lachrymose
lacklustre
lamentable
lamination
landlocked
landlubber
languorous
laryngitis
lascivious
laughingly
leadership
lectionary
legislator

legitimacy
legitimise
leguminous
lengthways
lengthwise
lenticular
leprechaun
letterhead
levigation
levitation
lexicology
liberalism
liberality
liberation
libidinous
librettist
licentiate
licentious
lieutenant
lifelessly
lifesaving
lighthouse
likelihood
limberness
limitation
linguiform
linguistic
liquidator
literature
lithograph
lithologic
litigation
littleness
liturgical
livelihood
liveliness

liverwurst
locomotion
locomotive
loggerhead
logistical
loneliness
lonesomely
loquacious
lordliness
loveliness
lubricator
lucklessly
luculently
lugubrious
lumberjack
luminosity
luminously
lusciously
lustration
lustreless
luxuriance

**M**
macadamise
mackintosh
magistrate
Magnificat
maidenhair
mainspring
mainstream
maisonette
makeweight
malapropos
malcontent
malefactor
maleficent

| | | | |
|---|---|---|---|
| malevolent | medicament | mignonette | monolithic |
| malignance | medication | militarise | monoplegia |
| malingerer | mediocrity | militiaman | monopolise |
| malodorous | meditation | millennial | monotheism |
| manageable | meditative | millennium | monotonous |
| management | melancholy | mimeograph | monstrance |
| managerial | membership | mineralogy | monumental |
| mandibular | memorandum | minestrone | moonshiner |
| manifestly | menacingly | miniseries | moonstruck |
| manifoldly | mendacious | minorities | moratorium |
| manipulate | mendicancy | miraculous | morbidness |
| manservant | meningitis | misadvised | mordacious |
| manuscript | mercantile | miscellany | morganatic |
| marginally | mercifully | misconduct | mortifying |
| marguerite | mesmeriser | misericord | motherhood |
| marionette | metabolise | misfortune | motherless |
| marketable | metabolism | misleading | motionless |
| marrowbone | metacarpal | mismeasure | motivation |
| martingale | metallurgy | misogamist | mouldiness |
| marvellous | metaphoric | misogynist | mountebank |
| masquerade | metastasis | missionary | mournfully |
| mastectomy | metatarsal | mistakenly | mouthpiece |
| mastermind | metatarsus | mizzenmast | muckraking |
| masterwork | methodical | moderately | muliebrity |
| matchmaker | Methuselah | moderation | mulishness |
| materially | methylated | modifiable | multimedia |
| matriarchy | meticulous | modulation | multiplier |
| maturation | metrically | Mohammedan | mumblingly |
| maturative | metropolis | moisturise | munificent |
| matureness | mettlesome | molybdenum | musicology |
| mayonnaise | Michaelmas | monarchism | mutilation |
| meagreness | microfiche | monastical | myocardium |
| measurable | micrometer | monetarism | mysterious |
| measurably | microphone | monochrome | mythically |
| mechanical | microscope | monogamist | mythologic |
| meddlesome | midshipman | monogamous | |

N
namelessly
Narcissism
nasturtium
naturalise
naturalism
naturalist
nautically
navigation
Neapolitan
nebulosity
necromancy
necropolis
needlework
negatively
neglectful
negligence
negligible
negotiable
negotiator
networking
neutralise
neutrality
newsletter
newsmonger
newsworthy
nightdress
nightshade
nihilistic
nimbleness
nincompoop
nomination
nominative
nomography
nonaligned
nonchalant

nosography
notability
noteworthy
noticeable
notifiable
nourishing
numeration
numerology
numerously
numismatic
nunciature
nurseryman
nutcracker
nutritious

O
obdurately
obediently
obligation
obligatory
obligingly
obliterate
obsequious
observable
observance
obsoletely
obstetrics
obstructor
obtainable
obtuseness
occasional
occultness
occupation
occurrence
oceanarium
oceangoing

octahedron
odiousness
odontology
oesophagus
officially
oligarchic
omnipotent
omniscient
omnivorous
ontologist
opalescent
openhanded
opensesame
operahouse
ophthalmic
oppositely
opposition
oppression
oppressive
opprobrium
optatively
optimistic
optionally
oracularly
oratorical
orchestral
ordination
originally
originated
originator
ornamental
orological
orthoclase
orthodoxly
oscillator
osculation

osculatory
ossiferous
ostensible
osteopathy
outbalance
outgeneral
outlandish
outpatient
outpouring
outrageous
outstation
outstretch
overactive
overburden
overcharge
overexpose
overshadow
overweight
oxidisable

P
paediatric
palindrome
pallbearer
palliative
pallidness
palpitated
paltriness
pancreatic
panegyrist
paniculate
pantograph
paperknife
paranormal
paraphrase
paraplegia

| | | | |
|---|---|---|---|
| paratroops | pennyroyal | peroration | pianoforte |
| pardonable | pennyworth | perpetrate | picaresque |
| pardonably | pensionary | perpetuate | pickpocket |
| Parisienne | pentagonal | perpetuity | piercingly |
| parliament | Pentateuch | perplexing | pigeonhole |
| paroxysmal | pentathlon | perplexity | piledriver |
| parramatta | peppercorn | perquisite | pilgrimage |
| partiality | percentage | persistent | pincushion |
| participle | perception | personable | pitilessly |
| particular | perceptive | personally | plagiarise |
| pasquinade | percipient | persuasion | plagiarist |
| passageway | percolator | persuasive | planchette |
| passionate | percussion | pertinence | plantation |
| pasteboard | percussive | perversion | plastering |
| pasteurise | peremptory | perversity | playground |
| patchiness | perfection | perversive | playwright |
| patentable | perfidious | pestilence | pleadingly |
| pathfinder | perfoliate | petitioner | pleasantly |
| pathologic | perforator | petulantly | pleasantry |
| patisserie | performing | phallicism | plebiscite |
| patriarchy | perihelion | pharisaism | pluperfect |
| patriotism | perilously | pharmacist | plutocracy |
| pawnbroker | periodical | phenomenal | pneumatics |
| peacefully | periosteal | phenomenon | poetically |
| peacemaker | peripheral | philistine | poignantly |
| peashooter | periscopic | philosophy | poinsettia |
| peccadillo | perishable | phlegmatic | politeness |
| peculiarly | peritoneum | phonograph | politician |
| pedestrian | periwinkle | photogenic | polyanthus |
| peduncular | permafrost | photograph | polychrome |
| peerlessly | permanence | phrasebook | polygamist |
| pejorative | permeation | phrenology | polygamous |
| pellicular | permission | phylactery | polyphonic |
| penetrable | permissive | physically | polytheism |
| penicillin | pernicious | physiology | polytheist |
| penmanship | pernickety | pianissimo | Pomeranian |

pomologist
ponderable
pontifical
popularise
popularity
population
populously
porousness
portamento
portcullis
portentous
portliness
Portuguese
positional
positively
positivism
possession
possessive
possessory
posthumous
postmaster
postscript
powerfully
powerhouse
practising
pragmatism
prearrange
precarious
precaution
precedence
preceptive
preciously
preclusion
precocious
precursory
predecease

predestine
predicable
prediction
predictive
predispose
prefecture
preferable
preference
preglacial
prehensile
prehistory
premarital
prepayment
prepossess
prepotency
presbyopia
presbytery
prescience
presidency
pressurise
presumable
presuppose
pretension
prevailing
prevalence
prevention
preventive
priesthood
primordial
principled
privileged
prizefight
proceeding
procession
proclivity
procreator

proctorial
procumbent
procurable
procurator
prodigious
production
productive
profession
proficient
profitable
profligacy
profundity
progenitor
prognostic
projectile
projection
prominence
promissory
promontory
promptness
promulgate
pronounced
propaganda
propagator
propellant
propensity
propertied
propitiate
propitious
proportion
proprietor
propulsion
prosecutor
prospector
prospectus
prosperity

prosperous
prosthesis
prostitute
protection
protective
Protestant
protoplasm
protracted
protrusion
provenance
proverbial
providence
provincial
prudential
psychiatry
psychology
psychopath
pubescence
publishing
pugilistic
pugnacious
puissantly
punctually
punishable
punishment
Puritanism
purposeful
purulently
putrescent

Q
quadrangle
quadruplet
quandaries
quarantine
queasiness

| | | | |
|---|---|---|---|
| quenchable | redemption | rendezvous | resumption |
| quiescence | rediscover | reorganise | resumptive |
| quintuplet | redundancy | reparation | resurgence |
| quizmaster | referendum | repatriate | retainable |
| | refinement | repeatable | retardment |
| R | reflecting | repeatedly | retirement |
| rabbinical | reflection | repentance | retraction |
| radiograph | reflective | repertoire | retrograde |
| radiometer | refraction | repetition | retrospect |
| ragamuffin | refractory | repetitive | returnable |
| ramshackle | refreshing | reportable | revelation |
| rancidness | refutation | repository | revengeful |
| ranunculus | regardless | repression | reversible |
| ravenously | regenerate | repressive | revertible |
| razzmatazz | regentship | republican | revitalise |
| readership | regimental | repudiator | revolution |
| realisable | registered | repugnance | rhetorical |
| reasonable | regression | reputation | rheumatism |
| reassemble | regularise | reschedule | rheumatoid |
| rebellious | regulation | resentment | rhinestone |
| receivable | regulative | reservedly | rhinoscope |
| receptacle | rejuvenate | resilience | riboflavin |
| recidivism | relatively | resistance | ridiculous |
| recidivist | relativity | resolution | rightfully |
| reciprocal | relaxation | resonantly | rigorously |
| recitation | relegation | resounding | ringleader |
| recitative | relentless | respectful | ringmaster |
| recklessly | relinquish | respective | roadrunner |
| recommence | reluctance | respirator | robustness |
| recompense | remarkable | respondent | Romanesque |
| reconsider | remedially | responsive | rotational |
| recreation | remittance | responsory | rotisserie |
| recumbency | remorseful | restaurant | rottenness |
| recuperate | remoteness | restlessly | roundabout |
| recurrence | remunerate | restrained | roundhouse |
| redeemable | renderable | restricted | rubberneck |

rubbishing
rubiginous
ruefulness
ruggedness
rumination
ruthlessly

S
sabbatical
saccharide
saccharine
sacerdotal
sacredness
sacrosanct
salamander
salivation
sallowness
salmonella
saltcellar
salubrious
salutarily
salutation
salutatory
sanatorium
sanctified
sandalwood
sanguinary
sanguinely
sanitation
sarcophagi
satisfying
saturation
sauerkraut
savageness
savourless
scabbiness

scandalise
scandalous
scantiness
scarceness
scarlatina
scattering
scepticism
schematise
schismatic
scholastic
schoolroom
scientific
scoffingly
scoreboard
scornfully
scrambling
screenings
screenplay
scriptural
scrofulous
scrupulous
scrutineer
scrutinise
sculptress
sculptural
sculptured
scurrility
scurrilous
scurviness
seamanship
seamstress
searchable
seasonable
secretness
secularise
secureness

sedateness
seducement
sedulously
seemliness
seersucker
seismology
semicircle
semiquaver
senatorial
separately
separation
separatism
septennial
sepulchral
sequential
sereneness
serpentine
serviceman
settlement
shagginess
shamefaced
shantytown
shellproof
shenanigan
shillelagh
shipmaster
shipwright
shirtdress
shockingly
shockproof
shoemaking
shopkeeper
shoplifter
shopsoiled
shortbread
shortening

shrewdness
shrewishly
shrillness
Shrovetide
shuddering
siderostat
sidewinder
silentness
silhouette
silverside
silverware
similarity
similitude
simoniacal
simplicity
simplistic
simulacrum
simulation
sinecurist
sinfulness
singularly
sinisterly
sisterhood
skateboard
skittishly
skyscraper
slanderous
sleepyhead
sleeveless
slightness
slipstream
sloppiness
slothfully
sluggishly
slumberous
smattering

smokestack
smuttiness
snapdragon
sneakingly
sneeringly
snivelling
snobbishly
snowplough
soldiering
solicitous
solicitude
solidarity
solitarily
solstitial
solubility
somatology
sombreness
somersault
somnolence
sonorously
soothingly
soothsayer
sordidness
sororicide
soundboard
soundproof
soundtrack
spacecraft
spaciously
sparseness
specialise
specialist
speciality
speciously
spectacled
spectrally

speculator
speechless
spellbound
sphericity
spiritedly
spiritless
spirograph
spirometer
splashdown
splendidly
spoilsport
spoliation
sponginess
spoonerism
sprinkling
spruceness
spuriously
squareness
stabiliser
stagecoach
stagecraft
staggering
stagnantly
stagnation
stalactite
stalagmite
stammering
starriness
statecraft
stationary
stationery
statistics
statuesque
steadiness
steakhouse
stealthily

steaminess
stentorian
stepfather
stereotype
stertorous
stigmatise
stipulator
stolidness
stomatitis
stormbound
straighten
strategist
stratified
strawberry
streamline
streetwise
strengthen
strictness
stringency
striptease
stroganoff
stronghold
strongroom
structural
structured
struthious
strychnine
stubbornly
studiously
stuffiness
stultifier
stupendous
sturdiness
subaqueous
subculture
subheading

subjection
subjective
subliminal
sublingual
submersion
submission
submissive
subscriber
subsequent
subsidence
subsidiary
subsistent
substitute
subterfuge
subtleness
subversion
subversive
succeeding
successful
succession
successive
succinctly
succulence
succussive
suddenness
sufferable
sufferance
sufficient
suffragist
suggestion
suggestive
sullenness
sultriness
superpower
supersonic
supervisor

supination
supplement
suppleness
supplicate
supposedly
suppressor
suprarenal
surgically
surpassing
surprising
surrealism
susceptive
suspension
suspicious
sustenance
suzerainty
swaggering
sweatshirt
sweepstake
sweetbread
sweetening
sweetheart
sweltering
sycophancy
sympathise
syncarpous
synonymous
synthesise
systematic

T
tabernacle
tablespoon
tabulation
tachometer
tactically

tambourine
tangential
tantamount
tarantella
taskmaster
tastefully
tattletale
tauntingly
tawdriness
taxidermic
technician
technology
telegraphy
telepathic
telescopic
television
temperable
temperance
temptation
temptingly
tenability
tenantable
tenderfoot
tenderness
tenebrific
tenemental
tentacular
tenterhook
terracotta
tessellate
testicular
tetchiness
textualist
thankfully
theatrical
theocratic

theodolite
theologian
theosophic
thereafter
thermionic
thermostat
thickening
thimbleful
thoroughly
thoughtful
threadbare
threadworm
threescore
thriftless
thrivingly
thrombosis
throneless
throughout
thumbscrew
thundering
thunderous
ticklishly
timekeeper
timeliness
timeserver
timorously
tinctorial
Tinseltown
tiresomely
tocopherol
tolerantly
toleration
tomfoolery
toothbrush
toothpaste
topgallant

topography
tormenting
torpidness
torrential
torridness
tortellini
touchiness
touchingly
touchstone
tourmaline
tournament
tourniquet
townhouse
toxicology
trafficker
tragically
traitorous
trajectory
trammelled
trampoline
tranquilly
transcribe
transcript
transgress
transience
transistor
transition
transitive
transitory
translator
transplant
transverse
traumatism
travelogue
travertine
treasuries

tremendous
trepanning
trespasser
triangular
trickiness
trifoliate
trifurcate
trigeminal
trilateral
trilocular
trimestral
tripartite
triplicate
trippingly
triumphant
troglodyte
troubadour
truculence
trustiness
trustingly
tryptophan
tsarevitch
tubercular
tumbledown
tumbleweed
tumultuous
turbidness
turbulence
turgidness
turpentine
turtleneck
typescript
typography
tyrannical

U
ubiquitous
ulceration
ultimately
ultrasonic
ultrasound
umbilicate
umbrageous
unaffected
unassisted
unassuming
unattached
unavailing
unbalanced
unbearable
unbeatable
unbecoming
unbeliever
unbuttoned
uncoloured
uncommonly
uncritical
unctuosity
undeniable
undeniably
underbelly
underbrush
undercover
underlying
underscore
undershirt
understand
understate
understudy
undertaker
undervalue

underwater
underworld
underwrite
undeterred
undisputed
undulating
undulation
uneasiness
uneconomic
unedifying
uneducated
unenviable
unequalled
unerringly
uneventful
unexpected
unexplored
unfairness
unfaithful
unfamiliar
unfeminine
unfettered
unfinished
unflagging
unforeseen
unforgiven
ungraceful
ungracious
ungrateful
unhampered
uniformity
unilateral
unimagined
unimpaired
unimposing
unimproved

uninspired
uninviting
university
unkindness
unlamented
unleavened
unlettered
unlicensed
unmeasured
unmerciful
unoccupied
unofficial
unpleasant
unpolished
unpolluted
unprepared
unprovoked
unpunctual
unpunished
unreadable
unrecorded
unreliable
unrequited
unresolved
unrewarded
unrivalled
unscramble
unseasoned
unsociable
unsteadily
unsuitable
unswerving
untenanted
unthankful
unthinking
untidiness

untillable
untroubled
untruthful
unwavering
unworthily
unyielding
upbraiding
upbringing
upholstery
uproarious
upstanding
usefulness
uxoriously

V
valorously
vanquished
variegated
vaudeville
vauntingly
vegetation
vegetative
vehemently
veneration
venialness
venomously
ventilator
ventricose
verifiable
vernacular

vertebrate
vertically
vesication
vesiculate
vespertine
veterinary
vibraphone
victorious
victualler
viewfinder
vigilantly
vigorously
villainous
vindicator
vindictive
virtuously
virulently
visibility
visitation
vituperate
vocabulary
vocational
vociferate
vociferous
volatility
volitional
voltameter
volubility
volumetric
voluminous

voluptuous
vulnerable

W
wainwright
wallflower
wanderlust
wastefully
wastepaper
watchmaker
watchtower
watercress
waterfront
watermelon
waterproof
waterspout
watertight
waterworks
wavelength
weathering
westernise
wheelchair
whispering
wholewheat
widespread
wildebeest
wilderness
wilfulness
willowherb

windjammer
windshield
wingspread
withdrawal
withholder
woefulness
wonderland
wondrously
workaholic
worshipful
worshipper
worthiness
worthwhile
wrathfully
wretchedly

X
xenophobia
xylography
xylotomous

Y
yardmaster
yearningly
yeastiness
youthfully

Z
zootomist

# TEN-LETTER MULTIPLE WORDS

**A**
able seaman
able-bodied
act of faith
act the goat
active duty
after-hours
aide-de-camp
air cushion
air hostess
air vesicle
alarm clock
all-purpose
alms-giving
altar cloth
altar-bread
Anglo-Saxon
Angora-wool
arbor vitae
arc-welding
art nouveau
arty-crafty
at a premium
at all costs
at odds with
atomic bomb
avant-garde
axe to grind

**B**
babe in arms
baby-boomer
bag of bones
baked beans
bar mitzvah
Barbary ape
barbed wire
bare-headed
base-minded
bathing-box
beat-hollow
beauty shop
beauty spot
bed of nails
bed of roses
behind bars
bell-turret
belly dance
better-half
big brother
bilge water
bill of fare
bird of prey
Black Death
black magic
Black Maria
black power
black sheep
black widow
blank verse
bleary-eyed
blind alley
blood count
blood donor
blood group
blood money

blood sport
Bloody Mary
blue ribbon
blue-collar
boat people
boll weevil
bond-holder
booby prize
book-hunter
bored stiff
bottom line
bowie knife
brain death
brain drain
brass tacks
break of day
breast bone
breast-feed
bring round
broken-down
broken-wind
browned-off
bucket seat
buffer zone
bulk buying
bull-necked
Bunsen lamp
bush-shrike
butter bean
butter-boat
by a whisker
by and large
by-election

**C**
cack-handed
café au lait
call it a day
camel's hair
can of worms
cannon-shot
carbon copy
casus belli
cat burglar
Cat scanner
cathode-ray
cattle show
cattle-grid
chain store
chain-smoke
chamber pot
charge card
check digit
cheesed off
chew the cud
child's play
chorus girl
clapped-out
claw hammer
clay pigeon
clean slate
clear as mud
close ranks
close shave
close thing
closed book
closed shop

cloven hoof
coat of arms
coat of mail
comic opera
comic strip
common time
cordon bleu
couch grass
country road
country town
crack a joke
crepe paper
cross-bones
cross-staff
crown glass
crown lands
cruet-stand
cut corners

**D**
daily-bread
daily-dozen
daisy-chain
damask plum
damask rose
dandy-brush
dapple-grey
de-escalate
dead letter
dead-ringer
death's head
death's-door
deckle edge
deep-rooted
deep-seated
disc jockey

dish aerial
ditto marks
dive bomber
diving suit
donkey-work
double-take
down-at-heel
down-market
draw-a-blank
drop-hammer
dry as a bone
duck-billed
dull-witted
dust-jacket
Dutch treat

**E**
ear-trumpet
emery board
emery paper
end product
epoxy resin
Euro-tunnel
ex cathedra
eyelet-hole

**F**
face-saving
fair-minded
fallow deer
false alarm
false start
family tree
fancy dress
far-fetched
far-sighted

field event
fifty-fifty
finger bowl
fire escape
firing line
first-class
flash flood
flat-footed
flea market
flesh wound
flick knife
flight-deck
floppy disk
fluid ounce
fly fishing
fly the coop
fly-by-night
fore-and-aft
forte-piano
forty-winks
four-poster
free-for-all
freight car
French horn
Frigid Zone
front bench
fuddy-duddy
full-bodied
fund-holder
funny-money

**G**
garage sale
gas chamber
Gatling gun
get-up-and-go

give a leg up
go down hill
go-go dancer
go-straight
goggle-eyed
golden calf
golden rule
good as gold
Good Friday
goody-goody
goose bumps
goose flesh
grand opera
graph paper
grass roots
grass snake
grass widow
gravy train
Greco-Roman
green thumb
grey-matter
grim-reaper
ground rule
guinea fowl
Gulf Stream

**H**
hand-maiden
hand-picked
hand-to-hand
hang-glider
hanky-panky
hard-bitten
hard-boiled
hard-headed
hark-back-to

hatchet job
hatchet man
head waiter
head-honcho
health farm
heart-throb
heavy metal
heavy water
heavy-going
heavy-laden
high and dry
high priest
high roller
high-ground
high-handed
high-minded
high-strung
hit the road
hobby horse
hocus-pocus
hodge podge
hoity-toity
hokey-pokey
holus-bolus
Holy Spirit
hopping mad
horse laugh
horse sense
hot-blooded
hubba-hubba
human being
hurdy-gurdy
hurly-burly

**I**
ill-advised

ill-founded
ill-natured
ill-starred
in absentia
in good time
in memoriam
in name only
in the wrong
Indian file
iron-maiden
ivory tower

**J**
jam session
job-sharing
joint stock
jump the gun

**K**
keep posted
keep tabs on
kick boxing
kidney bean
kiss of life
knock-kneed

**L**
lady-killer
lady's-smock
large-scale
last hurrah
Last Supper
law-abiding
left-handed
letter-bomb
life jacket

light opera
linseed oil
lion's-share
lip service
living room
long-winded
lord-it-over
lotus-eater
love affair
low tension
lower house

**M**
magnum opus
make do with
man-of-straw
martial-law
melting pot
Middle Ages
misery guts
mock-heroic
monkey-suit
motor-mouth
mumbo jumbo
Murphy's law

**N**
namby-pamby
name the day
natural gas
natural law
ne'er-do-well
nettle rash
never-never
night-light
nit-picking

Nobel prize
nom de plume
not-cricket
nudge-nudge
nulla-nulla

**O**
off-roading
off-the-cuff
old country
Old English
on a par with
on all fours
on the cards
on the house
on the level
on your bike
open-minded
out on a limb
out-of-order
out-of-sorts
out-of-touch
outer space
over the top
oxalic acid
oxygen tent

**P**
pack-animal
Palm Sunday
paper money
paper-tiger
pave the way
Peace-Corps
peeping Tom
penalty box

petit-point
pigeon-toed
pitch-black
plate glass
play-possum
plough-back
pocket-book
point-blank
polar angle
poles-apart
post office
prairie dog
pre-eminent
pre-emption
pre-emptive
prima donna
prima facie
prime-mover
private eye
proper noun
push button

Q
quid pro quo

R
rain forest
razor-shell
real estate
red herring
red-blooded
rising-damp
river basin
rock bottom
rose window
Rotary Club

rough stuff
round robin
royal flush
rubber tree

S
safari park
safari suit
safety belt
safety lamp
salmon pink
sand martin
Santa Claus
sash window
scaling wax
Scotch mist
Scotch tape
scratch pad
sea anemone
sea serpent
second best
second wind
second-hand
second-rate
self-denial
self-esteem
self-regard
self-styled
sense organ
septic tank
sewage-farm
sheep's eyes
sheet glass
sheet metal
sheet music
shell shock

shish kebab
short-lived
short-range
shrink-wrap
side effect
side-glance
side-saddle
signet ring
silk cotton
silk screen
silver-gilt
sine qua non
single file
singles bar
six-shooter
sixth sense
slave trade
slit trench
slow-motion
small hours
small print
small-scale
smart money
smoke alarm
snail's pace
sniffer dog
social work
soft option
soft palate
solar flare
solar power
solid-state
sour grapes
space probe
sperm whale
spin-doctor

spinal cord
spirit-away
split hairs
split-level
sponge cake
square meal
square root
square-deal
squeeze-box
starry-eyed
stock-still
stony-broke
strong-suit
sugar daddy
sui generis
surf the net
sweet-tooth

T
tailor-made
taken-aback
talk-turkey
tea service
terra firma
the-year-dot
Third World
thumb index
thumbs-down
ticker tape
ticking off
tie breaker
timber line
timber wolf
tongue-tied
topsy-turvy
trade union

tread water
tread-wheel
treble clef
trench coat
trench foot
troy weight
tub-thumper
twelfth man

U
up to a point
up-the-creek
up-the-spout

upper crust
upper house

V
vampire bat
vice consul

W
waffle iron
wage earner
walky-talky
watched-pot

water table
water tower
weather map
well-heeled
white paper
white sauce
white slave
white water
widow's peak
willy-nilly
wind tunnel
wing collar

wire-haired
wishy-washy
witness box
work-to-rule
world-weary
worry beads

Y
yackety-yak

Z
zero-option

# ELEVEN-LETTER WORDS

A
abandonment
abecedarian
abhorrently
abnormality
abomination
abracadabra
absenteeism
abstinently
abstraction
abusiveness
academician
accelerando
accelerator
accessional
accipitrine
acclamation
acclimatise
accommodate
accompanist
accordingly
accountable
accountably
accountancy
accumulator
achievement
acknowledge
acquiescent
acquisition
acquisitive
acquittance
acrimonious
acupuncture

adjournment
adjudicator
adolescence
adumbration
advancement
adventurous
adversarial
advertently
advertising
aeronautics
affectation
affectingly
affiliation
affirmation
affirmative
afterburner
aggravating
aggravation
aggregation
agnosticism
agoraphobia
agriculture
aimlessness
allegorical
alleviation
altercation
alternately
alternative
ambiguously
ambitiously
amiableness
amontillado
amorousness

amphetamine
anachronism
anaesthesia
anaesthetic
analogously
androgynous
angelically
Anglicanism
Anglophobia
animatingly
annihilator
anniversary
anonymously
antechamber
anthologise
antifebrile
antinuclear
antiquarian
antiqueness
antirrhinum
antitypical
anxiousness
aphrodisiac
apocalyptic
apologetics
apostleship
appallingly
appellation
application
applicative
appointment
appreciable
approbation

appropriate
approvingly
approximate
appurtenant
aquaculture
aquiculture
arbitrarily
arbitration
archaeology
archdiocese
Archimedean
archipelago
arduousness
aristocracy
arraignment
arrangement
arterialise
artlessness
assassinate
assertively
assiduously
assignation
association
associative
assuagement
astigmatism
astonishing
astringency
athleticism
atmospheric
atomisation
atrabilious
atrociously

attemptable
attentively
attenuation
attestation
attitudinal
attribution
audaciously
audiovisual
auscultator
austereness
autogenesis
autographic
avoirdupois
awkwardness

B
bacchanalia
baccivorous
backbencher
balefulness
balletomane
barbiturate
barefacedly
barquentine
bashfulness
beastliness
beauteously
beautifully
bedizenment
beguilement
believingly
belligerent
bellybutton
Benedictine
benediction
benefaction

beneficence
beneficiary
benevolence
benignantly
bereavement
bewitchment
biauricular
bibliolater
bibliomania
bibliophile
bicarbonate
bicentenary
bifurcation
biliousness
biodynamics
biofeedback
birdwatcher
bittersweet
blamelessly
blameworthy
blasphemous
blessedness
blockbuster
bloodlessly
bloodstream
bloodsucker
blunderbuss
bombardment
bookishness
boorishness
botanically
botheration
bottlenosed
boundlessly
bounteously
bountifully

bourgeoisie
boysenberry
braggadocio
brainteaser
breadbasket
breadthways
breadwinner
breastplate
brilliantly
brittleness
brotherhood
brusqueness
brutishness
bulbiferous
bulletproof
bullfighter
bureaucracy
bushwhacker
businessman
butcherbird

C
cabbalistic
cacophonous
calciferous
calcination
calculating
calculation
calefaction
calibration
calligraphy
callousness
calorimeter
calumniator
Calvinistic
camaraderie

campanology
candelabrum
candescence
candidature
candleberry
candlelight
candlepower
candlestick
cannibalise
cannibalism
canonically
capaciously
capacitance
captainship
captivating
carbuncular
carburettor
cardiograph
cardsharper
carefulness
caressingly
carnivorous
Carolingian
carriageway
cartography
castellated
castigation
cataclysmic
catastrophe
catchweight
categorical
caterpillar
catheterise
catholicise
Catholicism
catoptrical

| | | | |
|---|---|---|---|
| cauliflower | citizenship | commonality | conciseness |
| causatively | clairvoyant | commonplace | concomitant |
| caustically | clamorously | communalise | concordance |
| ceaselessly | clandestine | communalism | concubinage |
| celebration | classically | communicant | concurrence |
| celestially | cleanliness | communicate | condemnable |
| centenarian | cliffhanger | communistic | condensable |
| centrepiece | climacteric | commutation | conditional |
| centrically | climatology | commutative | conditioned |
| centrifugal | coagulation | compactness | conditioner |
| ceremonious | coalescence | comparative | condominium |
| certificate | cobblestone | compartment | condottiere |
| chalcedonic | cockleshell | competently | conductible |
| chamberlain | codicillary | competition | confederacy |
| chambermaid | coeducation | competitive | confederate |
| chanticleer | coefficient | compilation | conferrable |
| chaotically | coexistence | complacency | confidently |
| charlatanic | coincidence | complainant | confidingly |
| cheerleader | collaborate | compliantly | confinement |
| cheerlessly | collapsible | complicated | conflagrate |
| cheesecloth | collectible | comportment | conflicting |
| Chippendale | collusively | compositely | congealable |
| chiropodist | colonialism | composition | Congressman |
| chitterling | colonialist | compression | congruously |
| chlorophyll | combination | compromised | conjectural |
| choirmaster | combustible | comptroller | conjugality |
| cholesterol | comeuppance | compunction | conjugation |
| Christendom | comfortable | computation | conjunction |
| chronometer | comfortably | computerise | conjunctive |
| cinquecento | comfortless | comradeship | conjuration |
| circularise | commandment | concealable | connectedly |
| circularity | commemorate | concealment | connoisseur |
| circulating | commendable | conceitedly | connotation |
| circulation | commendably | conceivable | connubially |
| circumpolar | commentator | concentrate | consciously |
| circumspect | commiserate | conciliator | consecutive |

consentient
consequence
considerate
considering
consignment
consistency
consolation
consolidate
conspicuous
conspirator
constituent
constrained
constricted
consumerism
consumption
consumptive
containable
containment
contaminate
contemplate
contentedly
contentious
contestable
continental
contingency
continually
contractile
contraction
contractual
contraption
contravener
contredanse
contretemps
contributor
contrivance
controversy

conurbation
convenience
convergence
convertible
conveyancer
convivially
convocation
convolution
cooperation
cooperative
copiousness
copperplate
coppersmith
cornerstone
corporality
corporately
corporation
corporeally
corpulently
corpuscular
correctable
correctness
correlation
corroborate
corrosively
corrugation
corruptible
corruptness
cosignatory
cosmography
cosmologist
cotyledonal
counselling
countenance
counterfeit
counterfoil

countermand
countermove
counterpane
counterpart
counterplot
counterseal
countersign
countersink
countryside
courteously
crackerjack
credentials
credibility
credulously
crepuscular
crestfallen
criminology
crookedness
cruciferous
crucifixion
cryptograph
crystalline
crystallise
culmination
culpability
cultivation
cursoriness
curtailment
customarily

D
dauntlessly
debarkation
deceitfully
deceptively
declamation

declamatory
declaration
decollation
decolourise
decorticate
decrepitate
decrepitude
decrescendo
deductively
deerstalker
defalcation
defectively
defenceless
defensively
deferential
deficiently
defloration
defoliation
deformation
degradation
degradingly
dehydration
deification
delectation
deleterious
deliciously
delightedly
delightsome
delineation
delinquency
deliriously
delitescent
deliverable
deliverance
demagnetise
demarcation

democratise
demographic
demonstrate
denominator
dependently
deportation
depravation
deprecation
deprecatory
depredation
depredatory
deprivation
derangement
dereliction
dermatology
describable
description
descriptive
desecration
desegregate
deservingly
desiccation
desideratum
designation
desperately
desperation
despoilment
despondency
destination
destitution
destruction
destructive
desultorily
deteriorate
determinism
detestation

detrimental
Deuteronomy
devastation
development
deviousness
devolvement
devotedness
dexterously
diagnostics
dialectical
diametrical
dictatorial
differentia
differently
diffidently
diffraction
diffuseness
diffusively
dilapidated
dimensional
diplomatist
directional
directorate
directorial
direfulness
disaffected
disapproval
disarmament
disbandment
disbeliever
discernible
discernment
discontinue
discordance
discotheque
discourtesy

discrepancy
disencumber
disentangle
disgruntled
disguisedly
dishevelled
dishonestly
disillusion
disinclined
disjunction
disjunctive
dislocation
disobedient
disobliging
disorganise
dispensable
dispersedly
dispiriting
displeasure
disposition
disputation
disputative
disquieting
disquietude
dissectible
disseminate
dissentient
dissipation
dissolutely
dissolution
dissolvable
dissyllable
dissymmetry
distasteful
distensible
distinction

distinctive
distinguish
distracting
distraction
distressful
distressing
distributor
distrustful
disturbance
diversified
divertingly
doctrinaire
doctrinally
documentary
dolefulness
domesticate
domiciliary
domineering
downtrodden
draughtsman
dreadnought
dubiousness
duplication
dutifulness
dynamically
dysfunction

E
earnestness
earthenware
earthliness
eclecticism
edification
editorially
educational
effectively

| | | | |
|---|---|---|---|
| efficacious | enfranchise | etymologise | expectorate |
| efficiently | engineering | etymologist | expediently |
| effulgently | enhancement | euphemistic | expeditious |
| egalitarian | enlargement | eurhythmics | expenditure |
| egregiously | enlightened | evanescence | expensively |
| ejaculation | ennoblement | evangelical | experienced |
| elaborately | enslavement | evaporation | explanation |
| elaboration | entablature | evaporative | explanatory |
| elaborative | entertainer | eventuality | exploitable |
| elastically | enthralment | eventuation | exploration |
| electrician | entwinement | evolutional | exploratory |
| electrocute | enumeration | examination | explosively |
| electrolyse | enunciation | exceedingly | exponential |
| electrolyte | envelopment | exceptional | exportation |
| elementally | environment | excessively | expostulate |
| elephantine | epipetalous | exclamation | expressible |
| eligibility | epiphyllous | exclamatory | expropriate |
| ellipsoidal | epithetical | exclusively | expurgation |
| elucidation | equableness | excoriation | exquisitely |
| elucidative | equiangular | excorticate | extemporise |
| emancipator | equidistant | excrescence | extenuation |
| embarkation | equilateral | exculpation | exterminate |
| embarrassed | equilibrate | executioner | externalise |
| embroilment | equilibrium | executorial | extirpation |
| empirically | equivalence | exemplarily | extractible |
| encapsulate | equivocally | exfoliation | extradition |
| enchantment | equivocator | exhaustless | extrapolate |
| enchantress | eradication | exhortation | extravagant |
| encouraging | erratically | exhortative | extrication |
| encumbrance | erroneously | existential | exuberantly |
| endemically | eschatology | exoneration | |
| endlessness | esotericism | exorbitance | F |
| endorsement | essentially | expansively | fabrication |
| enfeoffment | established | expatiation | facetiously |
| enforceable | ethnography | expectation | faithlessly |
| enforcement | ethnologist | expectorant | fallibility |

familiarise
familiarity
fanatically
farinaceous
fascination
fashionable
faultlessly
fearfulness
feasibility
featureless
febriferous
fecundation
feloniously
ferociously
fidgetiness
filamentary
financially
fingerprint
finicalness
firecracker
fissiparous
flabbergast
flaccidness
flannelette
flatulently
flavourless
flexibility
flightiness
flirtatious
flocculence
florescence
flourishing
fluctuation
fluorescent
fomentation
foppishness

forbearance
foreclosure
foreshorten
forestation
forethought
forfeitable
forgiveness
formularise
formulation
fornication
forthcoming
fortunately
forwardness
fractiously
fragileness
fragmentary
frantically
fratricidal
fraudulence
freebooting
freemasonry
freethinker
fretfulness
frightfully
frivolously
frowardness
fruitlessly
frustration
fulguration
fulmination
fulsomeness
funambulist
functionary
fundamental
furiousness
furnishings

furtherance
furthermost

G
gallowglass
garnishment
garrulously
gendarmerie
genealogist
generalship
generically
genetically
genteelness
gentlemanly
gentlewoman
genuineness
geopolitics
germination
gerrymander
gesticulate
ghastliness
globularity
glomeration
godlessness
gormandiser
gracelessly
gradational
grammatical
grandfather
grandmaster
grandmother
grandparent
granulation
graphically
gravitation
greasepaint

grotesquely
guesstimate
guilelessly
guiltlessly
gullibility
gurgitation
guttersnipe
gynaecology
gyrocompass

H
haberdasher
habituation
haemoglobin
haemophilia
haemorrhage
hagiography
hagiologist
hallucinate
handicapped
handicapper
harbourless
harebrained
harmfulness
harpsichord
hatefulness
haughtiness
haustellate
hazardously
heartbroken
hearthstone
heartlessly
heavenwards
heavyweight
heedfulness
heinousness

| | | | |
|---|---|---|---|
| heliography | hydrogenous | immenseness | impulsively |
| Hellenistic | hydrography | immigration | inadvertent |
| hemipterous | hydrometric | impartially | inadvisable |
| hemispheric | hydropathic | impassioned | inalienable |
| heptahedron | hydrophobia | impassively | inalterable |
| herbivorous | hydrophobic | impatiently | inattention |
| hereditable | hydroponics | impeachable | inattentive |
| heretically | hydrostatic | impeachment | inaugurator |
| hermeneutic | hyperactive | impecunious | incalescent |
| hibernation | hyperbolise | impedimenta | incantation |
| hideousness | hypertrophy | impenitence | incarcerate |
| highfalutin | hypnologist | imperfectly | incarnation |
| highlighter | hypogastric | imperforate | incessantly |
| hippocampus | hypostasise | imperialism | incinerator |
| histrionics | hypostatise | imperiously | inclination |
| hobbledehoy | hypothesise | impermanent | inclusively |
| holographic | | impermeable | incoherence |
| homocentric | I | impersonate | incompetent |
| homoeopathy | identically | impertinent | incongruity |
| homogencity | ideographic | impetuosity | incongruous |
| homogeneous | idiomorphic | implausible | inconsonant |
| homomorphic | idiotically | implication | inconstancy |
| homoplastic | ignobleness | implicative | incontinent |
| honeysuckle | ignominious | imploration | incorporate |
| hopefulness | ignoramuses | importantly | incorporeal |
| horological | illogically | importation | incredulity |
| horseradish | illuminator | importunate | incredulous |
| hospitalise | illusionist | impractical | incremental |
| hospitality | illustrator | imprecation | incriminate |
| hospitaller | illustrious | imprecatory | inculcation |
| huckleberry | imagination | impregnable | indefinable |
| hullaballoo | imaginative | impressible | indentation |
| humiliation | imbrication | impropriety | independent |
| hunchbacked | imitability | improvement | indifferent |
| hyacinthine | imitatively | improvident | indigestion |
| hydrocarbon | immediately | imprudently | indignantly |

indignation
indivisible
indomitable
indubitable
indulgently
industrious
inebriation
ineffectual
inefficient
inelegantly
ineluctable
inequitable
inescapable
inessential
inestimable
inexcusable
inexpensive
infanticide
infatuation
inferential
inferiority
infertility
infestation
infinitival
influential
informality
informative
infracostal
infrangible
infrequency
ingeniously
ingenuously
ingratitude
inhabitable
inheritance
injudicious

injuriously
innocuously
innumerable
inoffensive
inoperative
inopportune
inquisition
inquisitive
inscription
inscrutable
insensitive
inseparable
insidiously
insincerity
insinuating
insinuation
insouciance
inspiration
instability
instigation
instinctive
instructive
insultingly
insuperable
integration
intemperate
intentional
interaction
interceptor
intercessor
interchange
intercostal
intercourse
interesting
interfacing
interfusion

interlineal
intermeddle
intermingle
interpreter
interracial
interregnum
interrogate
intersperse
intolerable
intolerance
intractable
intractably
intravenous
intricately
intrusively
intuitional
intuitively
intumescent
inventively
inventorial
investigate
investiture
invidiously
inviolately
involuntary
involvement
iridescence
irksomeness
irradiation
irreducible
irrefutable
irregularly
irrelevance
irreligious
irreparable
irreverence

irrevocable
isomorphism
isomorphous

J
jactitation
joylessness
judgemental
judiciously
justiciable
justifiable
juvenescent

K
kitchenette
kleptomania
knavishness

L
labefaction
labiodental
laboriously
labradorite
laconically
lactescence
lactiferous
lamentation
landgravine
landscapist
languidness
languishing
laryngotomy
latitudinal
leaseholder
leatherback
leatherneck

| | | | |
|---|---|---|---|
| lecherously | macroscopic | matrimonial | minesweeper |
| lectureship | magisterial | mawkishness | miniaturise |
| legerdemain | magnanimity | meadowsweet | ministerial |
| legionnaire | magnanimous | measureless | minnesinger |
| legislation | magnifiable | measurement | misanthrope |
| legislative | magnificent | mechanician | misbegotten |
| legislature | magnificoes | medicinally | miscarriage |
| lengthiness | maintenance | medievalism | mischievous |
| letterpress | maladjusted | medievalist | misconceive |
| libellously | malapropism | megalomania | misconstrue |
| libertarian | malediction | melancholia | misspelling |
| lickspittle | maleficence | melliferous | mockingbird |
| ligamentous | malevolence | mellifluent | molestation |
| Lilliputian | malfeasance | mellifluous | mollycoddle |
| lingeringly | malfunction | melodiously | momentarily |
| linguistics | maliciously | memorabilia | momentously |
| liquefiable | malignantly | memorandums | monarchical |
| liquescency | malpractice | mensuration | monasticism |
| liquidation | manipulator | mentionable | moneylender |
| literalness | manufactory | mercenarily | monographer |
| lithography | manufacture | merchandise | monographic |
| litigiously | marchioness | merchantman | Monseigneur |
| loathsomely | marginalise | mercilessly | monstrosity |
| loudspeaker | marketplace | mercurially | monstrously |
| lubrication | marshalling | meritorious | moonlighter |
| lucubration | marshmallow | metamorphic | mountaineer |
| ludicrously | masculinity | metaphysics | mountainous |
| luminescent | masterpiece | meteorology | movableness |
| lumpishness | mastication | methodology | munificence |
| lustfulness | masticatory | metrication | murderously |
| luxuriantly | matchlessly | microphonic | murmuringly |
| luxuriously | materialise | microscopic | musculature |
| | materialism | micturition | |
| | materialist | millionaire | N |
| M | matriarchal | mindfulness | naphthalene |
| machination | matriculate | mineraliser | narratively |
| macrobiotic | | | |

nationalise
nationalism
nationality
naturalness
naughtiness
Neanderthal
necessarily
necessitate
necessitous
neckerchief
necromancer
needfulness
needlepoint
nefariously
negligently
negotiation
neighbourly
neuropathic
neutraliser
nickelodeon
nictitation
nightflower
nightingale
noctivagant
nocturnally
noiselessly
nonchalance
nondescript
nonetheless
nonfeasance
nonsensical
northeaster
nosological
notableness
nothingness
notoriously

nourishment
noxiousness
numerically
numismatics

O

obfuscation
objectively
objectivity
objurgation
obliqueness
obliviously
obnoxiously
obsceneness
obscureness
obsecration
observantly
observatory
obsolescent
obstetrical
obstinately
obstipation
obstruction
obstructive
obtestation
obtrusively
obviousness
occultation
odoriferous
offensively
officialdom
officialese
officiously
ominousness
omnipotence
omnipresent

omniscience
ontological
opalescence
operational
operatively
opinionated
opportunely
opportunism
opportunist
opportunity
opprobrious
orchestrate
orderliness
organically
orientation
originality
originative
ornithology
ornithopter
orthopaedic
oscillation
ostentation
osteoplasty
outdistance
outstanding
overbalance
overbearing
overflowing
overweening
overwrought
oxygenation

P

pacifically
paediatrics
paedophilia

painfulness
painstaking
palpability
palpitation
pamphleteer
pandemonium
panegyrical
pantheistic
paperweight
parabolical
paradoxical
paragraphic
paramedical
parasailing
parasitical
parentheses
parenthesis
paripinnate
parishioner
parochially
participant
participate
participial
particulate
partitively
partnership
passionless
passiveness
paternalism
paternoster
pathologist
patronising
peculiarity
pedagogical
peevishness
pelargonium

| | | | |
|---|---|---|---|
| pellucidity | persistence | planetarium | potentially |
| penetration | personalise | planetoidal | powerlessly |
| penitential | personality | planisphere | practicable |
| pennyweight | perspective | playfulness | practically |
| pensiveness | perspicuity | pleasurable | prayerfully |
| penultimate | perspicuous | Pleistocene | precipitant |
| penuriously | pertinacity | plenipotent | precipitate |
| perambulate | pertinently | plenteously | precipitous |
| perceivable | perturbable | plentifully | preciseness |
| perceivably | pervertible | pliableness | preconceive |
| perceptible | pessimistic | ploughshare | precontract |
| perceptibly | pestilently | plutocratic | predecessor |
| percipience | pettifogger | pluviometer | predicament |
| percolation | pharyngitis | pocketknife | predication |
| peregrinate | philatelist | pointedness | predicative |
| perennially | philologist | pointillism | predicatory |
| perestroika | philosopher | poisonously | predictable |
| perfectness | philosophic | polarimeter | predominant |
| perforation | phonography | polariscope | predominate |
| performance | phosphorate | polemically | prehistoric |
| perfunctory | phosphorous | politically | prejudgment |
| pericardiac | photography | pollination | prejudicial |
| pericardium | photophobia | poltergeist | preliminary |
| peripatetic | phraseogram | polycarpous | prematurely |
| periphrases | phraseology | polystyrene | prematurity |
| periphrasis | physiognomy | polytechnic | premeditate |
| peristaltic | pictorially | pomegranate | premiership |
| peritonitis | picturesque | pompousness | premonition |
| permanently | pigsticking | ponderously | preoccupied |
| permissible | pipistrelle | pontificate | preparation |
| permissibly | piratically | pornography | preparatory |
| permutation | piscatorial | porphyritic | preposition |
| perpetrator | pitchblende | portability | prerogative |
| perpetually | pitifulness | portmanteau | presentable |
| persecution | placability | portraitist | presentment |
| persevering | plaintively | possibility | preservable |

prestigious
prestissimo
presumption
presumptive
pretentious
preterition
prevalently
prevaricate
preventable
prickliness
primateship
primitively
principally
privatively
probability
probationer
problematic
procreation
proctorship
procuration
procurement
prodigality
profanation
profaneness
proficiency
profuseness
progenitive
progression
progressive
prohibition
prohibitive
proletariat
proliferate
prominently
promiscuous
promisingly

promptitude
promulgator
pronouncing
propagation
propagative
propinquity
propitiable
propitiator
proposition
proprietary
proprieties
prorogation
prosaically
prosecution
proselytise
prospective
prostration
protagonist
protectoral
protractile
protraction
protractive
protuberant
providently
provisional
provocation
provocative
provokingly
provostship
proximately
prudishness
psychedelic
psychopathy
pterodactyl
publication
publishable

pulchritude
Punchinello
punctilious
punctuality
punctuation
purgatorial
purificator
puritanical
purposeless
putrescence
pyrotechnic
Pythagorean

Q
quacksalver
quadrennial
qualitative
quarrelsome
querulously
quicksilver
quiescently
quiveringly

R
radioactive
radiocarbon
radiography
rapaciously
rapscallion
rapturously
rarefaction
ratatouille
rationalise
rationalism
ravishingly
reactionary

readability
readmission
realisation
reassertion
reassurance
recantation
receptivity
reciprocate
reciprocity
reclaimable
reclamation
recognition
recondition
reconnoitre
reconstruct
recoverable
recriminate
recruitment
rectangular
rectifiable
rectilinear
rediscovery
redoubtable
redundantly
reflexively
reformation
reformative
reformatory
refrangible
refreshment
refrigerate
refulgently
regretfully
regrettable
regurgitate
reiteration

| | | | |
|---|---|---|---|
| reliability | restructure | sceptically | seriousness |
| religiously | resuscitate | scholarship | serviceable |
| reluctantly | retaliation | scholiastic | shallowness |
| remembrance | retardation | schoolchild | shamelessly |
| reminiscent | retentively | schoolhouse | shapeliness |
| remonstrate | reticulated | scintillate | shareholder |
| remorseless | retractable | scopolamine | shellacking |
| Renaissance | retribution | scragginess | shirtsleeve |
| repentantly | retributive | scrumptious | shiveringly |
| repetitious | retrievable | scrutiniser | shrinkingly |
| replenished | retroactive | scuttlebutt | shuttlecock |
| replication | reverberant | searchingly | sightliness |
| repressible | reverberate | searchlight | sightseeing |
| reproachful | reverential | secretarial | significant |
| reprobation | rhetorician | secretariat | silversmith |
| reprovingly | righteously | sectionally | simperingly |
| repudiation | riotousness | sedentarily | singularity |
| repugnantly | ritualistic | sedimentary | sinistrally |
| repulsively | romanticise | seditionary | sketchiness |
| requirement | romanticist | seditiously | skilfulness |
| requisition | Rosicrucian | seductively | skulduggery |
| resemblance | rudimentary | segregation | slaughterer |
| resentfully | rumbustious | seismograph | slenderness |
| reservation | | selfishness | slightingly |
| resignation | S | semiskilled | smithereens |
| resourceful | sacramental | sensational | smokescreen |
| respectable | sacrificial | senselessly | smorgasbord |
| respectably | sagaciously | sensibility | sociability |
| respiration | salesperson | sensitively | solemnities |
| respiratory | sarcophagus | sensitivity | soliloquies |
| resplendent | satirically | sententious | soliloquise |
| restitution | savouriness | sentimental | solvability |
| restiveness | scaffolding | sentinelled | soothsaying |
| restoration | scapularies | septicaemia | sorrowfully |
| restorative | scaremonger | sequestered | sovereignty |
| restriction | scenography | serendipity | spectacular |

speculation
speculative
spendthrift
spherically
spherometer
spondylitis
sponsorship
spontaneity
spontaneous
spreadeagle
spreadsheet
squalidness
squeamishly
stagflation
stalactitic
standardise
standoffish
stateliness
steadfastly
steeplejack
stereotyped
stethometer
stimulation
stipendiary
stipulation
stockbroker
strangulate
strenuously
stringently
stringiness
stuntedness
stylishness
stylography
subcontract
subdivision
subdominant

subjugation
subjunctive
sublimation
submergence
submersible
subordinate
subsequence
subservient
subsistence
substantial
substantive
suburbanite
sufficiency
suffocating
suffocation
suffragette
suggestible
suggestibly
suitability
sumptuously
superabound
superficial
superfluity
superfluous
superimpose
superinduce
superintend
superiority
superlative
supermarket
superscribe
supervision
supervisory
suppliantly
supportable
supposition

suppository
suppression
suppressive
suppuration
supremacist
surrounding
susceptible
sustainable
swarthiness
sweepstakes
switchblade
switchboard
sycophantic
syllabicate
syllogistic
symmetrical
sympathetic
symposiarch
symptomatic
synchronise
synchronism
synchronous
syncopation
syntactical
systematise

T

tachycardia
taciturnity
tagliatelle
talkatively
tangibility
tastelessly
tautologist
tediousness
teenybopper

teetotaller
teleprinter
temperament
tempestuous
temporality
tendentious
tentatively
termination
terminology
terraqueous
terrestrial
territorial
tessellated
testimonial
tetrahedron
thalidomide
theatricals
thenceforth
theoretical
theosophist
therapeutic
thermometer
thingumabob
thistledown
thoughtless
threatening
thriftiness
thunderbolt
tiddlywinks
tightfisted
toastmaster
tonsillitis
topographer
topographic
torchbearer
totalisator

totteringly
tracheotomy
traditional
traducement
tragedienne
tragicomedy
trailblazer
transaction
transfigure
transformer
transfusion
transiently
translation
translucent
transmittal
transmitter
transparent
transported
transporter
transsexual
transuranic
transversal
treacherous
treasonable
treasonably
tremblingly
tremulously
trendsetter
trepidation
tribulation
tributaries
tributarily
triennially
trifurcated
trimestrial
trituration

triumvirate
troublesome
truculently
truncheoned
trusteeship
trustworthy
tuberculose
tuberculous
tumefaction
turbulently
typographic
tyrannosaur
tyrannously

U
ultramarine
ultraviolet
unalterable
unambitious
unbefitting
unblemished
unceasingly
uncommitted
unconfirmed
unconscious
uncontested
undergrowth
underhanded
undertaking
undesirable
undeviating
undignified
undisguised
unemotional
unendurable
unfalteringly

unfermented
unflappable
unflinching
unfulfilled
unfurnished
ungodliness
unification
uniformness
uninhibited
universally
unknowingly
unluckiness
unmanliness
unmeaningly
unmindfully
unmitigated
unnaturally
unnecessary
unobservant
unobtrusive
unoffending
unorganised
unpalatable
unpatriotic
unperformed
unperverted
unpopularly
unpractised
unprintable
unpromising
unprotected
unpublished
unqualified
unreadiness
unreasoning
unreclaimed

unredressed
unrelenting
unremitting
unrepentant
unresisting
unsatisfied
unsaturated
unseaworthy
unsentenced
unshrinking
unsolicited
unsoundness
unspeakable
unspecified
unsupported
unsurpassed
unsuspected
untarnished
unteachable
unthinkable
untinctured
untouchable
untraceable
untravelled
unutterable
unutterably
unvarnished
unwarranted
unwholesome
unwillingly
unwitnessed
unwittingly
upholsterer
uranography
uselessness
utilitarian

**V**
vaccination
vacillating
valediction
variability
variegation
vellication
ventilation
venturesome
veraciously
verboseness
verisimilar
versatility
vertebrated
vexatiously
vicariously
viceroyship

viciousness
vicissitude
vinaigrette
vindication
viniculture
viridescent
visibleness
visionaries
viticulture
vivaciously
volubleness
voraciously
vulcanology

**W**
waggishness
wakefulness

waspishness
watercolour
waywardness
wearisomely
weighbridge
wheelwright
whereabouts
wherewithal
whimsically
wholesomely
widdershins
willingness
windsurfing
winsomeness
wishfulness

witlessness
womanliness
wonderfully
workmanlike
workmanship
worldbeater
worldliness

**X**
xylophonist

**Z**
zealousness
zinciferous
Zoroastrian

# ELEVEN-LETTER MULTIPLE WORDS

**A**
ad infinitum
addle-headed
after effect
agony-column
All Souls' Day
all-of-a-piece
all-that-jazz
armed forces
armour plate
arsenic acid
at a loose end
at face value
at the double
au contraire

**B**
back-draught
bag of tricks
baker's dozen
bald as a coot
ball bearing
banana split
bandy-legged
bank holiday
barley sugar
barley water
barrel organ
basset hound
battle royal
battlefield
beam-compass
beat the drum

beauty sleep
bed of thorns
below-stairs
beyond a joke
big business
bite the dust
black bryony
black comedy
black market
blank cheque
blaze a trail
blind as a bat
block letter
blood vessel
blue-eyed-boy
body politic
bolt-upright
booster shot
boracic acid
bottle brush
bottle glass
bottle green
bounden duty
brace and bit
brazen-faced
break the ice
breech birth
bring to heel
broad-minded
bronze-steel
brush-turkey
bucket-wheel
buffer state

build on sand
built-up area
bulk carrier
bull terrier
bull-baiting
bums on seats
burgess-ship
business-end
butter-knife

**C**
cabbage rose
cabbage-moth
cabbage-worm
cable stitch
call the tune
calling-crab
calling-hare
camphor tree
capital gain
carbon paper
career woman
carrion crow
carry the can
carry the day
carry weight
case history
casting vote
cat's whisker
catch phrase
cathode rays
caught short
caustic soda

cave-dweller
chain stitch
chain-bridge
change hands
chaos theory
check-string
cheek-by-jowl
chicken feed
chicken wire
child labour
chock-a-block
choir-screen
Cinque-Ports
circular saw
city fathers
city slicker
civil rights
Civvy Street
class-fellow
clear the air
clear-headed
cleft palate
clever-clogs
close at hand
close-fisted
clothes-moth
cloud-capped
clover-grass
cochin-china
cock-and-bull
cod-liver oil
coffee table
cold storage

cold-blooded
cold-comfort
cold-hearted
colour-blind
come to grief
come to light
come unstuck
comic relief
common chord
common sense
common-touch
compound eye
contour line
contra-tenor
cotton-press
courtesy car
crime-writer
crying shame
custom-built
cut and dried

D
danger-money
de-profundis
death rattle
depth charge
dirty old man
dish antenna
distaff line
diving board
divining rod
double agent
double entry
double-cross
double-Dutch
double-edged

down payment
down-to-earth
draw the line
drawing room

E
eager beaver
echo chamber
echo sounder
elbow grease
electric eel
electric eye
empty-headed
entrance fee
Eternal City
exhaust pipe

F
fiddle-de-dee
finger stall
firing-squad
fish-eye lens
flip one's lid
fool's errand
foot the bill
forget-me-not
forlorn hope
fountain pen
free-radical
freeze-frame
French fries
front runner
full of beans
full-blooded

G
gambrel roof
gate-crasher
germ warfare
get cracking
get the drift
gild the lily
give the bird
give the slip
give-and-take
give-what-for
go great guns
go to the dogs
go to the wall
go up in smoke
go-overboard
graphic arts
graven image
grizzly bear
ground cover
ground rules
ground swell

H
hair-raising
hairpin bend
halcyon-days
half-and-half
half-hearted
half-measure
hand-to-mouth
happy medium
hard as nails
hard-and-fast
hard-pressed
hard-put-to-it

harvest moon
have a stab at
have kittens
heavy-handed
heroic verse
high treason
high-pitched
home stretch
hominy grits
Homo sapiens
honours list
hors d'oeuvre
house arrest
house martin
house-broken
huff and puff
human-shield
humming-bird

I
I'll eat my hat
ill-disposed
ill-humoured
ill-mannered
in a nutshell
in cold blood
in the offing
in the saddle
in touch with
in two shakes
in-deep-water
into thin air
Irish coffee
iron-curtain

**J**
join the club
Judgment Day
jugular vein
jungle-juice

**K**
king's-ransom
kiss of death
kiss-and-tell
knock for six

**L**
large as life
laughing gas
leading lady
legal tender
let off steam
level-headed
lie detector
light-headed
lily-livered
limp-wristed
line drawing
lion-hearted
long-sighted
look the part
look-askance
loop-the-loop
loose cannon
Lord's Prayer
love-handles
love-in-a-mist

**M**
made-to-order
make a hole in
make a meal of
make light of
make-believe
make-headway
make-or-break
martial arts
meet-halfway
metric-scale
Mexican wave
mind-bending
mind-blowing
miss the boat
missing link
money market
morning star
morning suit
morris dance
mortar-board
mother's-ruin
mum's-the-word
muscle-bound

**N**
name-calling
near the bone
neck-and-neck
nerve centre
nether world
never-say-die
nip in the bud
nitty-gritty
no such thing
noble-savage

non sequitur
nothing to it
notice board
nuclear test

**O**
object-glass
odds and ends
odds and sods
off the rails
old-chestnut
olive branch
on cloud nine
on no account
open and shut
open-mouthed
opera bouffe
oral history
original sin
out-and-about
out-of-pocket
out-of-the-way
over-a-barrel
over-the-hill
over-the-moon

**P**
package tour
pampas grass
Pandora's box
panic attack
panic button
parlour game
party pooper
Passion play
pension plan

peptic ulcer
Peter's Pence
photo finish
pick holes in
piece of cake
pies in the sky
pineal-gland
plain-spoken
plaster cast
play for time
play it by ear
play-the-game
pocket-money
poison dwarf
prickly heat
pros-and-cons
public works
pull strings
pull through
purple-patch
purple-prose

**Q**
quantum jump
quantum leap
Queer Street
queue jumper
quick-witted

**R**
rabbit punch
radar beacon
rain or shine
range finder
rank and file
rant and rave

raw material
rear admiral
regular army
ride-shotgun
right as rain
right to life
right-minded
risk capital
rock the boat
role-playing
Roman candle
rubber-stamp
rule of thumb
running mate

S
safe cracker
safe keeping
safe-conduct
safe-deposit
safety glass
safety match
safety razor
safety valve
sailing boat
salmon trout
saving grace
savoir-faire
search party
second class
second sight
secret agent
see daylight
see the light
self-assured
self-centred

self-control
self-evident
self-induced
self-loading
self-raising
self-reliant
self-respect
self-seeking
self-service
self-serving
self-starter
set the scene
set-to-rights
share option
sharp-witted
sheath-knife
shed light on
sheet anchor
ship-biscuit
shock troops
short shrift
short-handed
short coming
show of hands
show the door
sick at heart
silicon chip
silly season
silver birch
single entry
sinking fund
sitting duck
sitting room
skeleton key
skin and bone
slave driver

slave labour
sleep-walker
slipped disc
small screen
small-minded
small-wonder
snow leopard
snowed under
soft landing
soft-hearted
solar plexus
solar system
son of a bitch
soup kitchen
spice of life
spirit level
split second
spring-clean
square dance
stage-manage
stage-struck
stake a claim
star-crossed
statute-book
stick insect
stiff-necked
stone's throw
stool-pigeon
straight man
strait-laced
street value
strip mining
strong point
sudden death

T
table tennis
take pot luck
take the piss
take umbrage
take-home pay
talent scout
talking book
talking head
talking shop
tennis elbow
the game is up
thin as a rake
thin-skinned
third degree
tight-lipped
time will tell
toffee-nosed
tour de force
track record
tree creeper
trench fever
two's company

U
up against it
up to scratch
up-and-coming
utility room

V
vacuum flask
vapour trail
variety show
vice admiral

W
war of nerves
warm as toast
warts and all
water-closet
water-logged
waxed-jacket
wear and tear
weather vane

well-founded
well-groomed
well-meaning
well-thumbed
whistle stop
white-collar
white-knight
whole number
winter sport

wisdom tooth
witch doctor
wolf whistle
word for word
words fail me
work station
worlds apart
wrapped up in

wrought iron

Y
yellow fever
yellow-belly

Z
zero gravity

# TWELVE-LETTER WORDS

A
abbreviation
absoluteness
abstemiously
abstractedly
abstractness
abstruseness
academically
acceleration
accidentally
accomplished
accumulation
accumulative
accurateness
accusatorial
acoustically
acquiescence
adaptability
adhesiveness
adjudication
adorableness
adulteration
advantageous
adventitious
aerodynamics
aeronautical
aestheticism
affectionate
aforethought
afterthought
agricultural
alliteration
alliterative

allusiveness
alphanumeric
alterability
amalgamation
ambidextrous
amelioration
amenableness
amicableness
amortisation
amphitheatre
anaesthetise
anaesthetist
analogically
analytically
anatomically
annihilation
announcement
Annunciation
antagonistic
antecedently
antediluvian
anthological
anthropology
anticipation
antiparallel
antiphrastic
apostrophise
appendectomy
appendicitis
appositional
appreciation
apprehension
approachable

appropriator
appurtenance
archipelagic
architecture
aristocratic
Aristotelian
arithmetical
aromatherapy
articulately
articulation
artificially
artistically
asphyxiation
assassinator
asseveration
assimilation
assimilative
astonishment
astringently
astrological
astronautics
astronomical
astrophysics
atmospherics
attractively
attributable
augmentation
augmentative
auscultation
auspiciously
Australasian
authenticate
authenticity

avariciously

B
bacchanalian
bachelorhood
bachelorship
backbreaking
backwardness
bacteriology
bantamweight
beatifically
behaviourism
beneficently
beneficially
benevolently
beseechingly
bewilderment
bewitchingly
bibliography
bibliomaniac
bicentennial
biochemistry
biographical
blackcurrant
blackguardly
blamableness
blandishment
blatherskite
bletherskate
blissfulness
blockbusting
bloodletting
bloodthirsty
boisterously
brackishness
breakthrough

breathalyser
breathlessly
breathtaking
brinkmanship
Brontosaurus
buccaneering
bullfighting
burdensomely
bureaucratic
businesslike
butterscotch

C
cabinetmaker
cadaverously
calamitously
calligrapher
calligraphic
callisthenic
calumniation
cancellation
canonisation
cantankerous
capitulation
capriciously
captiousness
caravanserai
carbohydrate
carelessness
caricaturist
catamountain
catastrophic
catechetical
cautiousness
censoriously
centennially

ceremonially
chairmanship
championship
chaplainship
characterise
chartography
chastisement
chauvinistic
cheerfulness
chemotherapy
childishness
chimerically
chirographer
chiropractic
chitterlings
chivalrously
choreography
Christianity
chronologist
churlishness
circuitously
circumcision
circumjacent
circumscribe
circumstance
cirrocumulus
cirrostratus
civilisation
clairvoyance
clairvoyants
clannishness
classicalism
classicalist
classifiable
climatically
clownishness

coalitionist
codification
cohabitation
cohesiveness
coincidental
coincidently
collaborator
collaterally
collectively
collectivism
colloquially
colonisation
combinations
commencement
commendation
commendatory
commensality
commensurate
commercially
commissarial
commissariat
commissioned
commissioner
commodiously
commonwealth
communicable
communicator
compensation
compensatory
complacently
complaisance
complemental
completeness
complexioned
complication
compressible

compulsively
compunctious
concentrated
conciliation
conciliatory
conclusively
concomitance
concomitancy
concordantly
concrescence
concreteness
concupiscent
concurrently
condemnation
condemnatory
condensation
conditioning
confabulator
confectioner
conferential
confessional
confidential
confirmation
confirmatory
confiscation
confoundedly
Confucianism
congeniality
conglomerate
congratulate
congregation
connectively
connubiality
conquistador
conscionable
conscription

consecration
consequently
conservation
conservatism
conservative
conservatory
considerable
consignation
consistently
consolidator
constabulary
constituency
constitution
constitutive
constriction
constrictive
constructive
consultation
consummation
contagiously
contaminate
contemporary
contemporise
contemptible
contemptuous
contiguously
contingently
continuation
continuously
contractible
contrariness
contrariwise
contributive
contributory
contriteness
controllable

contumacious
contumelious
convalescent
convectively
conveniently
conventional
conversantly
conversation
conveyancing
convincingly
conviviality
convulsively
coordination
coquettishly
corporeality
correctional
corroborator
cosmological
cosmopolitan
costermonger
counteragent
countercharm
countercheck
counterclaim
counterforce
countermarch
counterpoint
counterpoise
countertenor
courageously
covetousness
cowardliness
credibleness
crenellation
cryptography
culpableness

D
debilitating
debilitation
decapitation
decentralise
decipherable
decisiveness
decongestant
decreasingly
deducibility
defamatorily
definiteness
definitional
definitively
deflagration
degeneration
degenerative
dejectedness
deliberately
deliberation
delicateness
delicatessen
delightfully
delimitation
deliquescent
delusiveness
demilitarise
demonologist
demonstrable
demoralising
denomination
denunciation
departmental
depopulation
depreciation
depressingly

derivational
derivatively
desiderative
desirability
despairingly
despoliation
despondently
despotically
destructible
determinable
determinedly
dethronement
devotionally
diabolically
diagrammatic
dialectician
diaphanously
dictatorship
didactically
dietetically
differential
digressional
dilapidation
dilatability
dilatoriness
diminishable
diminutively
diploblastic
directorship
disadvantage
disaffection
disagreeable
disagreeably
disagreement
disallowable
disappointed

disassociate
disastrously
disbursement
discerningly
discipleship
disciplinary
discomfiture
discomposure
disconnected
disconsolate
discontented
discordantly
discouraging
discourteous
discoverable
discreetness
discretional
discriminate
discursively
disdainfully
disenchanted
disestablish
disgorgement
disgustingly
disharmonise
disincentive
disinfectant
disingenuous
disintegrate
disinterment
disobedience
disorganised
disorientate
dispensation
dispiritedly
displacement

displeasedly
disputatious
disreputable
dissatisfied
disseminator
dissertation
dissimilarly
dissociation
dissuasively
distillation
distinctness
distractedly
distribution
divisibility
doctrinarian
dogmatically
domestically
doubtfulness
dramatically
draughtiness
dreadfulness

E
eavesdropper
eccentricity
ecclesiastic
eclectically
econometrics
economically
ecstatically
educationist
effervescent
efflorescent
effusiveness
egoistically
Egyptologist

electrolysis
electroplate
elementarily
elliptically
elocutionary
emancipation
emasculation
embezzlement
embitterment
emblazonment
emphatically
encephalitis
enchantingly
encroachment
encyclopedia
encyclopedic
endomorphism
endoskeleton
enfeeblement
entanglement
enterprising
entertaining
enthronement
enthusiastic
entomologist
entrancement
entreatingly
entrepreneur
envisagement
epicycloidal
epidemiology
epigrammatic
episodically
epistemology
equalisation
equipollence

equivalently
equivocatory
escapologist
escutcheoned
esoterically
estrangement
etymological
euphoniously
evanescently
evisceration
evolutionary
exacerbation
exaggeration
exaggerative
exasperating
exchangeable
excitability
excruciating
executorship
exhaustively
exhilaration
exorbitantly
exoterically
expatriation
experiential
experimental
explicitness
exploitation
expostulator
exterminable
exterminator
extinguisher
extortionate
extramarital
extramundane
extraneously

extravagance
extravagancy
extravaganza
extroversion

F
factiousness
factitiously
faithfulness
fallaciously
fancifulness
farcicalness
fastidiously
fearlessness
featherbrain
feminineness
fenestration
fermentation
feverishness
fibrillation
fictitiously
flagellation
flatteringly
flexibleness
flittermouse
fluorescence
forbiddingly
forcibleness
formaldehyde
fortuitously
fountainhead
frankincense
fraudulently
freestanding
frontispiece
functionally

G
gamesmanship
gastronomist
genealogical
genuflection
geographical
geologically
geometrician
gesticulator
gladiatorial
globetrotter
gluttonously
gobbledegook
gobbledygook
gossipmonger
governmental
governorship
gracefulness
graciousness
gratefulness
gratuitously
gregariously
grievousness
groundlessly

H
haberdashery
hagiographer
hallucinogen
harlequinade
harmoniously
headmistress
headquarters
headshrinker
heartstrings
heliocentric

heliotropism
henceforward
hermetically
hesitatingly
heterogenous
heterosexual
hieroglyphic
highfaluting
hindquarters
hippopotamus
historically
homoeopathic
homomorphous
horizontally
horticulture
housebreaker
housekeeping
humanitarian
hydrochloric
hydrographer
hydrostatics
hydrotherapy
hygienically
hyperbolical
hypertension
hypnotherapy
hypochondria
hypocritical
hypostatical
hypothetical
hysterectomy
hysterically

I
identifiable
idiosyncrasy

illegitimate
illumination
illustration
illustrative
immaculately
immatureness
immemorially
immoderately
immutability
impartiality
impenetrable
impenitently
imperatively
imperfection
imperishable
imperishably
impersonally
impersonator
impertinence
imperviously
imponderable
impressively
imprisonment
inaccessible
inaccurately
inadequately
inadmissible
inadvertence
inadvertency
inapplicable
inapplicably
inappositely
inarticulate
inauspicious
incalculable
incalculably

incandescent
incapacitate
incautiously
incendiarism
incidentally
incineration
incommodious
incommutable
incomparable
incomparably
incompatible
incompetence
incomputable
inconclusive
inconformity
inconsequent
inconsistent
inconsolable
inconstantly
incorrigible
indebtedness
indecisively
indecorously
indefensible
indefinitely
indelibility
independence
indicatively
indifference
indigestible
indiscretion
indisputable
indissoluble
indoctrinate
ineradicable
inexpedience

inexplicable
infectiously
infiltration
inflammatory
inflationary
infringement
inhabitation
inhospitable
inosculation
insalubrious
insolubility
inspectorate
installation
instrumental
insufferable
insurrection
intellectual
intelligible
intemperance
intercession
interconnect
interdictory
interjection
interlocutor
intermediary
interminable
intermission
intermittent
interpellate
interpleader
interruptive
interstellar
intervention
intimidation
intolerantly
intoxicating

intransigent
intransitive
introduction
introductory
introversion
invalidation
inveiglement
invertebrate
investigator
invisibility
invulnerable
irascibility
irrationally
irredeemable
irredeemably
irregularity
irremediable
irremediably
irrepealably
irresistible
irresolvable
irrespective
irresponsive
irreverently
irreversible
irritability
isolationism
isolationist

J
journalistic
jurisdiction

K
kaleidoscope
kleptomaniac

L
lasciviously
laudableness
laureateship
legitimately
legitimation
legitimatise
lexicography
licentiously
lifelessness
likeableness
liquefaction
listlessness
lithographer
localisation
lonesomeness
longitudinal
longshoreman
loquaciously
lugubriously
lukewarmness
luminousness

M
machicolated
mademoiselle
magnetically
magnetometer
magnificence
magniloquent
maintainable
majestically
malevolently
malformation
malleability
malnutrition

maltreatment
manipulation
manslaughter
Marseillaise
marvellously
meditatively
melodramatic
mercantilism
mercifulness
meretricious
metamorphism
metaphysical
methodically
metropolitan
microbiology
middleweight
minicomputer
ministration
miraculously
mirthfulness
misadventure
misanthropic
misbelieving
miscalculate
misdemeanour
misdirection
misinterpret
misplacement
mispronounce
misrepresent
misstatement
mobilisation
modification
monastically
monosyllabic
monumentally

morphologist
mournfulness
muddleheaded
multifarious
multiformity
multilateral
multilingual
multiplicate
multiplicity
municipality
mysteriously

N
narcotically
naturalistic
navigability
needlessness
neglectfully
neighbouring
Neoplatonism
neurasthenia
neurosurgery
nevertheless
Newfoundland
nidification
noctambulist
nomenclature
nonchalantly
noneffective
nonflammable
notification
nutritionist
nutritiously

O
obdurateness

obligatorily
obligingness
obliteration
obscurantist
obsequiously
obsolescence
obsoleteness
obstreperous
occasionally
oceanography
octogenarian
omnipotently
omnipresence
omnisciently
opinionative
oppressively
oratorically
organisation
orienteering
ornamentally
orthodontist
orthopaedics
ossification
ostentatious
osteoporosis
otherworldly
outmanoeuvre
outrageously
overpowering
overwhelming
oxyacetylene

P
paramilitary
parasitology
parenthesise

parochialism
parsimonious
participator
particularly
partisanship
pathetically
pathological
patriarchate
peacefulness
penitentiary
pentagonally
peradventure
perambulator
peregrinator
peremptorily
perfidiously
pericarditis
periphrastic
permanganate
permeability
perpetration
perplexingly
perseverance
persistently
perspicacity
perspiration
perspiratory
persuasively
pertinacious
perturbation
pestilential
petrifaction
pettifoggery
pharmacology
philanthropy
philharmonic

Philhellenic
philistinism
philosophise
phonetically
phosphoresce
photographic
photogravure
phrenologist
pigmentation
pitiableness
pitilessness
pleasantries
Plesiosaurus
polarisation
policyholder
polysyllabic
polyurethane
populousness
portentously
positiveness
possessively
postgraduate
postmeridian
potentiality
practicality
practitioner
praiseworthy
preciousness
precociously
precognition
precondition
predestinate
predilection
prefabricate
preferential
premaxillary

preparedness
preponderant
preposterous
prerequisite
presbyterial
prescription
presentation
presentiment
preservation
preservative
presidential
presumptuous
prevailingly
preventative
primogenitor
principality
probationary
processional
proclamation
prodigiously
productivity
professional
professorial
profoundness
prolifically
prolificness
prolongation
promulgation
propagandise
prophylactic
propitiation
propitiously
proportional
proscription
prosperously
protectorate

protestation
protoplasmic
protuberance
proverbially
providential
prudentially
pseudonymous
psychiatrist
psychologist
pugnaciously
pumpernickel
purblindness
purification
putrefaction
pyrotechnics

Q
quadrangular
quadraphonic
quadriplegia
quadrivalent
qualmishness
quantitative
questionable
questionably
quinquennial
quintessence

R
radiotherapy
rambunctious
ramification
ratification
readjustment
readmittance
reappearance

rebelliously
recalcitrant
recapitulate
receivership
receptionist
reciprocally
recklessness
recognisance
recollection
recommitment
reconcilable
reconstitute
reconveyance
recrudescent
recuperation
recuperative
redistribute
reflectively
refractorily
refreshingly
refrigerator
regardlessly
regeneration
registration
rehabilitate
reimposition
reinvestment
reinvigorate
rejuvenation
relationship
relativeness
relentlessly
reliableness
reminiscence
remonstrance
remorsefully

removability
remuneration
renouncement
renunciation
repercussion
repercussive
reprehension
repressively
reproachable
reproduction
residentiary
resoluteness
respectfully
respectively
resplendence
responsively
restaurateur
restrainedly
resurrection
resuscitable
resuscitator
reticulation
retractation
retrenchment
retrocession
retroversion
revengefully
rheumatology
rhinoplastic
ridiculously
romantically
ruthlessness

S
sacrilegious
salesmanship

| | | |
|---|---|---|
| salubriously | simultaneous | streetwalker |
| salutariness | skullduggery | streptomycin |
| sanguineness | slanderously | stubbornness |
| sarsaparilla | sledgehammer | studiousness |
| satisfaction | slovenliness | stupefaction |
| satisfactory | sluggishness | stupendously |
| scandalously | smallholding | stylographic |
| scatterbrain | snobbishness | subcommittee |
| schoolmaster | solicitation | subconscious |
| scornfulness | solicitously | subcontinent |
| screenwriter | solitariness | subcutaneous |
| scripturally | somnambulate | subjectively |
| scriptwriter | somnambulist | subjectivity |
| scrupulosity | sonorousness | submaxillary |
| scrupulously | sophisticate | submissively |
| sculpturally | spaciousness | subscription |
| scurrilously | specialities | subsequently |
| sectarianism | specifically | subservience |
| sedulousness | spiritedness | substantiate |
| segmentation | spiritualise | substitution |
| seismologist | spiritualism | subterranean |
| selenography | spirituality | successfully |
| semidetached | spitefulness | successively |
| semiliterate | sporadically | succinctness |
| sensibleness | spotlessness | sufficiently |
| septennially | spuriousness | suggestively |
| shamefacedly | stalwartness | superannuate |
| shamefulness | statistician | superciliary |
| sharecropper | steeplechase | supercilious |
| sharpshooter | stenographer | supernatural |
| shatterproof | stereophonic | superstition |
| sheepishness | stockbroking | supplication |
| shillyshally | straitjacket | suppositious |
| shrewishness | stranglehold | suppressible |
| shudderingly | stratosphere | surmountable |
| simultaneity | strawberries | surprisingly |

surroundings
surveillance
susceptivity
suspiciously
symbolically
synonymously
synoptically

T
talismanical
tangentially
tangibleness
tastefulness
technicality
technologist
teleological
teleprompter
teleshopping
tercentenary
thanksgiving
theatrically
theocratical
theoretician
theosophical
therapeutics
thoroughbred
thoroughfare
thoughtfully
thriftlessly
ticklishness
torrefaction
tortuousness
totalitarian
toxicologist
traitorously
tranquillise

tranquillity
transferable
transgressor
transitional
transitorily
translucency
transmigrant
transmission
transmutable
transmutably
transoceanic
transparency
transpontine
transposable
transudation
transversely
transvestism
trigonometry
tripartitely
triumphantly
tropological
truthfulness
tuberculosis
tumultuously
tyrannically

U
ubiquitously
ultramontane
umbrageously
unacceptable
unaccustomed
unacquainted
unanswerable
unappeasable
unassailable

unauthorised
unbecomingly
unbelievable
unchallenged
unchangeable
uncharitable
uncommercial
unctuousness
uncultivated
underachieve
underclothes
undercurrent
underdressed
undergarment
underpinning
understratum
underwriting
undeservedly
undischarged
unemployable
unexpectedly
unfaithfully
unfathomable
unfavourable
unfranchised
unfrequented
unfruitfully
ungenerously
ungovernable
ungracefully
ungraciously
ungratefully
unhesitating
unhistorical
unimportance
unimpugnable

universalist
universities
unkindliness
unlawfulness
unlikelihood
unlikeliness
unmanageable
unmarketable
unmercifully
unmistakable
unmistakably
unobstructed
unparalleled
unpatronised
unpleasantly
unpopularity
unprejudiced
unpretending
unprincipled
unprivileged
unproductive
unprofitable
unpropitious
unquenchable
unquestioned
unreasonable
unregistered
unreservedly
unrestrained

unrestricted
unsatisfying
unscrupulous
unseasonable
unseemliness
unstableness
unsteadiness
unstratified
unsuppressed
unsuspecting
unsuspicious
unsystematic
untenantable
unthinkingly
untowardness
untrammelled
unwieldiness
unworthiness
uproariously

V

vainglorious
valetudinary
valuableness
variableness
verification
veterinarian
victoriously
vigorousness

vilification
villainously
vindictively
vitalisation
vituperation
vocabularies
vocalisation
vociferously
voluminously
voluptuaries
voluptuously

W

warehouseman
weatherboard
weatherglass
weatherproof
welterweight
whimsicality
whisperingly
wholehearted
whortleberry
worshipfully
wrathfulness
wretchedness

Y

youthfulness

# TWELVE-LETTER MULTIPLE WORDS

## A
absent-minded
Achilles' heel
adrenal gland
Afro-American
all and sundry
angel of death
angel of mercy
animal rights
anti-aircraft
anything goes
argue the toss
armour bearer
armour plated
artesian well
ascorbic acid
Ash Wednesday
assembly line
at arm's length
at death's door
atomic energy
atomic number
atomic theory
atomic weight
auld lang syne

## B
baby carriage
baby snatcher
back of beyond
balance wheel
barbette ship
bear the brunt

beat a retreat
bedding plant
better part of
bill of health
bird's-eye view
birthday suit
black and blue
black economy
black pudding
blast furnace
blood brother
blood pudding
bloody-minded
body stocking
boiling point
bomber jacket
book learning
bow and scrape
bowling alley
bowling green
break dancing
break the bank
bride-chamber
bridging loan
bring to a head
Brussels lace
bunch of fives
Bunsen burner
burial ground
buyer's market
by a short head

## C
cabin cruiser
call of nature
call the shots
camp follower
candid camera
candle-holder
candy-striped
cannon fodder
capital goods
carbon-dating
cardinal-bird
carpenter bee
carpet-knight
carte blanche
cartridge box
case the joint
case-hardened
cash and carry
cat-o'-mountain
cattle plague
caveat emptor
century plant
chaise longue
chimney piece
chimney stack
chimney sweep
chimney-shaft
clear as a bell
clear-sighted
clearing bank
climb the wall
clinging vine

clinker-built
closed season
cloven footed
cloven hoofed
coaxial cable
cold as marble
cold-shoulder
Cologne water
come a cropper
common market
compos mentis
concert pitch
conic section
conning tower
console table
control panel
control tower
conveyor belt
cook the books
cooling tower
copying press
cost of living
cost the earth
count the cost
court martial
crack a bottle
crack the whip
credit rating
creepy-crawly
cross-country
cross-current
cross-examine
cross-grained
cross-purpose
cross section
culture shock

cupboard love
cut and thrust

D
danger signal
death warrant
decimal point
deer-stalking
devil may care
dinner jacket
do the honours
dolman sleeve
donkey engine
donkey's years
double-dealer
down the drain
drawing board
dressing-down
drop a clanger
drop-in centre
drunk as a lord
Dutch auction
Dutch courage

E
ear-splitting
earth science
easy on the eye
end of the road
essential oil
even-tempered
exchange rate

F
fait accompli
family circle

fault-finding
feeble-minded
feel the pinch
field-glasses
flame-thrower
flying doctor
flying saucer
folding stuff
for a rainy day
for the asking
for the record
force of habit
fourth estate
Freudian slip
fully-fledged

G
gasp one's last
gastric-juice
get the bullet
get the hang of
gift of the gab
give the lie to
glass ceiling
gloom and doom
gold standard
golden fleece
good riddance
good-humoured
goose pimples
green fingers
grind to a halt
growing pains
guiding light

**H**
habeas corpus
habit-forming
hair of the dog
hair's-breadth
hand over fist
happy as a lark
happy-go-lucky
haute couture
haute cuisine
have a crack at
have a head for
have a nose for
have a stake in
have an eye for
have it coming
heart and soul
heart failure
heart-rending
heart-to-heart
hidden agenda
high fidelity
high-sounding
high-spirited
highly strung
hit a bad patch
hit the bottle
Holy of holies
Holy Thursday
home from home
home straight
house warming
house-husband

**I**
in a cold sweat
in at the death
in the hot seat
in the long run
in the running
it's a dog's life

**J**
jack-in-the-box
jump the queue

**K**
keep the peace
knight-errant
know the ropes
know the score

**L**
labour of love
laissez-faire
launching pad
lay it on thick
leading light
learn by heart
let well alone
level pegging
lie of the land
life sentence
light-hearted
lightning rod
little people
little tin god
long drawn out
long-standing
looking glass
low frequency
lumbered with

lunar eclipse

**M**
mad as a hatter
magnetic pole
magnetic tape
maid of honour
maiden speech
maiden voyage
make a play for
make ends meet
make good time
make the grade
make up leeway
man about town
man of his word
marline spike
master stroke
master-at-arms
matter-of-fact
meat and drink
melting point
merchant bank
merchant navy
merchant ship
mezzo-soprano
mind-boggling
mine detector
minstrel show
mixed economy
monkey wrench
moral support
moral victory
morning after

**N**
narrow-minded
National Park
national debt
national grid
nautical mile
nerve-racking
New Testament
noncommittal
none the wiser
not cut out for
not turn a hair
notary public
nothing doing
nuclear power
nuclear waste
nuts and bolts

**O**
object lesson
oblique angle
of the essence
off the record
Old Testament
old school tie
old wives' tale
old-fashioned
on a knife edge
on bended knee
on one's mettle
on the rampage
on the rebound
on the streets
on the up and up
on the warpath
one jump ahead

one track mind
one-horse race
opera glasses
optical fibre
organ-grinder
out in the cold
out of the blue
out on one's ear

**P**
palette knife
Pan-Hellenism
passion fruit
pat on the back
patent office
pay on the nail
pecking order
petty larceny
petty officer
pick up the tab
pigs might fly
pip at the post
plain clothes
plane sailing
play ball with
playing field
Plimsoll line
poet laureate
pole-position
post meridiem
powers that be
pride of place
primrose path
public health
public sector
public spirit

push one's luck
put a damper on
put a sock in it
put on the spot
put the bite on
put the boot in

**Q**
queue-jumping

**R**
rabble-rouser
racing driver
rags-to-riches
rainbow trout
raise the ante
raise the wind
random-access
razzle-dazzle
red corpuscle
red-letter day
return ticket
rhesus factor
rhesus monkey
rhyming slang
Richter scale
ride the tiger
right-hand man
ring-side-seat
rip-off artist
roaring drunk
rocking chair
rocking horse
rolling stock
rolling stone
Roman holiday

Roman numeral
rough diamond
round the bend
rub shoulders
rule the roost
run its course
run of the mill
run the risk of

S
safe and sound
safe as houses
same old story
scarlet fever
scarlet woman
Scotland Yard
second fiddle
second nature
second string
second to none
security lock
security risk
sedge warbler
see the back of
self-educated
self-employed
self-interest
self-portrait
self-reproach
selling point
serial number
sharp-tongued
Shetland pony
ship chandler
ship's-biscuit
shock therapy

shoot through
shooting star
short-circuit
short-staffed
shot in the arm
show business
show the ropes
Siamese twins
side whiskers
silver lining
silver screen
simple-minded
single-decker
single-handed
single-minded
six of the best
sliding scale
slow handclap
smash and grab
snake charmer
sock it to them
soda fountain
song and dance
sound barrier
sound effects
space shuttle
space station
speak volumes
spick-and-span
spinal column
spine-chiller
spiral galaxy
squeaky-clean
stage whisper
stained glass
stand-up comic

standing army
status symbol
staying power
steal the show
steer clear of
sticky wicket
stony-hearted
storm trooper
stormy-petrel
straight face
strike a chord
strike it rich
strip cartoon
strong-minded
stuffed shirt
sweet and sour

T
take a shine to
take as gospel
take for a ride
talking point
tartaric acid
tax avoidance
tax therapist
temporal lobe
ten-gallon hat
tenant farmer
the bare bones
the die is cast
the real McCoy
the red carpet
the very thing
there's the rub
thick and fast
thick-skinned

throw a wobbly
time exposure
time-honoured
tip the scales
toggle switch
top of the tree
trace element
tracing paper
train-spotter
training ship
treasure hunt
trick or treat
trigger-happy
truth-will-out
tunnel vision
turn of phrase
turn up trumps
Twelfth Night
twenty-twenty
two-way mirror
typhoid fever

U
ugly duckling
unwritten law
urban renewal
user-friendly

V
vestal virgin
visiting card
vote of thanks

W
walkie-talkie
wandering Jew
water boatman
water buffalo
water spaniel
water-company
water-soluble
watering hole
ways and means

weather-bound
Welfare State
well-disposed
well-grounded
well-informed
well-mannered
whale of a time
what's cooking
whipped cream
white feather
wicketkeeper
will-o'-the-wisp
willing horse
witching hour
with open arms
within reason
working party
World-Wide-Web
writer's cramp

Y
yellow streak

# THIRTEEN-LETTER WORDS

## A
absorbability
accessibility
accommodating
accommodation
accompaniment
accoutrements
acidification
acquisitively
acrimoniously
administrator
admirableness
admissibility
adventurously
advertisement
advisableness
aesthetically
affirmatively
afforestation
agglomeration
agglutination
aggravatingly
agreeableness
agriculturist
algebraically
allegorically
alternatively
ambassadorial
ambidexterity
amniocentesis
amplification
anachronistic
anagrammatise

antichristian
anticlimactic
anticlockwise
anticorrosive
antihistamine
antilogarithm
antimonarchic
antipersonnel
apostolically
appellatively
appendiculate
applicability
apportionment
appropriately
appropriation
approximately
approximation
arbitrariness
arboriculture
archaeologist
architectural
argentiferous
argumentation
argumentative
arithmetician
ascertainable
ascertainment
assassination
assiduousness
asthmatically
astonishingly
atrociousness
attainability

attentiveness
attributively
audaciousness
authentically
authoritarian
authoritative
autobiography
availableness
axiomatically

## B
baccalaureate
barefacedness
beatification
believability
bibliographer
biodegradable
biotechnology
blamelessness
blasphemously
bloodcurdling
bombastically
bougainvillea
bouillabaisse
boundlessness
bountifulness
brotherliness
bumptiousness
butterfingers

## C
calcification
callisthenics

candidateship
capaciousness
carbonisation
categorically
cauterisation
ceremoniously
certification
challengeable
changeability
changefulness
characterless
Christmastide
chronographer
chronological
chrysanthemum
cicatrisation
cinematograph
circumference
circumfluence
circumspectly
circumvention
clamorousness
clandestinely
clarification
collaboration
collectedness
colloquialism
combativeness
commemorative
commensurable
commercialise
commercialism
commiseration
communication
communicative
commutability

companionable
companionably
companionless
companionship
comparatively
compassionate
compatibility
compendiously
complainingly
complaisantly
complimentary
comprehension
comprehensive
conceitedness
concentration
conceptualise
concomitantly
concupiscence
condescending
condescension
conditionally
conduciveness
confabulation
confectionery
confederation
configuration
conflagration
confraternity
confrontation
congressional
conjecturally
conjugational
consanguinity
conscientious
consciousness
consecutively

consequential
conservatoire
considerately
consideration
consolidation
conspicuously
constableship
constellation
consternation
consumptively
contamination
contaminative
contemplation
contentiously
contortionist
contraception
contradiction
contradictory
contravention
contributable
controversial
convalescence
convocational
convulsionary
correlatively
correspondent
corroboration
corrosiveness
counteraction
counteractive
counterattack
counterfeiter
countersignal
counterstroke
counterweight
courteousness

craftsmanship
creditability
credulousness
crossbreeding
crotchetiness
cylindrically

D
dastardliness
decaffeinated
deceitfulness
deceptiveness
decomposition
decontaminate
defectiveness
defencelessly
deferentially
deliciousness
deliriousness
dematerialise
demonstration
demonstrative
depersonalise
deprecatingly
dermatologist
descriptively
desirableness
destructively
desultoriness
deterioration
determination
determinative
detrimentally
dexterousness
dialectically
diametrically

dictatorially
differentiate
diffusibility
diffusiveness
digestibility
disadvantaged
disappearance
disconnection
discontinuity
discretionary
disengagement
disfiguration
disfigurement
disgracefully
dishonourable
disjunctively
dismemberment
disobediently
disparagement
disparagingly
dispassionate
dispossession
disproportion
disrespectful
dissemination
dissimilarity
dissimilitude
dissolubility
dissoluteness
distastefully
distinctively
distinguished
distressfully
distressingly
distributable
distrustfully

diversifiable
dramatisation

E
eccentrically
educationally
effectiveness
effervescence
efficaciously
efflorescence
egotistically
elaborateness
electrocution
embarrassment
embellishment
embryological
encompassment
encouragement
encouragingly
encyclopaedia
endurableness
energetically
enigmatically
enlightenment
entertainment
entomological
epiphenomenon
equidistantly
equitableness
equivocalness
establishment
estimableness
evangelically
everlastingly
exceptionable
exceptionally

excitableness
exclusiveness
excommunicate
excortication
exhibitionism
exhibitionist
expansibility
expansiveness
expectoration
expeditionary
expeditiously
expensiveness
expostulation
expressionism
expressionist
expropriation
exquisiteness
extemporarily
extensibility
extensiveness
extermination
extragalactic
extrajudicial
extraordinary
extravagantly
extrinsically

F
facetiousness
falsification
fantastically
featherweight
ferociousness
fertilisation
floricultural
foolhardiness

foreknowledge
forgetfulness
fortification
fossilisation
fractiousness
frequentative
frightfulness
frivolousness
fundamentally

G
galvanisation
geometrically
gesticulation
gesticulatory
glorification
gracelessness
grammatically
granddaughter
grandiloquent
gratification
grotesqueness
gubernatorial
guiltlessness

H
hairsplitting
hallucination
hallucinatory
harmonisation
heartlessness
hemispherical
hermaphrodite
hermeneutical
heterogeneous
horticultural

hydrodynamics
hypercritical
hypochondriac

I
idiomatically
idiosyncratic
ignominiously
illustriously
immovableness
immutableness
impartibility
impassiveness
impeccability
impecuniosity
imperceptible
imperfectness
impermissible
impersonation
impertinently
imperturbable
impetuousness
implacability
importunately
impossibility
impracticable
impressionism
improvability
improvisation
inadvertently
inappropriate
inattentively
incandescence
incarceration
incombustible
incommunicado

incompetently
inconceivable
inconceivably
incongruously
inconsiderate
inconsistency
inconspicuous
incontestable
incontestably
incontinently
inconvenience
inconvertible
incorporation
incorrectness
incorruptible
incredibility
incredulously
incurableness
indefatigable
independently
indescribable
indeterminate
indifferently
indiscernible
indispensable
indistinctive
individualise
industrialise
industriously
ineffectively
ineffectually
inefficiently
ineligibility
inexhaustible
inexpediently
inexpensively

inexperienced
inexpressible
inferentially
infinitesimal
inflexibility
influentially
injudiciously
inoffensively
inopportunely
inquisitively
insatiability
insensibility
insidiousness
insignificant
insinuatingly
instantaneous
instinctively
institutional
instructively
insubordinate
insubstantial
insufficiency
insupportable
insusceptible
intangibility
intelligently
intemperately
intentionally
interestingly
international
interpolation
interpretable
interrelation
interrogation
interrogatory
interruptedly

interspersion
intrinsically
introspection
intrusiveness
investigation
investigative
invidiousness
invincibility
inviolability
invisibleness
involuntarily
irascibleness
irrationality
irrecoverable
irreligiously
irreplaceable
irrepressible
irrepressibly
irresponsible
irretrievable
irretrievably

J

judiciousness
justification

K

kaleidoscopic
knowledgeable

L

lackadaisical
languishingly
laughableness
lecherousness
lethargically

lexicographer
librarianship
litigiousness
loathsomeness
ludicrousness
luxuriousness

M
Machiavellian
magnanimously
magnetisation
magnification
magnificently
magniloquence
maliciousness
malleableness
manifestation
manufacturing
masculineness
materialistic
mathematician
matriculation
matrimonially
mellifluently
mellifluously
melodiousness
mercenariness
merchandising
mercilessness
meritoriously
metamorphosis
metaphysician
meteorologist
ministerially
misanthropist
miscellaneous

mischievously
misconception
miserableness
misgovernment
mismanagement
misunderstand
mollification
monarchically
monstrousness
mortification
mountainously
mouthwatering
multicoloured
multinational
multiplicable
multitudinous
mummification
mystification

N
necessitously
negotiability
neighbourhood
niggardliness
nightwatchman
noiselessness
nonconforming
nonsensically
notoriousness
nullification

O
objectionable
objectiveness
obliviousness
obnoxiousness

observational
obstinateness
obstructively
odoriferously
offensiveness
officiousness
ophthalmology
opportuneness
opprobriously
orchestration
ornamentation
ornithologist
osteomyelitis
overqualified
overstatement
oversubscribe
overvaluation
ovoviviparous
oystercatcher

P
paediatrician
palaeontology
palatableness
panegyrically
parabolically
paradoxically
parallelogram
paraphernalia
parasynthesis
parliamentary
participation
particularise
particularity
paterfamilias
patriotically

patronisingly
peaceableness
penetrability
penitentially
pennilessness
penuriousness
perambulation
percussionist
peregrination
perfectionism
perfunctorily
perishability
perpendicular
perseveringly
perspectively
perspicacious
perspicuously
petrification
petrochemical
pharmaceutics
pharmacopoeia
phenomenalism
philanthropic
philosophical
photochemical
phraseologist
phrenological
physiological
physiotherapy
picturesquely
plaintiveness
platitudinous
plausibleness
plenteousness
pneumatically
poisonousness

poliomyelitis
polliniferous
ponderability
ponderousness
powerlessness
practicalness
pragmatically
prayerfulness
precautionary
precipitantly
precipitately
precipitation
precipitously
preconception
predicability
predicatively
predominantly
prefiguration
prefigurement
prehistorical
prejudicially
preliminarily
prematureness
premeditation
premeditative
preoccupation
preordination
preponderance
prepositional
prepossessing
presidentship
presumptively
pretentiously
preternatural
prevarication
primitiveness

primogeniture
prismatically
privatisation
probabilities
problematical
procrastinate
professoriate
prognosticate
progressional
progressively
projectionist
promiscuously
pronounceable
pronouncement
pronunciation
prophetically
proportionate
prospectively
prostaglandin
protectionism
protectionist
protectorship
provincialism
provisionally
psychoanalyse
psychoanalyst
psychological
psychosomatic
psychotherapy
punctiliously
puritanically
pusillanimous
pyrotechnical

Q
quadrilateral

quadruplicate
qualification
qualitatively
quartermaster
querulousness
questionnaire
quincentenary
quintuplicate

R
rapaciousness
rapprochement
rationalistic
realistically
reappointment
rearrangement
reciprocation
recommendable
reconcilement
recrimination
recriminatory
recrudescence
rectification
reduplication
refrigeration
regimentation
regurgitation
reimbursement
reincarnation
reinforcement
reinstatement
reinvestigate
rejuvenescent
remissibility
remonstrative
remorselessly

replenishment
reprehensible
representable
reproachfully
repulsiveness
resolvability
resplendently
restrictively
restructuring
resuscitation
retentiveness
retrogression
retrogressive
retrospection
retrospective
reverberation
reverentially
reversibility
revolutionary
revolutionise
righteousness

S
sacramentally
sadomasochism
sagaciousness
salaciousness
sanctimonious
sarcastically
scandalmonger
scarification
schizophrenia
scholasticism
scintillating
secretiveness
sedentariness

sedimentation
seditiousness
seismographic
semiautomatic
semiconductor
semiconscious
senselessness
sensitiveness
sententiously
sentimentally
separableness
sequestration
Shakespearean
shamelessness
shapelessness
significantly
signification
socioeconomic
somnambulator
sophistically
sophisticated
sorrowfulness
spasmodically
specification
spectroscopic
speculatively
splendiferous
splenetically
spontaneously
sportsmanship
sprightliness
stalactitical
statesmanship
statistically
steadfastness
strangulation

strategically
stratocumulus
strengthening
streptococcus
subcontractor
subordinately
substantially
substantively
superabundant
superannuated
superficially
superfluities
superfluously
superlatively
supernumerary
superstitious
supplantation
supplementary
suppositional
surreptitious
swashbuckling
symmetrically
syntactically
synthetically

T
tablespoonful
tantalisation
tastelessness
telegraphical
temperamental
temperateness
tempestuously
tenaciousness
terrestrially
territorially

theatricality
thenceforward
theologically
theoretically
therapeutical
thermonuclear
thoroughgoing
thoughtlessly
threateningly
thunderstruck
tolerableness
tonsillectomy
topographical
tortoiseshell
traditionally
tranquilliser
transatlantic
transcendence
transcription
transgression
transientness
transitionary
translucently
transmittable
transmutation
transnational
transparently
transpiration
transportable
transposition
transversally
triangularity
tricentennial
typographical
tyrannosaurus

U
umbelliferous
unaccompanied
unaccountable
unadulterated
unappreciated
unassimilated
unceremonious
uncertainties
uncomfortable
uncomplaining
unconditional
unconquerable
undercarriage
underemployed
underestimate
undergraduate
understanding
undiscernible
undisciplined
unembarrassed
unenlightened
unexceptional
unfamiliarity
unfashionable
unfashionably
unforgettable
unfortunately
ungrammatical
unguardedness
unimpeachable
unimpressible
uninhabitable
uninterrupted
unjustifiable
unmentionable

unmindfulness
unnecessarily
unneighbourly
unobtrusively
unprecedented
unpresentable
unpretentious
unrecompensed
unrepresented
unrighteously
unsavouriness
unserviceable
unsightliness
unskilfulness
unsubstantial

unsurpassable
unsymmetrical
untrustworthy
unwarrantable
unwillingness
unworkmanlike
unworldliness

V
valedictorian
vegetarianism
venerableness
ventriloquial
ventriloquism
versification

vexatiousness
vivaciousness
voluntariness
voraciousness
vulcanisation
vulnerability

W
wearisomeness
wholesomeness
wonderfulness
worthlessness

Y
yachtsmanship

# THIRTEEN-LETTER MULTIPLE WORDS

## A

acquired taste
active service
African violet
after a fashion
agree to differ
all in good time
all in one piece
alpha and omega
amusement park
an eye for an eye
analogue clock
angry young man
animal kingdom
anybody's guess
aqueous humour
armed services
ask for the moon
assault course
at a snail's pace
at crack of dawn
at dead of night
at full stretch

## B

back to the hilt
bag and baggage
bamboo curtain
baptism of fire
beside oneself
beyond compare
big bang theory
bird of passage

bite the bullet
black-and-white
bleeding heart
blind man's-buff
blood pressure
blood relation
blood relative
blotting paper
blow the lid off
boarding house
Bob's your uncle
booking office
break the mould
breech loading
bring into play
broad-spectrum
broken English
bubonic plague
bucketing down
bulletin board
burnt offering
bush telegraph
business class
by all accounts

## C

calendar month
carbon dioxide
cardboard city
cardiac arrest
carpenter moth
carrier pigeon
cat-o'-nine-tails

catch in the act
catch on the hop
catchment area
cerebral palsy
chain reaction
chance one's arm
change of heart
Channel Tunnel
charge account
chop and change
Christmas card
clear one's name
clear the decks
clearing house
clincher-built
clip one's wings
closed circuit
coarse-grained
cock of the walk
cog in the wheel
cold as charity
come to nothing
command module
commercial art
common measure
complex number
computer virus
concavo-convex
confidence man
cook one's goose
corps de ballet
Corpus Christi
cost-effective

cottage cheese
cotton-spinner
counting house
country cousin
crazy like a fox
cruise missile
crystal gazing
cultured pearl
curtain-raiser
cut down to size
cut to the quick

D
daddy longlegs
dead and buried
dead as the dodo
dead reckoning
death struggle
decimal system
deep in thought
dice with death
double-dealing
double-jointed
double-meaning
draggle-tailed
dressed to kill
dyed-in-the-wool

E
eat like a horse
esprit de corps

F
fall from grace
fine-tooth comb
fit like a glove

flashing point
flesh and blood
floating voter
flying colours
follow through
fool's paradise
foot in the door
fortune hunter
fortune-teller
fresh as a daisy
fringe benefit
from the word go

G
Geiger counter
gentian violet
get the message
get to the point
give the bullet
give the creeps
global warming
go the distance
go the whole hog
good Samaritan
good-naturedly
grappling hook
grappling iron
grief-stricken
grin and bear it
ground control
guided missile
gum up the works

H
half the battle
hang by a thread

hard-luck story
have a field day
have a hold over
have high hopes
have the edge on
head in the sand
head over heels
heads will roll
heart-breaking
hedge one's bets
helter-skelter
heritage trail
heroic couplet
high and mighty
high frequency
high-fibre diet
Highland fling
highwater mark
hit rock bottom
hit the ceiling
hit the jackpot
hole in the wall
Holy Communion
home economics
homeward bound
human interest

I
ill-considered
in a weak moment
in cahoots with
in the abstract
in the doghouse
in the pipeline
in the same boat
inverted comma

**J**
Jekyll and Hyde
just the ticket

**K**
kangaroo court
keen as mustard
keep in the dark
kick the bucket
kinetic energy
knockout drops
know what's what
knuckle-duster

**L**
lance corporal
latchkey child
laughing stock
lay down the law
leap in the dark
learning curve
level crossing
life preserver
light-fingered
like clockwork
like grim death
live like a lord
long-suffering
look daggers at
lose the thread
lotus position
lunatic fringe

**M**
mad cow disease
magic mushroom

magnetic field
magnetic north
make the most of
man of the world
mind-expanding
mint condition
mixed blessing
mixed marriage
mixed metaphor
moment of truth
moral majority
mortality rate
mother-of-pearl
motion picture
muddle through

**N**
name of the game
nervous system
next to nothing
no alternative
no great shakes
no holds barred
not before time
not for a moment
not on your life
nuclear energy
nuclear family
nuclear fusion

**O**
of unsound mind
old as the hills
on a shoestring
on pain of death
on tenterhooks

on the safe side
once and for all
one for the road
one in a million
one night stand
order of the day
ordinal number
out of the woods
owner-occupier

**P**
pain in the neck
panic-stricken
par excellence
Parkinson's Law
parrot-fashion
part and parcel
Passion Sunday
peace offering
pick and choose
place in the sun
play havoc with
poetic justice
poetic licence
police officer
pooper-scooper
power steering
pre-Raphaelite
pressure group
pressure point
primary school
prime minister
princess royal
private sector
profit sharing
pull the plug on

put new heart in
put out to grass

**Q**
quick-tempered
quotation mark

**R**
rack and pinion
radio spectrum
rag and bone man
read like a book
reference book
remote control
retaining wall
rhythm section
riotous living
rite of passage
rogues' gallery
roller coaster
Roman numerals
rough-and-ready
round the clock
round the twist
run a tight ship
run out of steam

**S**
sabre-rattling
sandwich board
satellite dish
search warrant
secret service
self-assertion
self-confessed
self-confident

self-conscious
self-contained
self-deception
self-inflicted
self-possessed
self-propelled
self-righteous
self-satisfied
senior citizen
sergeant major
serve a purpose
seventh heaven
sharp as a razor
short and sweet
short-tempered
sick to death of
side-splitting
sign the pledge
signature tune
silver service
silver wedding
silver-tongued
sitting pretty
skirting board
slap in the face
sleep like a log
sleep like a top
sleight of hand
slippery slope
smear campaign
smoke detector
social climber
social science
soft in the head
solid geometry
soul-searching

sounding board
sparks will fly
speed merchant
spending spree
spike one's guns
spill the beans
spine-chilling
spinning wheel
spiny anteater
spit and polish
spitting image
splinter group
spring balance
spring chicken
square measure
St Patrick's Day
stab in the back
standing order
starting block
starting price
stay the course
steady as a rock
steering wheel
step out of line
stepping stone
stick out a mile
stick-in-the-mud
stiff upper lip
stone the crows
stop at nothing
straight angle
straight flush
straight-laced
street fighter
stretch a point
strike it lucky

string quartet
submachine gun
sulphuric acid
sweep the board
sweet nothings

**T**
take a back seat
take a hard line
take liberties
take lying down
take the mickey
take the plunge
talk of the town
tear a strip off
telephoto lens
the cat's mother
the penny drops
think better of
time out of mind
time-consuming
tip the balance
to coin a phrase
to good purpose
to kingdom come
to say the least
tongue in cheek
tongue-twister
track-and-field

traffic lights
treasure-trove
treat like dirt
trial and error
turn on the heat
turn the corner
turn the tables

**U**
umbilical cord
up to the minute
urban guerilla

**V**
value for money
value judgment
vexed question
vice president
vicious circle
video cassette
video recorder

**W**
walls have ears
water softener
watering place
way of all flesh
weak as a kitten

weather-beaten
wee small hours
weeping willow
weight watcher
well-appointed
well-connected
well-preserved
well-thought-of
wheeler-dealer
white as a sheet
white elephant
whooping cough
wide of the mark
with kid gloves
with one accord
within an ace of
wood engraving
word blindness
word processor
work like magic
work the oracle
worn to a shadow

**Y**
yeoman service

**Z**
zebra crossing

# FOURTEEN-LETTER WORDS

**A**
abominableness
acceptableness
accomplishment
accountability
acknowledgment
administration
administrative
advantageously
adventitiously
affectionately
aforementioned
aggrandisement
aggressiveness
alphabetically
alphanumerical
antidepressant
aphoristically
apologetically
apprehensively
apprenticeship
arboricultural
archaeological
arithmetically
aromatherapist
astronomically
attainableness
attractiveness
auspiciousness
authentication
autobiographer
autosuggestion

**B**
bacteriologist
beautification
biographically
blithesomeness
boisterousness
breathlessness

**C**
capitalisation
capriciousness
cardiovascular
censoriousness
censurableness
centralisation
chancellorship
changeableness
characteristic
charitableness
cinematography
circuitousness
circumambulate
circumlocution
circumnavigate
circumspection
circumstantial
classification
claustrophobia
cognoscibility
commensurately
commensuration
commissionaire
commodiousness

comprehensible
comprehensibly
conceivability
concentrically
conclusiveness
confidentially
conglomeration
congratulatory
congregational
conjunctivitis
constitutional
constructional
constructively
consubstantial
consuetudinary
contagiousness
contemptuously
contiguousness
continuousness
contradictable
contraindicate
contraposition
controvertible
contumaciously
contumeliously
conventionally
conversational
convertibility
correspondence
corruptibility
counterbalance
countermeasure
courageousness

creditableness

**D**

deceivableness
definitiveness
degenerateness
deliberateness
delightfulness
demisemiquaver
demobilisation
democratically
demoralisation
denominational
deplorableness
derogatoriness
despicableness
despitefulness
destructionist
detestableness
diagrammatical
diminutiveness
diplomatically
disappointedly
disappointment
disapprobation
disapprovingly
disarrangement
disciplinarian
disconsolately
discontentedly
discontentment
discontinuance
discouragement
discourteously
discretionally
discriminately

discrimination
discriminatory
disdainfulness
disembarkation
disembowelment
disenchantment
disenfranchise
disinclination
disingenuously
disinheritance
disintegration
disjointedness
disorderliness
disrespectable
dissertational
distinguishing
distractedness
diverticulitis
divertissement

**E**

ecclesiastical
educationalist
electioneering
electrotherapy
emblematically
enterprisingly
etymologically
excruciatingly
existentialism
existentialist
expressionless
expressiveness
extemporaneous
extinguishable
extortionately

**F**

fallaciousness
fastidiousness
favourableness
figurativeness
formidableness
fortuitousness
fraternisation
friendlessness
fundamentalist

**G**

genealogically
generalisation
geocentrically
geographically
grandiloquence
gregariousness
groundlessness

**H**

hallucinogenic
harmoniousness
histrionically
horticulturist
hyperbolically
hypersensitive
hypocritically
hypostatically
hypothetically

**I**

identification
illegitimately
illustratively
impassableness

imperviousness
implacableness
impoverishment
impressibility
impressionable
impressiveness
inalienability
inapproachable
inarticulately
inauspiciously
incapacitation
incommensurate
inconclusively
inconsequently
inconsiderable
inconsistently
inconveniently
incoordination
indecipherable
indecorousness
indefiniteness
indemonstrable
indestructible
indestructibly
indeterminable
indiscreetness
indiscriminate
indistinctness
indivisibility
indoctrination
inexpressively
infectiousness
infelicitously
inflexibleness
infrastructure
inharmoniously

inordinateness
insatiableness
inseparability
insignificance
instrumentally
insufficiently
insuperability
insuppressible
insurmountable
intangibleness
intelligentsia
interplanetary
interpretation
interpretative
intoxicatingly
invariableness
invincibleness
inviolableness
irrecognisable
irreconcilable
irreparability
irreproachable
irresoluteness
irrespectively

L
latitudinarian
libertarianism
libidinousness
licentiousness
lithographical
longitudinally

M
macadamisation
mathematically

meretriciously
mesdemoiselles
metaphysically
meteorological
microprocessor
miraculousness
misapplication
misappropriate
miscalculation
misinformation
multifariously
multiplication
mysteriousness
mythologically

N
naturalisation
nitroglycerine

O
obsequiousness
obstreperously
opinionatively
oppressiveness
ostentatiously
osteoarthritis
outrageousness
overpoweringly
overproduction

P
pachydermatous
parsimoniously
passionateness
pathologically
perfectibility

perfidiousness
perishableness
permissibility
perniciousness
persuasiveness
pertinaciously
pharmaceutical
pharmacologist
philanthropist
photochemistry
photosynthesis
popularisation
practicability
precariousness
precociousness
predestination
predeterminate
preferentially
preponderation
preposterously
presumptuously
procrastinator
productiveness
professionally
prognosticator
prohibitionist
propitiousness
proportionable
proprietorship
prosperousness
providentially
psychoanalysis
psychoneurosis

Q
quantification

quantitatively
quintessential

R
reasonableness
recapitulation
recommendation
reconciliation
reconnaissance
reconstruction
redistribution
refractoriness
rehabilitation
reimprisonment
reintroduction
rejuvenescence
relentlessness
relinquishment
remorsefulness
reprehensively
representation
representative
resolvableness
respectability
responsibility
responsiveness
retrogradation
revengefulness
revivification

S
sacrilegiously
salubriousness
sanctification
satisfactorily
scholastically

schoolmistress
scientifically
scrupulousness
scurrilousness
seasonableness
secularisation
sensationalism
sentimentalism
sentimentalist
sentimentality
simplification
simultaneously
slaughterhouse
sociopolitical
solicitousness
somnambulation
sophistication
specialisation
speechlessness
stenographical
stigmatisation
stratification
subconsciously
submissiveness
substantiation
sufferableness
superabundance
superannuation
supercelestial
superciliously
superficiality
superincumbent
superintendent
supernaturally
superphosphate
supersensitive

superstructure
supposititious
susceptibility
suspiciousness
systematically

T
tatterdemalion
tautologically
teleologically
telescopically
teletypewriter
terminological
thermodynamics
thermoelectric
thoughtfulness
traditionalist
traitorousness
transcendental
transitoriness
transverberate
tridimensional
troubleshooter

tumultuousness

U
ubiquitousness
unacknowledged
unapproachable
unappropriated
uncompromising
unconscionable
uncontrollable
unconventional
underdeveloped
undermentioned
undernourished
understatement
undiscoverable
unfaithfulness
ungratefulness
unintelligible
unmentionables
unostentatious
unpremeditated
unprofessional

unquestionable
unquestionably
unreliableness
unrestrainedly
unsatisfactory
unscrupulously
unsociableness
unsuccessfully
unsuitableness

V
valetudinarian
verisimilitude
villainousness
vituperatively
vivisectionist
vulnerableness

W
weightlessness

Z
Zoroastrianism

# FOURTEEN-LETTER MULTIPLE WORDS

**A**
above suspicion
Achilles' tendon
across the board
action stations
against the odds
ahead of the game
all in a day's work
all over the shop
and all that jazz
armed to the hilt
as the crow flies
at a rate of knots
at the expense of
automatic pilot

**B**
babes in the wood
back-seat driver
backs to the wall
banana republic
be-all and end-all
beg the question
behind the times
belle of the ball
beside the point
bird of paradise
blood poisoning
blow hot and cold
boa constrictor
bread-and-butter
break the back of
break the record

breathing space
broad in the beam
Buckley's chance
bulimia nervosa
burst the bubble
bury the hatchet
by the same token

**C**
calico-printing
carbon monoxide
cardinal points
carry a torch for
cash on delivery
cast a cloud over
catch one's death
catch red-handed
Catherine-wheel
cathode-ray tube
cauliflower ear
chalk and cheese
chamois-leather
change one's mind
chicken-hearted
chicken-livered
Chinese lantern
circuit-breaker
class conscious
clear as crystal
cloak-and-dagger
close to the wind
clutch at straws
coconut matting

collective noun
come full circle
communion table
contract bridge
covering letter
credibility gap
crocodile tears
cross-fertilise
cross-reference
cry one's eyes out
culture vulture
current account
cut one's teeth on
cystic fibrosis

**D**
darken one's door
dead to the world
devil's advocate
do the spadework
double entendre
double standard
doubting Thomas
down in the mouth
dress rehearsal
drink like a fish

**E**
ears are burning
electric guitar
electronic mail
emperor penguin
expense account

extended family

**F**
faint-heartedly
fair to middling
fall on deaf ears
family planning
fellow-creature
fighting chance
figure of speech
finders keepers
flog a dead horse
Flying Dutchman
follow one's nose
for all the world
for good measure
for the life of me
free enterprise
freedom fighter
from the year dot

**G**
general-purpose
get it in the neck
get one's own back
get the better of
get the brush-off
get to first base
get to grips with
give a wide berth
give free rein to
give the heave-ho
give up the ghost
go like hot cakes
go out of one's way
go out on the town

good-for-nothing
good-humouredly
grasp the nettle
grease one's palm
great white hope

**H**
hard nut to crack
have been around
have it both ways
heart-searching
hit the bull's-eye
hold all the aces
hold no brief for
hold one's breath
hold one's tongue
holier-than-thou
hunt high and low

**I**
I'm all right, Jack
icing on the cake
identical twins
identity crisis
ill-gotten gains
in one fell swoop
in the good books
in the limelight
indirect speech
into the bargain
it's a small world

**J**
jobs for the boys

**K**
keep a tight rein
keep an open mind
keep one's hand in
keyhole surgery
knock into shape
knock on the head
know one's onions

**L**
large intestine
larger than life
law unto oneself
lay it on the line
leading article
let the side down
let them eat cake
letter of the law
lie in one's teeth
line one's pocket
live and let live
live by one's wits
loaded question
long in the tooth
Lutheran Church

**M**
magnetic needle
maidenhair-fern
make the running
man in the street
man of the moment
marching orders
market gardener
market research
mass production

men in grey suits
mend one's fences
merchant marine
monkey business

N
national anthem
natural history
natural science
Neanderthal man
never-never land
new lease of life
nineteenth hole
noblesse oblige
northern lights
nuclear fission
nuclear reactor
number-cruncher

O
Oedipus complex
off one's trolley
offset printing
on one's last legs
on the breadline
on the grapevine
on the off chance
one of those days
one that got away
one-armed bandit
opposite number
order of the boot
ordinary seaman
out for the count
out of this world
over my dead body

Oxford movement

P
package holiday
passive smoking
photo-engraving
pick one's brains
pinch and scrape
pins and needles
pituitary gland
plaster of Paris
plastic surgery
platinum blonde
pleased as Punch
pluck up courage
pop the question
presence of mind
president-elect
pressure cooker
prima ballerina
printed circuit
put in a good word
put on a pedestal
put the screws on
Pyrrhic victory

Q
quite something

R
radio frequency
radio telescope
rational number
rattle one's cage
read the riot act
rear-view mirror

record-breaking
recreation room
registered post
registry office
Remembrance Day
rhesus negative
rhesus positive
rheumatic fever
rhubarb, rhubarb
rhythm and blues
riding for a fall
ring the changes
rough and tumble
run the gauntlet

S
Saint Elmo's fire
salt of the earth
saved by the bell
scatter-brained
science fiction
second thoughts
security police
self-abnegation
self-effacement
self-expression
self-importance
self-indulgence
self-interested
self-sufficient
self-supporting
send to Coventry
Sergeant-at-Arms
set one's heart on
shaggy dog story
share of the cake

sheet-lightning
shepherd's purse
shock treatment
shotgun wedding
sign of the cross
silent majority
simple fraction
simple interest
skate on thin ice
slap on the wrist
slice of the cake
small intestine
social contract
Society of Jesus
Socratic method
sodium chloride
soul-destroying
southern lights
speak for itself
special effects
sporting chance
sports medicine
stage direction
stainless steel
stamping-ground
stand corrected
standard-bearer
starting stalls
storm in a teacup
straw in the wind

strawberry-mark
streets ahead of
strike a balance
strike a bargain
stumbling-block
surgical spirit
swallow the bait
systems analyst

T
take a dim view of
take a rise out of
take in good part
take the edge off
Tasmanian devil
the cat's pyjamas
thick as thieves
think nothing of
three point turn
thrilled to bits
throw the book at
throw to the dogs
time immemorial
to feel the pinch
train of thought
Turkish delight
turn a deaf ear to
turn upside-down
two-dimensional

U
up to one's elbows
upwardly mobile

V
vending machine
vent one's spleen
vested interest
vice-chancellor
virtual reality

W
watch like a hawk
water-resistant
wave a magic
wand
wet one's whistle
what's eating you
whipper-snapper
white blood cell
whoopee cushion
wild-goose chase
wind-instrument
window shopping
with a vengeance
word processing
work like a charm
working capital

# FIFTEEN-LETTER WORDS

## A
acclimatisation
accountableness
acquisitiveness
adventurousness
antepenultimate
anthropocentric
anthropological
anthropomorphic
appropriateness
argumentatively
authoritatively

## B
bibliographical

## C
ceremoniousness
chronologically
circumscribable
circumscription
circumspectness
circumstantiate
combustibleness
communicability
communicatively
compassionately
comprehensively
compressibility
conceivableness
condescendingly
conscientiously
consequentially

considerateness
conspicuousness
contemplatively
contemporaneous
contemptibility
contentiousness
contractibility
contradictorily
controversially
conventionality
correlativeness
correspondently
correspondingly
corruptibleness
crystallisation

## D
decalcification
defencelessness
demonstrability
demonstratively
departmentalise
descriptiveness
destructibility
destructiveness
differentiation
disadvantageous
discontinuation
discretionarily
disentanglement
disgracefulness
disinterestedly
disorganisation

dispassionately
disrespectfully
dissatisfaction
distastefulness
distinguishable
distrustfulness
diversification
draughtsmanship

## E
efficaciousness
electrification
electrodynamics
electromagnetic
emancipationist
enfranchisement
entomologically
epidemiological
exchangeability
excommunication
exemplification
experimentalist
experimentation
externalisation
extrajudicially
extraordinarily

## F
flibbertigibbet
formularisation

## G
gastroenteritis

gentlemanliness

**H**
historiographer
homogeneousness
humanitarianism
hydrostatically
hypercritically
hypochondriacal

**I**
ideographically
impenetrability
inaccessibility
inapplicability
inappropriately
inattentiveness
incommensurable
incommunicative
incompatibility
incomprehension
inconsequential
inconsiderately
inconspicuously
incorrigibility
indemnification
indeterminately
individualistic
indomitableness
inefficaciously
inexcusableness
inexplicability
inflammableness
injudiciousness
inoffensiveness
inquisitiveness

inquisitorially
inscrutableness
inseparableness
insignificantly
instrumentalist
instrumentality
instrumentation
insubordination
intelligibility
intemperateness
interchangeable
interconnection
intolerableness
intractableness
intussusception
invulnerability
irreligiousness
irresistibility

**L**
lexicographical

**M**
marginalisation
Mephistophelian
microscopically
mischievousness
misconstruction
morphologically

**N**
nationalisation
notwithstanding

**O**
ornithorhynchus

**P**
palaeontologist
parliamentarian
perpendicularly
personification
perspicaciously
perspicuousness
phosphorescence
photosynthesise
physiologically
picturesqueness
plenipotentiary
pleuropneumonia
polyunsaturated
practicableness
prepositionally
prestidigitator
pretentiousness
procrastination
professionalism
prognostication
promiscuousness
proportionately

**R**
reproachfulness
retrogressively

**S**
straightforward
superficialness
supernumeraries
sympathetically
symptomatically

**T**
transfiguration
transliteration
transmutability
transparentness
transplantation
transpositional
treacherousness
treasonableness
trigonometrical
troublesomeness
trustworthiness

**U**
unceremoniously
uncommunicative
unconditionally
unconsciousness
unconstrainedly
undemonstrative
underprivileged
unexceptionable
unexceptionably
ungrammatically
unparliamentary

unphilosophical
unprepossessing
unpronounceable
unrighteousness
unsophisticated

**V**
vicissitudinous

**Z**
zoogeographical

# FIFTEEN-LETTER MULTIPLE WORDS

## A
against the clock
against the grain
ahead of one's time
alimentary canal
alive and kicking
all along the line
alternate angles
ambush-marketing
anabolic steroid
animal magnetism
animated cartoon
anorexia nervosa
anti-monarchical
any port in a storm
armed to the teeth
at close quarters
at cross-purposes
at the drop of a hat
aurora australis

## B
back to square one
because it's there
behind the scenes
blood and thunder
blow one's trumpet
bolt from the blue
brake horsepower
breach of promise
bubble and squeak
building society
by hook or by crook

## C
cable television
calm as a millpond
cardinal numbers
cardinal virtues
castles in the air
centre of gravity
chapter and verse
chemical warfare
Chinese checkers
clean as a whistle
coffee-table book
collision course
colour-blindness
come to grips with
confidence trick
contraband of war
convenience food
cool as a cucumber
corporate raider
cosmetic surgery
costing the earth
cottage industry
cross swords with
cross the Rubicon
crossword puzzle
curriculum vitae
curry favour with

## D
daylight robbery
delirium tremens
deliver the goods
dig one's own grave
digital computer
diplomatic corps
displaced person
do a roaring trade
do one's dirty work
do one's level best
double-barrelled
draw in one's horns
dual carriageway

## E
eternal triangle
evening primrose
extra-curricular

## F
feather one's nest
feel in one's bones
fine-toothed comb
finishing school
fluorescent lamp
fly off the handle
foundation stone

## G
gentleman-at-arms
get into the swing
get off one's chest
get off the ground
get on an even keel
get on one's nerves
give the game away

give the once-over
go like clockwork
go off at a tangent
go one better than
go to rack and ruin
golden handshake

H
hang on one's words
hang up one's boots
have designs upon
have no truck with
have over a barrel
have the last word
have two left feet
higher education
hit the headlines
hope against hope

I
in a blue moon on
in all conscience
in apple-pie order
in black-and-white
in broad daylight
in mint condition
in seventh heaven
in the altogether
in the first place
in the last resort
in the melting pot
in the nick of time
incidental music
indecent assault
infant mortality
it takes all sorts

J
jack of all trades
jumping-off point

K
keep a low profile
keep one's shirt on
know a thing or two
knuckle sandwich

L
lateral thinking
laugh out of court
lead a double life
lead a merry dance
leading question
learn the hard way
leave high and dry
leave in the lurch
leg before wicket
let it all hang out
let one's hair down
light of one's life
like a drowned rat
like the clappers
lily of the valley
long arm of the law
look the other way

M
mad as a March hare
magnetic equator
make a beeline for
make a break for it
make a clean sweep
make mincemeat of

make short work of
manic-depressive
manna from heaven
merchant service
middle-of-the-road
money is no object
much of a muchness

N
natural resource
night on the tiles
non-profit-making
not by a long chalk
not the done thing
nouvelle cuisine

O
of one's own accord
on speaking terms
on the never-never
on the right track
on the wrong track
on top of the world
open-and-shut case
over and done with

P
paint the town red
par for the course
pass the hat round
pay lip service to
personal trainer
physical therapy
pin back one's ears
pipped at the post
poison-pen letter

polar coordinate
poverty-stricken
press conference
prick up one's ears
public relations
punctuation mark
put back the clock
put in the picture
put the mockers on

Q
quick off the mark

R
rain cats and dogs
rattle one's sabre
rear its ugly head
regius professor
return to the fold
right-mindedness
rise with the lark
risk life and limb
rooted to the spot
Russian roulette

S
safety in numbers
scrape the barrel
second childhood
see eye to eye with
select committee
self-approbation
self-explanatory
self-opinionated
self-pollination
self-realisation

self-reproachful
set great store by
set one's sights on
settle old scores
shoulder to cry on
shrinking violet
silence is golden
since the year dot
singing telegram
situation comedy
slip of the tongue
snake in the grass
sparring partner
specific gravity
spitting image of
stand one's ground
stew in one's juice
stick to one's guns
storage capacity
straight talking
stretch one's legs
stubborn as a mule
surf the Internet
surrogate mother
sweat of one's brow
swim with the tide

T
take advantage of
take exception to
take it on the chin
take one's chances
talk one's head off
the bird has flown
the cat's whiskers
the coast is clear

the plot thickens
the sky's the limit
think the world of
third degree burn
throw in the towel
throw to the lions
thumb one's nose at
tighten one's belt
tilt at windmills
time is getting on
time on one's hands
tip of the iceberg
Tom, Dick and Harry
tower of strength
tracking station
tread on one's toes
turn a blind eye to

U
under lock and key
under the aegis of
under the counter
under the weather
unknown quantity

V
venereal disease
vital statistics

W
walrus moustache
wash one's hands of
wear the trousers
weather the storm
well-intentioned
wet the baby's head

whited sepulchre

wishful thinking

with a heavy heart

with bated breath

wither on the vine

work like a beaver

**Y**

you never can tell